A TREASURY OF
SHOLOM
ALEICHEM
Children's Stories

Other Translations of Sholom Aleichem
by Aliza Shevrin

Children's Short Stories

Holiday Tales of Sholom Aleichem
Around the Table: Family Stories of Sholom Aleichem

Novels

Marienbad
In the Storm
The Nightingale
The Bloody Hoax

A Treasury of
SHOLOM
ALEICHEM
Children's Stories

selected and translated by
ALIZA SHEVRIN

JASON ARONSON INC.
Northvale, New Jersey
London

This book was set in 12 pt. Berkeley by Alpha Graphics of Pittsfield, New Hampshire.

Library of Congress Cataloging-in-Publication Data

Sholem Aleichem, 1859–1916.
   [Short stories. English. Selections]
   A treasury of Sholom Aleichem children's stories / selected and translated by Aliza Shevrin.
      p. cm.
   Summary: A collection of stories which capture the life and experience of a Jewish child living in Eastern Europe during the late nineteenth and early twentieth centuries.
     ISBN 1-56821-926-1 (alk. paper)
    1. Jews—Europe, Eastern—Juvenile fiction. 2. Children's stories, Yiddish—Translations into English.   [1. Jews—Europe, Eastern—Fiction. 2. Short stories.]   I. Shevrin, Aliza.
II. Title.
PZ7.S55863Tr   1996
[Fic]—dc20   96-14590
                                       CIP
                                       AC

Manufactured in the United States of America. Jason Aronson Inc. offers books and cassettes. For information and catalog write to Jason Aronson Inc., 230 Livingston Street, Northvale, New Jersey 07647.

To My Grandchildren
    Ilene
    Julie
    Ariel
    Eric
    Suzannah
    Rachel Emma

Contents

Contents

Acknowledgments

My deepest thanks, for their help in translating the "untranslatable," go to Rabbi Robert Dobrusin, Professor Herb Paper, Avram Lis, Professor Maurice Freidberg, Isaac Norich, and my daily walking companion of so many years, Rivka Rubinfeld. To Bel Kaufman and Sidney Gluck of the Sholom Aleichem Memorial Foundation go my gratitude for their devotion to perpetuating Sholom Aleichem's legacy. My husband, Howie, has been my indispensable "second set of ears," in-house editor, polisher, translator of poems, and careful, critical reader of every page translated. I am deeply grateful for his generosity of time and talent and, I must add, we have had great fun working together.

Translator's Introduction

The year 1996 will commemorate the eightieth anniversary of the death of Sholom Aleichem. It is with great pleasure that I offer a collection of this beloved Jewish writer's children's stories as a tribute to the master for whom children were a source of joy and inspiration. In selecting the stories for this volume, I considered not only those in the two volumes of Sholom Aleichem's collected *Mayses far Yidishe Kinder* (Stories for Jewish Children), but those sprinkled throughout his other works; stories for and about children, covering a surprising range of childhood experiences well beyond those we are accustomed to reading in our highly sanitized contemporary literature for young children. They accurately capture the life and experience of a Jewish child living and growing up in the harsh circumstances of the Jewish Pale of eastern Europe during the latter part of the nineteenth and early twentieth centuries. Yet the stories' sensitivity to the universal experiences of childhood remind us that growing up even under our own more favored circumstances is still no picnic.

It has been remarked that if all the records of Jewish *shtetl* life were to disappear, it could easily be reconstructed from Sholom Aleichem's work alone. Although many of his stories and novels take place in large European cities and some in America, his renditions of Jewish *shtetl* life are the ones most treasured and most evocative for modern readers. Sholom Aleichem spent the most formative years of his life, until the age of twelve, growing up in a *shtetl*. It is not surprising that his memories of that time provided him with the most direct link to the Jewish experience. The children's story, in particular, in which he created his dearest and most intimate world, was the genre that allowed him to achieve not only profoundly personal goals but also literary and political aims as well.

Modern children's literature in Yiddish began in 1886 with Sholom Aleichem's first literary success and masterpiece, "The Penknife." Not written originally as a children's story but later rewritten in 1901–1903 for children, it was to become his most popular and most often translated story. It already possessed the hallmarks of the many Sholom Aleichem children's stories to come: the everyday experiences of a young boy, an exposé of the constricted, narrow, and often mean and dispiriting *cheder* (school) environment with its feared and hated rebbes, while at the same time weaving a universal tale of youthful initiation in the unlikely world of the *shtetl*. (For further discussion of this subject and its literary importance, I highly recommend the chapter "A Bridge of Longing," in David Roskies' book, *Mythologist of the Mundane: Sholom Aleichem* [Harvard University Press, 1995].)

Maurice Samuels describes Sholom Aleichem's children's world as utterly honest, *sui generis*. How his child protagonists dreamed, suffered, prevailed, and most of all, *talked*, is unlike "the priggishness of Horatio Alger, the falsity and sentimentalism of 'A Christmas Carol,' or even the pure fantasy of Grimm and Anderson." Samuels suggests they can best be likened to "some of the privations of Oliver Twist." These were children who were often oppressed, imbued with guilt, often hungry and deprived of physical comfort, humiliated and beaten by teachers, parents, and other children. Yet their lives were enriched with learning, religion, family, and community loyalty. However stringent and rigorous life was, their spirits seemed not to have been broken or crushed. Indeed many of the children come through in these narratives as imaginative, resourceful, vital, resilient, with surprising capacity for humor, magic, romance, and innocence in the midst of poverty, persecution, and isolation.

How did they manage this? Several themes emerge in the stories that might give us an answer: the role of nature and fantasy as sources of release, and regeneration of spirit.

Nature, the world beyond the confines of home and school, was a magnet drawing the child beyond the stifling constraints of the shtetl. Yet the fields and forests surrounding the shtetl were considered off-limits, forbidden for Jewish children as unsafe and a distraction from talmudic studies. Except for special holidays, or as an act of defiance, escape, or, as in the "Song of Songs" stories, a romantic adventure, children rarely ventured "beyond the borders of the town," "past the mills," "on the other side of the river." In the open country, under the "canopy of sky" (often likened to a blue skullcap!), freed from school for a day for a special outing as on Lag B'Omer, or escaping humiliation, a child could temporarily enjoy what the rest of the world took for granted—fresh air, green grass, a pond—and revel in nature's bounty. Most of these forays outdoors led to disaster, guilt, atonement, and return. Sholom Aleichem's work is replete with pastoral, idyllic scenes that Jews could savor only rarely and not without consequences. The Jew's place was at work, at home, in school, in the study house. Out-of-doors were dogs, perilous rivers, gentile peasants, and bandits.

Fantasy, often exercised in those forbidden out-of-doors, was also a powerful regenerative force in a child's life. To possess a penknife, to play a violin, to own the most impressive flag, to be part of a travelling troupe, to wage a battle with garden vegetables as the imagined enemy, to make money, to take revenge on a cruel teacher, to love a young girl—these dreams consumed and distracted the young lads (and they are all boys, except in "Two Purim Pastry Gifts") in these stories from the harsh realities of their existence. But even wealthier boys were not immune to these fantasies, notably in "With King Ahashuerosh" and "Song of Songs." Again, invariably, the actions taken to achieve the fantasies led to disaster, humiliation, punishment, or illness of a parent or even the child himself, who often languished with a high fever after a disappointment or unexpected reversal in fortune, like the heroes in "The Penknife" and "The Simkhas Torah Flag." It is difficult to accept, from the perspective of our own time, the necessity to squelch, suppress, or even punish ambition, fulfillment, pleasure, and creativity, but the political insecurities and financial constraints of the time left little energy for adults to consider what children needed emotionally or creatively. Survival was all, at any cost, and a child had better learn early what was in store for him in the future, rather than waste time with what was considered trivial and eventually detrimental to the community. Hence the prohibitions, the strict values, and the adherence to harsh parental and scholarly discipline.

It was the celebration of the Jewish holidays that made it possible for Jewish families to direct their energies to happier pursuits. The majority of Sholom Aleichem's stories, adult as well as children's, are centered around a particular holiday. Rich and poor alike were obliged and entitled to enjoy and observe the holidays. Holidays served both as religious education and as an opportunity to gather the family together, as the family members prepared and then celebrated the holiday, usually centering around a festive meal, as on Passover. For children, it was a time for playing games. Each holiday had its own traditions, such as putting on Purim plays, playing with tops on Chanukah, having competing teams during Lag B'Omer, having flag-decorating competitions at Simkhas Torah, or rolling nuts on Passover. Clearly this is Sholom Aleichem at his best, showing Judaism as equally available to all. But even on those festive occasions, dreams and expectations were often shattered as reality prevailed—the flag was destroyed, the nut game turned vicious, a teacher was humiliated by his vengeful students, or a kindly tenant farmer's vegetable garden was demolished.

The compassion lacking in adults is often attributed in many of these stories to the children; that is, until they become adults, hardened to life's cruel twists of fate, illness, madness, and need. The child asks the eternal question, "Why?" The adult answers, "It is God's will." Pity, innocence, kindliness, and empathy are natural to the sensitive child reacting to an adult world. Often Sholom Aleichem depicts acts of cruelty toward an animal that elicit pity and compassion. There are three such stories in this collection, all giving animals Jewish traits to an almost comedic degree, but making a moral point in each case ("Robchik [A Jewish Dog]," "Methusaleh [A Jewish Horse]," and "No More *Kapores*"). Other stories describe pitiful, deformed children ("Pity for Living Things," and "Creature"), or seemingly demented people ("David, King of Israel," and "Getzel").

Several stories are about orphans (the Mottel and Elyahu stories, "With King Ahashuerosh," and "The Youngest Seder King"). With the release from the authority of the father, with the father-son conflict removed, an often pathetic and defiant boy becomes a cheerful, liberated, doted upon, spoiled, and well-fed recipient of lavish maternal affection as well as sympathy coming from the entire community. Mottel, the cantor's orphan son, cannot be punished, doesn't go to *cheder*, is included in many adult situations from which a child is normally excluded, and has the time of his life.

Mothers figure strongly in these stories. The range of temperaments is wide. Some are cold and punitive, some weepy, always worried and prayerful, many are seen as the "good" parent protecting the boy from the father's anger, some are overprotective, others too preoccupied to care. Fathers, too, are seen as both ineffectual or dictatorial, sickly, or as attractive role models. Whenever a father is described as praying in synagogue, it is invariably done with love, respect, and honor. Nevertheless, every boy is happiest away from home and school, with friends, outdoors, or indulging in happy dreams.

It is important to mention the *cheder*, the one-room schoolhouse, since it plays such an important role in so many of Sholom Aleichem's children's stories. Twenty or thirty little boys, some as young as three, were crowded into a small, dark, airless, overheated or freezing space from morning till night, sitting at primitive tables, chanting their Talmud and Torah studies over and over. The room was generally in the home of the rebbe, the religious school teacher, and usually the rebbe's family would be present at the periphery of the room as they went about their daily routine. Whipping was the accepted form of discipline and students would frequently have faces slapped and ears twisted "for their own good." The stern rebbe is referred to by the boys in several stories ("Bandits," "Lag B'Omer") as the "Angel of Death" (*malakh hamoves*), and much effort is spent in placating, outfoxing, tricking, avenging, and finally stoically accepting this most powerful figure in a boy's life. The *Haskalah*, the movement of Enlightenment which sought to bring secular learning and knowledge of other languages to Jews, was to become highly critical of the narrow stringencies of the *cheder*. As a *maskil*, or follower of the *Haskalah*, Sholom Aleichem pressed for educational reform by accurately depicting, and sometimes satirizing, the *cheder* experience through the eyes of a child (himself).

The eternal child in Sholom Aleichem comes to the surface in his writing style, which strikes a direct, personal, intimate, almost naive or child-like tone. Each story is narrated in the first person: an adult recalling his childhood and telling his story to young children, drawing them into his world as he lived and saw it. The very first story of the collection begins with, "Children! Let me tell you a story . . . " Other stories end with warnings to other children (don't do as I did), or encouragement (do as I did). (For further discussion of Sholom Aleichem's contribution to Yiddish literature for children, please read Khoneh Shmeruk's important paper, "*Sholem-Aleykhem un di onheybn fun der yidisher literatur far kinder*," *Di goldene keyt* 112 (1984): 39–53.)

There are several references to boys who, at a young age, are already engaged to be married and who then wear a silver pocket watch on a silver chain to designate their new status. Once a boy was *bar mitzvah*ed at thirteen, he was considered marriageable, an adult with adult responsibilities. The marriages were always arranged by the boy's family and the prospective bridegroom sometimes had to prove his scholarly worth by mastering a Talmudic passage. Transgressions, or what we would call normal adolescent behavior, could lead to the breaking of the engagement. Red hair and freckles did not bode well for girls ("Pesseli the Rabbi's Daughter").

To those who will read these stories to their children and grandchildren, I say, "Be prepared to laugh, cry, become incensed at injustice, saddened by tragedy, lifted by soaring imagination, healed by profound compassion, and —most of all—be prepared to relive the pains, joys, and secrets of your own childhood, and to see them reflected in the eyes of your young listeners."

The Simkhas Torah Flag

A

hildren! Let me tell you a story about a Simkhas Torah flag. How a poor man's son like myself managed to get a flag for Simkhas Torah, how hard it was to get it and how easy it was to lose it. God punished me. That flag brought me untold suffering!

When I was young, just like you, they called me "Topele Tootaritoo," but my name was really "Kopele Kookarikoo." Do you know why? Because first of all, I had a thin, squeaky little voice like a half-grown rooster that has just begun crowing, and second of all, I couldn't pronounce the sounds "k" or "g", and wouldn't you know, my father was named Kalman, my mother—Gittl Kalman's, I—Kopel Gittl Kalman's, and the rabbi—Gershon Gorgel Dardaki from Galaganovka.

"Little boy! What is your name?"

"Me? Topel Dittl Talman's . . ."

"A little louder!"

"Topel Dittl Talman's! . . ."

"Louder!"

I shouted even louder, "To-pel! Dit-tel! Tal-man's!"

"And with whom do you study?"

"With whom do I study? With Dershon Dordel Dardati from Daladanovka!"

The crowd laughed.

The crowd laughed—and I wept.

I wept not because they were laughing at me, but because they also hit me. Everyone who had God in his heart hit me: my father, my mother, my sisters, the rabbi, my classmates. That's how they undertook to teach me to talk "like a normal person."

The rabbi once stuck a flat wooden stick down my throat and told my classmates to spit down my throat—perhaps that would cure me. But Reb Zyame the carpenter, who shared a house with the rabbi, intervened.

"Why are you tormenting a poor child for no reason? Just let me at him for one minute and you will see how he will speak 'like a normal person . . .'

Reb Zyame the carpenter called me over, grasped me by the chin and instructed me,

"Look at me, little boy, and repeat after me word for word, 'Can you catch a crook with a candle' . . ."

I looked at him and repeated after him word for word, 'Tan you tatch a troot with a tandle' . . ."

"Not like that!" exclaimed Reb Zyame. "Look right at my lips and say with me together, 'Go gather the geese and give them greens' . . ."

I looked right at his lips and said along with him, "Do dather the deese and dive them dreens."

"No, little fool," Reb Zyame said to me, "Don't say dreens; say greens! Greens! Greens!"

"Dreens! Dreens! Dreens!. . . ."

Reb Zyame waved his hand in disgust. "Do you know what I just figured out? It's a waste of time. Nothing will ever help him. He'll always talk funny."

B

To own a Simkhas Torah flag, a real flag, a flag attached to a fine straight stick, topped by a red apple, and in the apple a candle, seemed to me then such bliss, such joy that I dared not even think about it. Certainly there were many other good things in the world. There were children in school who had money to buy a penknife, a purse, or a cane. There were boys who ate candy every day, had nuts to crack, and that wasn't counting bagels and pancakes. And there were those who even ate *white* rolls on *weekdays* . . . what luck!

Oy, children! I have never, never eaten white rolls on weekdays! I would have been satisfied to eat my fill of black bread. We were, may it not happen to you, miserable poor folk, paupers, though every one of us worked hard. My father, of blessed memory, was the assistant sexton at the small study house of the Butcher's Synagogue. My mother, may she be remembered, was an expert baker of honey cakes, and my sisters mended stockings. You can truly believe me. There was never a time when I finished eating and was not still hungry enough to eat again.

Today no one even gives a second thought to having a kopek in one's pocket—one's very own kopek. I never so much as dreamed of it.

So just imagine when I, Kopel Kookarikoo, suddenly became wealthy and possessed my very own kopeks!

If you think a miracle happened, like a rich man losing some coins and I finding them, you're wrong. Or perhaps you think I simply filched them somewhere, stole them from a charity box? God save you from such thoughts! I swear to you, I earned them, honestly earned them, toiled for them with my own . . . legs.

It was Purim, and my father sent me to distribute the pastry trays to the elders of the small study house of the Butcher's Synagogue. Up to now the pastry trays had been distributed by one of my older sisters, but since I had grown up a bit, my father said that I might also be of some help. I took the trays of pastries, carrying them from house to house to all the elders of the small study house of the Butcher's Synagogue, slogging through the cold slippery mud with my bare feet, and earned for my services a silver forty kopek coin plus four groshens.

C

Having suddenly acquired a small fortune, I became preoccupied with what to do with all that money. Then my Bad and Good Impulses arrived on the scene. The Bad Impulse said,

"Why hold on to those groshens, little fool? Buy something. Buy poppy seed cookies, like those sweet ones on Pirondischky's stand. Buy little delicious pastries with honey crumbs or at least a frozen apple, something you can lick your chops over."

"And let my appetite get the better of me?" I said, "I'll eat up all my money in one day. I won't do it!"

"Right you are!" said my Good Impulse, "Better to lend your mother the few kopeks! She can really use them."

"Very smart!" I said, "I'll never see them again. Where will she get money to pay me back?"

"But she struggles so, poor thing," said my Good Impulse, "and she does pay your tuition."

"What's that to you—tuition?" said my Bad Impulse. "Better buy a shiny tin whistle with red decorations on it, a sharp penknife with two blades and a brass case, or a little purse with a good clasp."

"What will you keep in that little purse?" said my Good Impulse, "Your poverty?"

"Buttons!" said my Bad Impulse, "You'll stuff the purse full of buttons so people will think its money and all the boys will envy you . . ."

"Where will that get you?" said my Good Impulse, "You listen to me, hand out the money to poor folks, give charity and you will be doing a good deed. Poor people are starving."

"Poor people?" my Bad Impulse said to me, "You yourself are a poor man's son. You yourself are always hungry. Everyone is generous with other people's money. How come no one ever gave *you* anything when you needed it?"

D

Once my Bad Impulse very nearly won me over.

I had a friend in school—Yoylik, a rich man's son. He always had pockets full of treats, but he hated to give anything to anyone. You could beg on bended knee—not a crumb! Then one day Yoylik began cozying up to me, smiling too much, becoming too friendly.

"Do you know what?" he said to me, "You're a good kid, as I am a Jew. I like you because you don't beg like the others, 'Please give me a piece! Please, please give me a tiny piece!' I can't look at those beggars! Would you like a piece of candy?"

"A piece of tandy?" I said, "Why not?"

"Well," he said, "And wouldn't you like to have a nut or two to crack?"

"A nut or two?" I said, "Why not? If I had, I would trat them."

Yoylik put his hand in his pocket. I thought this meant he was going to give me something. But instead he said to me:

"I'll give you half a piece of marmalade candy and three nuts if you trade with me. Will you trade?"

"Trade?" I said, "What will I trade you?"

"I'll give you," he said, "my penknife. You know my white penknife? A real antique, one of a kind!"

What a question, did I know Yoylik's penknife! Who didn't know Yoylik's penknife? How many times had I envied him for it! How often had I seen it in my dreams!

"And I," I said, "What will I dive you for it?"

"And you," he said, "will give me your silver coin."

"Take it!" said my Bad Impulse, "Take it, it's a gem of a knife. All the boys will envy you . . ."

I was about to take out my money, but something made me stop.

"Some smart aleck you are!" I said. "For a silver toin you tan buy a new penknife."

"A penknife like mine?" said Yoylik, "Not on your life! Listen, do you know what? I'll throw in a half dozen bone buttons."

"For toins," I said, "you tan buy ten thousand dozen buttons."

"Well," he said, "and candy and buttons aren't worth anything? I promise you, whenever you ask me I will give you anything, as I am a Jew. Here I have an iron nail, do you see? I'll give you the nail for free. Do you see what a nail this is?"

"What do I need nails for?" I said.

"Silly," he said, "It will come in handy. You can hammer it in wherever you want. You can dig a hole with it."

"What do I need to did holes for," I said.

"I'll let you," he said, "pray from my little prayer book."

"Why do I need," I said, "to pray from other people's prayer books?"

"I'll let you," he said, "try on my *Shabbos* hat."

"Why do I need," I said, "to try on other people's *Shabbos* hats?"

"You don't want anything? Take this!" said Yoylik and gave me a jab in the side. "What do you think of this no-good cheapskate? I offer him all these things: a penknife, buttons, candy, nuts, a nail, a prayer book and trying on a hat—and he doesn't want any of them! A greedy belly—no matter how much you stuff in it, it's not enough! He thinks because he has a silver coin, he's a big shot! Just wait, Topele Tootaritoo, someday you'll come to me and you know what you'll get! Nehemiah! Here, I'm giving you the nail!"

Yoylik gave the nail to Nehemiah (a poor boy who had a limp), and from then on he was no longer my friend.

E

You may well ask: For what reason was I holding on to the money?

First of all, for the Lag B'Omer party. Every year for the Lag B'Omer party all the children would bring something to school: money or food or snacks. But I would always come with my very same poor boy's snack: a piece of bread and garlic. My face burnt with shame. And though they always invited me into the circle along with all the other boys, I still felt it was out of pity, and I couldn't enjoy the celebration. Now, I thought, I don't care, I am, thank goodness, a person with my own money. If a rich man's son like Yoylik could chip in four kopeks, I could certainly think of donating one kopek. How can I compare myself to him? I'm a nobody! On the other hand, where is the law that says that I can't give *five* kopeks as my share? So, I decided to give *ten* kopeks and let them know who Kopele Kookoorikoo was!

I laid aside ten kopeks for the Lag B'Omer party and saved the rest.

Later, during the summer, when vegetables and fresh fruit were in Piranditschky's stand, my Bad Impulse again visited me.

"See," he said, "those green gooseberries? Those red currants?"

"Dreen fruit," I said, "just put your teeth on edge."

"Say a prayer over the fruit," my Good Impulse said to me, "that will be a blessing."

"I've got plenty of time to say a blessing; there's the whole summer still ahead. There'll still be another crop of currants and plums, apples and pears, pumpkins and watermelons. I had better save my money, God willing, for Sukkos—to buy myself a flad."

And it was agreed that I would save the money for Sukkos to buy myself a flag.

F

With God's help, Sukkos came and I bought myself a flag, a large yellow "two-sided" flag. On one side were painted two beasts with cat faces who were really lions with open mouths and long tongues. Whistles and shofars were painted right on their tongues and underneath in large letters, it said: *B'HATZUTZROT V'KOL SHOFAR*—WITH TRUMPETS AND RAM'S HORN.

Beneath the lions, in the right hand corner was written: *DEGEL MAKHANEH YEHUDAH*—FLAG OF THE TRIBE OF JUDAH. In the left hand corner: *DEGEL MAKHANEH EFRAIM*—FLAG OF THE TRIBE OF EPHRAIM.

That was only one side of the flag. On the other side it was even nicer. There were portraits of Moses and Aaron, looking absolutely lifelike. Moses had a large peaked hat on his head, and Aaron had a golden circlet on his blonde head. In the center, between Moses and Aaron, stood a crowd of

Jews, packed almost one on top of the other, holding little Torah scrolls in their hands. All had one face, as if one mother had borne them. All wore the same long kaftans, all wore the same shoes, stockings, and rope belts reaching just below the thigh. The men, with one knee raised, were dancing and singing: "*Sisu v'simkhu b'simkhas torah*— Be merry and rejoice. Let us celebrate Simkhas Torah."

Once you've acquired a flag, you have to find a stick for it, for which one had to apply to Reb Zyame the carpenter, actually that same Reb Zyame who had once tried to teach me to talk "like a normal person."

"What do you want, Topele Tootaritoo?"

"A stit for my flad . . ."

"What do you mean, a stit?" he said.

"A stit," I said, "from a piece of wood, so I tan tarry my flad."

Reb Zyame teased me until I finally broke into tears. Then he softened, put down his work, took a piece of wood, whittled it here, cut it there—and it was soon finished.

Now I lacked only an apple and a candle, made of wax, of course, not of tallow. If tallow dripped on the apple, it would be ruined for eating because it would no longer be kosher. But wax was kosher.

Well, wax happens to be something I had more of than any other boy. In fact, if a boy needed any wax, to whom would he go for it? To me, of course! Because my father was the assistant sexton of the small study house of the Butcher's Synagogue, whatever was left of the candles after Yom Kippur belonged to him—that was his to keep. He would melt it down for Chanukah candles and Saturday night Havdalah candles or plain wax tapers.

What then dripped down from the Havdalah candles was mine to keep.

In short, I had everything that I needed!

G

I fastened the flag to the stick, stuck a red apple on its point and lit the wax candle on top of the apple and set out for the synagogue for Shemini Atzeres evening, the eighth day of Sukkos, for the *hakofes* procession around the synagogue. I was in the happiest frame of mind, feeling like a fortunate prince, the son of a king to whom no one is equal.

I imagined I was already in shul, seated up front in the eastern pew with all the wealthy children. Candles were burning brightly. My flag was nicer than all the other flags. My apple was redder than all the apples. My candle was larger than all the candles. The synagogue was tightly packed, the heat stifling. The women folk approached to kiss the Torah. Leading the procession, like a general-field marshal, was Reb Melekh, the cantor, his prayer shawl flying out behind him. Following him, the wealthy men of the town. Reb Melekh in his high, tinny vibrato voice warbled: "*O-zar da---lim, hoshea na!*—hel-per of the po-or and weak, sa-ave us!"

The women folk all leaped forward to kiss the Torah and shrieked in high-pitched voices, "May we all live till next year! May we all live till next year!" "The same to you! The same to you!"

But before reaching the small study house of the Butcher's Synagogue where I pray, you must first pass many other synagogues and study houses: the Cold Shul, the Litvish Shul, the Tailors' Shul, the Great Shul, the smaller study house, the Old study house, the First prayer house, the Chasidic prayer house, the *Misnaged* Shul, the New Shul, and the Yellow Shul—till finally you reached the Butcher's Synagogue, and then you walked down to the study house below.

All these study houses and synagogues I've just enumerated for you are not situated far from one another, as in Yehupetz. Here in Kasrilevka it's much more convenient. Here they are all jammed together on one street, on one small piece of earth, almost in one courtyard—and it is known as the *Shulhoif*—the Shul Square.

It was almost as if it were one big shul on our Shul Square. During the summer when the windows were open and you happened to walk by during services, so many different fragments of prayers and chanted texts would reach your ears that you didn't know what to do first: should you stop and rise on your toes three times for *k'dushah*, should you bow your head for a *borkhu*, or should you respond, "*Amen yehai sh'mai rabah*" for the mourner's prayer? While hearing from one side the singing of, "*Oz yishir moshe*—then Moses sang," someone on the other side could be heard shouting, "*E-kh---od*—the Lord is One!" Suddenly someone chimes in with a chant from the Gemorah: "*Mikhalel shehu tzarikh lifrat umifrat shehu tzarikh l'halel.*" But someone else interrupts with the chant, "*Yiskadal v'yiskadash sh'mai rabah*," part of the Kaddish. And now here's a third who comes out with still another chant, "*Hallelujah! Hallelujah!*"

Our shul square had two different moods: during the week it was entirely different from the way it was on Sabbaths and holidays. During the week it was a lively market-place for Jewish books, prayer shawls, ritual fringes, and *mezuzos*, ripe apples, unripe pears, sunflower seeds, and beans, poppy seed cookies, bagels, and sugar honeycakes. Goats sprawled on the ground, making themselves at home, chewing their cud as their little beards went up and down. But come the Sabbath and holidays—gone was the market, gone was the trading, gone were the goats. Jews, may they always thrive, gathered together in small groups, chatting and gossiping. They exchanged news of the week, of the year, and from the whole world. Schoolchildren of all grades ran, leaped about, and weaved in and out like fish in water; God had granted them a Sabbath gift—they were free! They checked out each others' new little kaftans to see whose was longer, compared holiday caps to see whose head was larger, and they measured with their fingers to see whose earlock was shorter. In the meantime, as usual, there would be enough jabs, pokes, and flicks on the nose—it was lively!

But the liveliest time of all was the evening of the eighth day of Sukkos, Shemini Atzeres, just before the procession, when all the schoolchildren from all grades gathered with their flags. They grouped themselves according to grade, the older boys separate from the younger boys. They checked out each others' flags to see whose stick was longer, whose apple redder, whose candle made of tallow or whose of wax. Along the way slurs, insults, and jokes were exchanged. One played a trick on another: this one blew out another's candle, another sneaked a bite of an apple, thereby earning himself a slap as a punishment—until it was time for each one to go to his own shul.

H

"*Mazel-tov*! Topele Tootaritoo has a flag! Greetings, *sholom aleykhem*, what a good Jew! Look how he's blushing . . ."

With that generous welcome I was greeted by my comrades when I arrived in the shul square holding my flag.

I checked out all the other flags and then glanced at my own. No question about it. No comparison. My flag won hands down.

First of all, there was the flag itself. No one else's was attached as straight as mine to its stick so that both sides of the flag could be seen. No one else's stick was as straight and smoothly carved as mine. No one else had such a red shiny apple. No one else had such a proper candle because no one else had as much wax as I. But who else got as many slaps and blows as I when I was caught by my father under the bench gathering the pieces of wax from the melted Yom Kippur candle stumps? As I compared my flag with all the other flags, my heart swelled with pride. I imagined I was growing taller and taller, bigger and broader, my legs floating along beneath me. I felt like laughing, shouting, dancing . . .

"Hey, let's see!" called out Yoylik, the rich man's son in astonishment.

He examined my flag. I examined his flag. 'Not much of a flag!' I thought to myself. 'Not much of a stick! As crooked as a pretzel!' I saw that he was boiling, but I pretended not to notice and looked off to the side.

"Kopel!" he said to me, "Where did you get that fine stick?"

"What?" I said and turned my face toward him.

"Where did you lay your hands," he said again, "on such a terrific stick?"

"What of it?" I said to him, "Do you want to trade it for your nail?"

Yoylik understood the dig. His eyes glinted, he sniffed, thrust his hands in his pockets and moved off. I watched him and gloated, full of satisfaction. I saw him as he called Nehemiah with the crooked leg to the side and whispered to him, winking in my direction. I saw very well what he was up to but I pretended not to notice. A moment later Nehemiah with the crooked leg came over to me, holding Yoylik's flag with the bent stick and said to me,

"Let me light my candle. Mine went out."

"Is it *your* flad?" I say to him, bending my flag with the candle to his, "I know whose flad that is . . ."

And before I knew what happened, Nehemiah touched his lit candle to my flag and in a twinkling it was on fire. My flag went up in flame, flickered, f-f-fu—my flag was no more!

* * *

Had a stone dropped on my head from the sky, had a wild beast attacked me and tried to devour me, had I seen a corpse in white shrouds in the middle of the night wanting to strangle me—my horror would not have been as great as it was when I saw my naked stick and the charred flag. A cry rent my heart:

"Oy vey, my flad! My flad! My flad! . . ."

The tears gushed from my eyes. The whole world turned black. The stick with the apple and the candle fell from my hands and I let myself run, whereto I did not know. I ran and wept hot, bitter tears. I wrung my hands and mourned my flag as one mourns a dead person. I came home, all alone, without a flag and crept into a dark corner where I sat, my head between my knees, and sobbed silently so that no one would see, no one would hear, and I questioned God,

"Why, why, God Almighty? Why did I deserve this? Why, oh why?"

EPILOGUE

You know, children, that all stories must come to a happy or sad ending. Most Jewish stories have sad endings. We have a saying that a Jew, and especially a poor one, can never enjoy anything. There's a lot to be said for that. When you grow up, you'll find out for yourselves. Meanwhile, I must tell you that the story about my flag did not end the way I just finished telling you. I suffered long and hard, lay in a burning fever, saw weird, strange images before my eyes, snakes and scorpions with fiery tongues, and wild animals in the form of humans. I heard crazy wild shrieks of cats and dragons. I tossed and ranted in a fever, was almost as good as gone. They thought I might not make it. In the small study house of the Butcher's Synagogue they had already begun to recite the psalms on my behalf. I was more dead than alive.

But as it is holiday eve, and at holiday time, especially on Simkhas Torah, we need to be happy, I also wish to end this story about my flag happily.

First of all, as you can see, with God's help, I did not die.

Second of all, know that the following year I had an even better flag, with a better stick, with a better apple. At the synagogue, I even sat up front in the eastern pew with all the rich children. The candle shone. My flag glowed. Jews marched in the procession. Reb Melekh the cantor with the flying prayer shawl went first, like a general-fieldmarshal. He warbled in his tinny, contralto voice, "*O-zar da—lim, hoshea na!*" The women folk kissed the Torahs, sprang before one's face and screamed, "May we all live another year! May we all live another year!" "The same to you! The same to you!"

Children, THE SAME TO YOU!

With King Ahashuerosh

A

When I was a little boy, do you know whom I envied most?

Ahashuerosh.

Not the Ahashuerosh who ruled over a hundred and twenty-seven provinces from India to Ethiopia. I mean Koppel the tailor wearing a gold crown, really a paper hat, and holding a long yellow broomstick for a scepter.

I also greatly envied Mordecai, the king's minister (Levi the shoemaker) with his coat turned inside-out and his tufted flaxen beard.

I envied Queen Vashti (Mottel the carpenter), a dress worn over his kaftan and a kerchief hiding his beard so he would look like a woman. And how can I forget Queen Esther (Ozar the assistant sexton) with his green apron? And how about Haman (Yosske the assistant), a clay pot on his head serving for a helmet?

But more than anyone I envied Feivel the orphan, who always wore a red shirt when he played the part of Joseph the Righteous in that wonderful play, "The Selling of Joseph," performed by the troupe. His brothers would rip off his red shirt, fling him into the lion's den, and Joseph the Righteous (Feivel, that is) would fall on his knees, clasp his hands in prayer, and implore the wild beasts not to hurt him as he sang a doleful song whose words touched the heart:

> Vipers and scorpions,
> Clamp your mouths shut!
> Clamp your mouths shut
> Know you not,
> Know you not,
> Know you not who I am
> I am Joseph the Righteous,
> Grandson of Isaac,
> Son of Jacob,
> Son of Jacob!

And though Joseph the Righteous was an orphan, a poor lad who made a home of sorts in the lower study house, living from hand-to-mouth, and I, a rich man's son, the grandson of Reb Meier, nevertheless I would gladly have traded places with him for just that one day of Purim.

When the long-awaited beloved day of Purim arrived, from early on in the morning I kept an eye out for the troupe of actors who were going from house to house, followed by a gang of kids running after them barefoot in the snow. Why couldn't I be part of that gang? No! I was forbidden because I was a rich man's son and Reb Meier's grandchild. I was obliged to keep to the house all day like a dog, and accompany the grownups to Grandfather Reb Meier's house for the Purim feast.

"Why are you walking as slow as molasses?" my father kept complaining as I spotted the troupe from afar on our way to Grandfather Reb Meier's Purim feast.

"You are, *kayn eyn horeh*, a big boy, you can walk a little faster!" urged my mother. "God willing, the Sabbath before Passover you'll be eight years old, may you live to be a hundred and twenty."

"Leave him alone, he wants to see the comedians!" piped up my elder brother, Moishe'le, who was also eager to stop and take in the actors.

"Go on, move a little faster!" said my teacher Reb Itzi, my nemesis, nudging me from behind.

I lowered my eyes and walked along with the others, absorbed in mournful thoughts: "Always I have to be with the grown-ups, always I have to be with the teacher! . . . Mornings, nights, Sabbath, and holidays! . . . May Reb Itzi's red, tobacco-stained nose fall off!"

B

My grandfather Reb Meier was the richest man in town. He lived like a king. He had a huge front room with enormous silver chandeliers hanging from the center of the ceiling. Elegant tapestries bedecked the walls. A large, heavy, silver candelabrum graced the table, holding many silvery candles that Grandmother Nehama displayed only twice a year—at the Passover seder and at the Purim feast. The candelabrum brightened every corner of the room.

At the head of the table, in a large green upholstered armchair, sat my Grandfather Reb Meier himself, a small man with a sparse beard, a slightly bent nose, silver hair, and dark, youthful eyes. He was garbed in a long, silk kaftan tied about the waist with a woven belt and wore the traditional holiday fur-trimmed hat on his head. In front of him on the table reposed an enormous, impressive braided Purim challah, risen high, sprinkled with saffron and studded with raisins.

Seated at the middle of the table was Grandmother Nehama, a tall woman and still quite attractive, looking regal in her gold-hued silken dress printed all over with white apples, wearing a jewel-ornamented headcloth, and exquisite pearls at her neck, as well as earrings and rings. In front of her was a huge platter with hot, sweet-smelling, sweet-and-peppery fish smothered in onions, raisins, and other spices. Grandmother served the fish, the fine silk kerchief tucked behind her ears with its two ends poking out, the diamonds and jewels sparkling and glittering as her face beamed and smiled.

All around the table sat the uncles and the aunts together with their children—boys and girls, each one named after the same grandmothers, grandfathers, uncles, and aunts. First there was Uncle Tzaduk and Aunt Tzivia and their three sons: Moishe'le, Hershe'le, and Velve'le, and two daughters: Sara'le and Foige'le. Next came Uncle Naftali and Aunt Dvoira'le with four sons: Moishe'le, Hershe'le, Velve'le, and Note'le, and three daughters: Sara'le, Foige'le, and Roche'le. And so on and on . . .

Enough of the family head count. Some people are superstitious about counting. Once, out of curiosity, Grandfather wanted to tally how many were seated at the table.

He picked up a silver beaker and pointing with it, began counting, "Not one, not two, not three, not four, not five, not six, not seven." Grandmother wrenched the beaker from his hand and wouldn't allow him to count further. "On my enemies' heads! What are you counting, hah? Thank God we have plates enough for everyone!"

Now that we were all gathered for the feast, Grandfather himself assigned our seats. Grandfather Reb Meier loved to have things neat and orderly—just so: an uncle sitting next to an uncle, an aunt next to an aunt, and we kids seated so that a brother would not sit next to a brother nor a sister next to a sister, because siblings are known to tease one another. So a Moishe'le had to sit next to a cousin Hershe'le, another Hershe'le sat next to a cousin Velve'le, another cousin Velve'le with his second cousin, Note'le, and so on. And the same went for the girls. I alone was left without a partner, so they seated me next to my nemesis, Reb Itzi. Reb Itzi was not only a scholar and a teacher, but also a tutor, a mentor, a sort of male governess meant to teach me manners—how to behave myself at the table and how to eat.

"When you sit at the table," my 'governess,' Reb Itzi, would lecture, "you must sit like a respectable person. You must look straight ahead, your hands must be folded on your lap, and you must not speak while eating. And when you eat noodles with soup, you must fill the spoon with as much noodles as soup. A sip of soup—and the spoon is laid down so you can wipe your lips. And again a sip of soup—and again the spoon is laid down and the lips wiped. Do not gulp one spoonful after another, like a peasant."

Reb Itzi seated himself next to me, made the blessing on the bread, removed a red handkerchief from his bosom pocket, and shook out the snuff right into my plate. Then he began to blow his nose with a loud snort that sounded for all the world like a shofar, winding up with the final *T'kiyah Gedola*—the long, powerful blast of the ram's horn—all the while keeping an eye on me to make sure I was sitting like a respectable person.

Shoshanas Ya-a-a-kov!

So Grandfather began singing in his very pleasant voice immediately after drinking the first glass of wine, snapping his fingers to the beat, and the assembled family followed with *Tzehala v'sameykha!* in all different voices, louder and louder. And my teacher, Reb Itzi, who had a small hooting voice like an owl, also chimed in, that is to say, he opened his mouth wide, shut his eyes, still keeping half an eye on me to make sure I was sitting like a respectable person, held his head a bit to the side, and kept time on the table with his middle finger—all to show Grandfather he was joining in the singing. Then came the part where you bless Mordecai and curse Haman, may one tenth of what we wish them both come true.

C

"The Purim players are here!" announced Tankhum the butler, a Jew wearing a red kaftan who always addressed everyone in the familiar way, except for Grandfather and Grandmother.

Hearing the words, "Purim players," we youngsters all sprang at once from our seats and were soon surrounding King Ahashuerosh in his gold crown.

"*Goot yontev,*" the troupe shouted joyfully, and lined up in two rows. On a golden chair sat King Ahashuerosh, while Memukhan (Chaim the coachman), hopped out on one leg singing a German tune:

A Persian I am, my name is Memukhan.
You can tell from my face that I'm not an old man.
In my sweet voice I sing
As on one foot I spring.
Ahashuerosh, the king, then inquires of Memukhan:
Memukhan, dear slave, please let me know,
Who in my kingdom is friend or foe?
Memukhan, the Persian, replies to the king:
Let King Ahashuerosh be pleased to observe
How some of his people neither bow nor serve.
Ahashuerosh, the king, waxed furious and wroth:
Who dares refuse to obey my commands
That I have commanded over all my lands?
Memukhan, the Persian, replied to the king:
He who keeps the Sabbath and wears a gaberdine,
He who circumcises sons—the cursed Jew, that fiend!
Ahashuerosh, the king, commanded Memukhan, the Persian:
If such are his crimes, bring him here to me,
We will soon see him hung from the highest tree!
Memukhan, the Persian, sang in a loud voice:
Hurry, hurry, hurry, brother Mondrish, you have no choice!
In came Mondrish with his tufted beard and began reciting his lineage to Ahashuerosh the king:

"Abraham, Isaac, and Jacob were my ancestors, and the
    613 commandments are my witnesses."
He let out in song:
    Woe, woe unto our Jewish souls,
    Haman, that bag of wind, is building hanging poles!

* * *

"Aren't you Joseph the Righteous?" I said to Feivel the
orphan, who was standing to one side with a tired, mournful face.

"Joseph the Righteous," Feivel confirmed.

"Are you also going to perform?" I asked.

"If they ask me to, I will," said Joseph the Righteous
and bent down to whisper in my ear: "Get me a piece of
your Purim challah."

"They'll catch me and then they'll be mad," I replied
in a whisper.

"Tear it off so nobody will see," he said, his eyes aglow.

"Steal it?"

"You call that stealing?" he countered.

"What else do you call it? Borrowing?"

"I'm starved," he said in a whisper, devouring the
bread with his eyes, "haven't had anything to eat since early
morning."

While the crowd was absorbed in the Purim play, I
snuck over to the table, and lowering my hand and making sure not to be seen, I tore off a piece of challah and
passed it into his hand. Joseph the Righteous craftily slipped
the piece of bread into his pocket and gratefully squeezed
my hand.

"You're a good fellow. May God give you the best of
everything!"

D

"Would you like us to put on 'M'khiras Yosef—The Sale of Joseph,' for you too?" said King Ahashuerosh, removing his gold crown and donning an ordinary hat.

"Enough! Enough!" said Grandfather, as he placed a silver coin in King Ahashuerosh's palm and asked Tankhum the butler to sweep away the mud the comedy troupe had tracked in. A commotion ensued in the room as chairs were moved back in place, and while the family was finding their seats again, I snuck out for a moment to see the troupe off.

"Come!" Joseph the Righteous said to me, taking me by the hand. "Listen to me, come along with us. I like you, you're a great kid, a fine lad."

"Where to?" I asked, my heart pounding.

"To King Ahashuerosh's," he said. "We're through performing for today. Now we're going to King Ahashuerosh's for our Purim feast."

Joseph the Righteous took my hand and we leaped across the mud.

Night was drawing closer and closer, and the mud became deeper and deeper. I imagined I had wings, I was being wafted in the air. I felt I was flying, floating . . .

"I'm afraid," I said to Joseph the Righteous, squeezing his hand more tightly.

"What is there to be afraid of, silly?" he consoled me as he chewed the piece of challah I had given him. "There's a feast waiting, silly. You'll hear us sing songs. Yum, what delicious challah! Out of this world! Melts in your mouth like butter! I can't understand how you can see this wonder before you without gobbling it all up."

"What's so special about it?" I said disdainfully, "At our house we eat challah all week long."

"Every day challah?" said Joseph the Righteous, licking his chops. "And meat, too?"

"Every day!" I said.

"Every day?" he said, swallowing, "I only eat meat once a week, on the Sabbath, and not every Sabbath at that because I'm not always invited to eat at a rich family's table every week. And if, with God's help, I wind up at a poor man's table, I eat aches and pains."

"What do you mean you eat aches and pains?" I asked.

"You don't know about aches and pains? You eat worms," he explained. "There's nothing to eat so you eat worms. I survive on handouts. Ozer, the sexton, long may he live, helps me out when he can, sometimes with a crust of bread, sometimes with a little potato. Ozer is a fine man, a jewel of a soul! Do you know him? He plays Queen Esther."

"Where is your father?" I asked.

"I don't have a father."

"Where is your mother?"

"I don't have a mother."

"Your grandfather? Your grandmother?"

"I don't have a grandfather, I don't have a grandmother."

"An uncle? An aunt?"

"I don't have an uncle, I don't have an aunt."

"A brother? A sister?"

"I don't have a brother, I don't have a sister. I have no one, no one, I'm an orphan is what I am!"

I glanced at his face and at the moon, and I imagined that he and the moon were the same color. I moved closer to him and we ran after the troupe, our little legs carrying us along.

E

"This is where King Ahashuerosh lives," said Joseph the Righteous and we stepped down into a small, dark hovel with an earth-covered floor.

"Freide-Ettl, sleepy head, get yourself out of bed!" King Ahashuerosh called to his wife, a sickly, tubercular woman who clutched her head with one hand and her heart with the other whenever she coughed. The troupe had spent most of the day singing and were so accustomed to rhyming that it was impossible for them to speak without rhyming.

"Bring in the fish, that delectable dish!" said Memu-khan. "There's bread enough, so enjoy the stuff, and three-cornered haman-toshn that are good for noshin', Purim puddings and cakes, the best anyone makes, and a flask of whisky to make you frisky."

"Mondrish, untie the sack that's on your back, or I'll tweak your cheek!"

"Instead of a tweak of the cheek, let's eat till we're weak," said Mondrish tossing off a triple rhyme.

"You're eating as if everything is sweet as honey, and in the meantime you've forgotten the money!" said Vashti.

"Vashti is no fool, it's the money that counts as a rule!" cried Haman.

But when it came to dividing the money, they stopped their rhyming and spoke plain, as people do when it's a matter of money. The largest portion went, naturally, to King Ahashuerosh. That was the custom with them every year. But when it came to the other troupe members, a bit of a quarrel broke out. Memukhan wondered why Vashti got more than he did. He, Memukhan, had to work harder than anyone, hopping about on one foot, sprinkling his speech with impromptu rhymes. But when the money was divvied up, Vashti suddenly was the star! How come? Because he and King Ahashuerosh were bosom buddies—a tailor and a carpenter always see eye to eye . . .

"Be quiet!" King Ahashuerosh chastised them both, "You no-good coachman, you horse-whipper, you wagon-greaser, you broken axle, you splintered spoke, you cracked bolt, you yoked ox! You have the nerve to contradict King Ahashuerosh? I'll paste you in the mouth so hard your teeth will be knocked out!"

Memukhan was silenced. The artists respected King Ahashuerosh because he was the director of the troupe, the entrepreneur. Mondrish was still grumbling under his breath, as were the others. Only Queen Esther dropped his few coins into his pocket, making light of the situation, and the troupe again became lively and cheerful and were soon speaking again in rhyme.

"May the rich earn as much in their lives as we will be able to bring home to our wives!" said Memukhan.

I looked around King Ahashuerosh's dwelling. In the center stood a large table covered with a coarse, dark cloth. On one side was a workbench and tools, on the other side was a wooden bed piled with many pillows reaching almost to the ceiling. Opposite the oven stood a cot upon which a black tomcat lay snoozing, its paws tucked under its body. From the top of the oven peered out several little pairs of black, gray, and blue eyes.

"Come down, you scamps!" said Joseph the Righteous, wagging his finger at the eyes. No further invitation was needed. The owners of the black, gray, and blue eyes slid down one at a time from the top of the oven. Their torn shirts barely reached below the bellybutton. Joseph the Righteous was apparently quite a familiar figure to them because the barely-clad children came up to him like little lambs and bent their curly heads for him to stroke.

"Are you hungry?" Joseph the Righteous said to them, "We'll soon be eating. We've brought you lots of goodies to eat."

And he listed for them all the goodies they had brought back and the little lambs looked at one another, their mouths watering in anticipation. And Joseph the Righteous stroked their curly heads as his own mouth watered in anticipation as well. They were all growing impatient to begin feasting. God answered their prayers as King Ahashuerosh raised a flask, poured himself a tumbler of whisky and drank the first gulp in honor of the blessed Purim holiday. All the others followed suit, downing tumblers of whisky, after which they seated themselves at the table, everyone, young and old, except Freide-Ettl, who was busy cooking at the oven. Even the black tomcat awoke, arched his back as he yawned, sidled up to the table, and stood by in the hope there might be a crumb or two for him from the feast. Joseph the Righteous and I and the half-naked little lambs with their curly heads sat ourselves on a long, wobbly bench which made the children laugh as if it were the greatest comedy in the world. At this point the troupe noticed me for the first time and wondered who this new, unfamiliar person was.

"Who is that little gooseberry?" asked King Ahashuerosh.

Joseph the Righteous explained to them who I was and how I had come there. His story tickled the crowd. Everyone came up to me, clapped me on the back, pinched my cheek, and said something to me, in rhyme, of course, and soon the feast began. Freide-Ettl brought over from the oven a tray of highly seasoned fish with roasted potatoes, and though they weren't as richly spiced as those at my Grandfather Reb Meier's, they were nevertheless quite tasty. The only fault was that the fish was very bony! What pleased me most was that everyone ate from the same platter, making for a very lively time as each person jabbed his fork into the food! After the fish, the troupe began sipping more whisky and toasting *l'khayim*, and things really livened up. They rose from the table, joined hands, and began to dance and sing:

> What we are
> Is what we are,
> Jews we are,
> That's what we are!
> What we have
> Is what we have,
> It's troubles we have,
> That's what we have.

"Sing another one!" shouted Mondrish, "Let's hear another one!"

And the troupe sang a Russian song, dancing and clapping their hands:

> *Nado znot*—You need to know
> *Kok gulyat!*—How to take a walk!

Pered bogom—Before God
Otvetshot!—To Answer!
Mi pyom, mi gulyayem,—We sing, we walk,
You are the King, live and be great!
Let us, Jews, drink *l'khayim!*
Next year in *Yerushelayim!*

"Say, isn't this the life?" said Joseph the Righteous, who by now had satisfied his hunger and felt like a new person. He drank some more whisky, offered me some, and pulled me into the circle to dance. I don't know why I was feeling so overjoyed, but I was truly elated. I felt happy, infinitely happy! When suddenly . . .

F

Suddenly the door opened and there stood my father with my teacher, Reb Itzi. The world darkened before my eyes. What my father must have thought when he saw me dancing with the troupe in the circle, I will never know. I only saw him standing there frozen in his tracks, staring at me, at the troupe, and at the rabbi. The rabbi glared at me, at the troupe, and at my father. I looked at my father, at the troupe, and at the rabbi and the troupe stared at my father, at the rabbi, and at me. No one could utter a word. It was Memukhan who stepped forward with a rhyme, as was his way.

"Why are you all looking with such dismay? Don't you know today is a holiday? A big tumbler of whisky is what we need. And the bigger the better, yes indeed! Eat up your pastries, a treat for a King, for who knows what tomorrow will bring!"

And Memukhan brought my father a tumbler of whisky and a piece of cake. My father pushed him away without a word. Memukhan's feelings weren't hurt in the least and he went on,

"My lord Reb Asher, son of Reb Meier! Don't you know me, the Purim player? Then I will have to drink alone. Amen I say to everyone!"

And Memukhan drained his tumbler of whisky and sang:

> The poorer they are
> The more they revel,
> The richer they are
> The more they drink!
>
> The poorer they are
> The more they sing,
> The richer they are
> The more they're mean!

"Mondrish, say something! Recite a blessing for our wealthy visitors from town and let's drink in their honor!"

And Mondrish poured himself a glass of whisky and recited a blessing in honor of the wealthy visitors from town,

"Here's to your health! May you always have wealth! May worms eat you, but nothing defeat you! God forget you, nothing fret you! Drunk as a skunk, etc.!"

"Why don't you say something, Reb Asher'l" said Reb Itzi, taking a deep snort of snuff and snapping his fingers.

"Can't you see they're all drunk?" said my father, beside himself with rage, grabbing me by the hand so tightly that it hurt. The three of us left King Ahashuerosh's house without so much as a farewell and once outside, my father stopped, looked sternly at me, and let me have two smart slaps.

"This," he said, "is just a down payment. The rest you will collect from your teacher when we get home. Listen carefully, Reb Itzi! I am putting him in your hands! You can do whatever you wish with him—let him learn his lesson! Let the blood flow! A boy almost nine years old! Let him remember what it's like to chase after Purim players, comedians, low-life! Ruining everyone's holiday!"

I didn't shed a tear but I felt my cheek flaming while my heart felt heavy as a stone. I wasn't even thinking of the punishment I would be receiving at home from Reb Itzi. My mind was elsewhere. My thoughts were with King Ahashuerosh, with Joseph the Righteous, with the little half-naked lambs with their curly heads, and in my ears I could not stop hearing the sound of that sweet Russian song:

> You need to know
> How to take a walk!
> Before God
> To answer!
> We sing, we walk,
> You are the King, live and be great!
> Let us, Jews, drink *l'khayim*!
> Next year in *Yerushelayim*!

Lag B'Omer

A

hildren, come here, I have great news for you!" said our rebbe Reb Yudel Angel of Death the day before Lag B'Omer and we perked up our ears to hear what great news our rebbe had for us.

I see, children, that you want me first to describe my rebbe, to tell you what he looked like—and I will, but only if you don't press me to tell you how he came to be called Angel of Death. A clever boy would figure it out for himself: it was because we feared him as much as the Angel of Death. But then you will ask *why* did we fear him as much as the Angel of Death? It was because he used to whip us till the blood ran. Well, why did he whip us till the blood ran? We probably deserved it; we didn't want to study. Why didn't we want to study? We were probably great trouble-makers. I tell you, it's a long story. He was called "Reb Yudel Angel of Death" and you can be sure he earned that title honestly, although in appearance he didn't look like an Angel of Death at all. He was slight, short, dried-up like a fig. His face was the dark greenish-yellow color of last year's Sukkos palm branch, and lined like a matzo. His cheeks were sunken and a little goatee barely sprouted from his chin, and even that in patches. The nose, I tell you, was rather large, starting off thin and ending up thick and bent like a ram's horn. And his Adam's apple, like a knob, slid up and down as if a mouse were scurrying around in there.

"What day do we have tomorrow?" the rebbe intoned in a sing-song, inclining his head and shutting one eye.

"Lag B'Om—er!" we all shouted in unison, like little goats who cry, "Meh-eh-eh!"

"When is Lag B'Omer?" he continued in the same chant.

"Thirty-three days before Shevuos," we answered.

"What do schoolboys do on Lag B'Omer?"

"Schoolboys get together and have a picnic on Lag B'Omer."

"What else do you do on Lag B'Omer?"

"You arm yourselves with bows and arrows and sling-shots, and you go singing into battle far, far beyond the village."

"That's the way," said the rebbe and opened his eye. "That's the way I like you! That's the way to be good boys! And that's why I am letting you free for almost a day and a half."

Hearing the word "free," followed by, "a day and a half," we were all about to spring from our seats ready to run home. But one look from the rebbe's little eyes was enough to glue us to our seats.

"Aha!" said the rebbe, now with a different intonation, "Just look at that! Ready to make a run for it! You just hear the word 'free' and already you've forgotten what school means and are ready to jump up like wild goats—hutz-hutz-hutz! I'm warning you, if you dare . . . you know very well what I mean? If I see one of you with a tear in his kaftan, or a scratch on his face, or any sign of mischief, I will give you . . ."

Reb Yudel removed his little whip from the cabinet and said to us, "Do you know what, children? Why waste words? Why lecture? Why threaten?—Nonsense! You will *certainly* not obey me and then I will *certainly* have to whip you. I'll tell you what, just lie down, one at a time, let me give you a few lashes in advance, alright? And what if it isn't enough? Don't worry, after Lag B'Omer you can be sure I'll make up the difference. So, children, don't dilly-dally, I beg you, start unbuttoning your trousers, it's a shame to waste time, time doesn't stand still!"

And the rebbe examined the strands of the little whip quite calmly, as one might examine, let us say, the tassels of the under prayer shawl on the eve of the Sabbath, first straightening them out, then testing them out in the air. Then he rose from his seat, approached the long bench, took a deep sniff of snuff, and was ready to go to work. We didn't wait too long to be asked, like Isaac when Abraham our Patriarch led him to the sacrificial altar. We stood up one at a time, went over to the bench, pulled down our trousers, and lay down quietly, without a word, shirts up, faces down, as if saying: "Here, dear rebbe, is what you asked for."

"That's the way I like you, Yossele!" said the rebbe to me as he applied a few light swipes because I was the first one to lie down. "That's the way, little kitten: one . . . two . . . three . . . four . . . five . . . you see? See, when the rebbe gives you a thrashing, you become an altogether different person. Now, Mottele," he said to my brother, Mottel, "Come here! I love these Yosseles and Motteles because you don't have to beg them. When you tell them 'Lie down,' they lie down. Shmulik'l, my soul, lie down, lie down, silly, it won't last long! The Jewish diaspora should last as long! And you, Leybe'nyu, what's taking you so long to unbutton yourself? Make it quick! Avrem'ele, my dear, I owe you a few from yesterday. We'll be even now. Shimele! How is that goat you were riding? Did you think I forgot? Little Hershl! Tell Big Hershl to do us a favor and please roll up his shirt. Don't worry, there are only males here. Come on over here, Topele Tootaritoo! Don't feel bad that you're the last one. Your father, the sexton, isn't accustomed to greater honors . . ."

Having finished whipping Kopel, the rebbe straightened up, placed his thumb on his Adam's apple like a cantor, and sang out in the chant in which they call the groom to the altar, warbling away just like Hersh-Ber the cantor:

"*Ya-amod ha-khosn yom-tov Lipman b'reb Sholom-Isaac maf-tir*!—Rise up, O bridegroom, this happy day, Lipman son of Sholom-Isaac, to recite the Maftir prayer! It's all right, don't be embarrassed, Reb Lipa, you're a *bar-mitzvah* boy already and engaged to be married, too, with a pocketwatch and a silver watchcase, but one thing has nothing to do with another. In honor of Lag B'Omer please be so kind and lie right down here on the bench. I certainly won't hurt you, God forbid, I'll just whip you some, nothing more! I promise you that by your wedding day it will be healed. Lipa, lie still, Lipa, don't make a fuss, I don't have the strength to fuss with a big lad like you! That's the way, you'll be fine! Now button up real good, children, wash your hands, pray the *minkha* evening service, and go on home. But quietly, nicely, well-behaved, the way I like it. And, God willing, the day after tomorrow bright and early you will all be right here in place, everything in order as it should be! Do you hear what I'm saying to you? If I see so much as a speck, a hair out of place!! Good night, be well, and have a happy holiday!

B

On the following morning, God brought forth the sun from its butterbarrel and granted us a beautiful, bright, joyous summer day, one of those beautiful, bright summer days that even in dark, bleak Kasrilevka, lying near Lake Shtunkayla, the air is fragrant, fresh, and delightful. The sky was pale blue. The birds sang. One longed to be out-of-doors in the fresh air. One was drawn to be out there, far, far from the muddy town, where a blade of grass sprouted, where the trees were covered with little green leaves, where God's birds danced and hopped, chirped and warbled. That morning my brother, Mottel, and I made sure to wake up early, sped through our prayers, grabbed our lunches, and ran off to Lipa Sholom-Isaac's. Why to Lipa Sholom-Isaac's? Because, first of all, Lipa Sholom-Isaac's was the oldest of the students, a *bar mitzvah* boy and engaged to be married as well, with a pocketwatch and a silver watchcase; and second of all, there was a large courtyard nearby where we always spent Friday afternoons, hopping around on one foot, playing *Kutzibaba, Ekakh and Mekakh, Kamerkamerhoiz,* and Hide-and-go-seek.

When my brother and I arrived at Lipa Sholom-Isaac's, we found the whole gang already there (altogether we were forty-four of us, students from two classes: Reb Yudel Angel of Death's and Reb Efraim Talin's).

"Here come the 'Yosseles' and the 'Motteles'! Show us, what did you bring?" said Lipa Sholom-Isaac's and began unwrapping the packages each of us had brought for the picnic, describing out loud each contribution and calling out our names in rhyme:

"Mendl-fendl, show us what you've got there! Two egg bagels, a piece of honey cake, an egg, and six groshen."

"Itzik-shpitzik, nodl-teshl! Go to the store, get some more! I see here, *kayn eyn horeh,* a treasure: two kikhl, three eggs, a piece of dried kishka, some sugar cookies, an almond bagel, a bunch of hazel nuts—aha! And ten groshen, ·too, as I am a Jew!"

"Yenkele-benkele-fleshele—bul-bul-bul! Show us what you have, you're no fool: a whole roll, a quarter chicken, some goose fat, too. What's this? A flask of mead? You little devil you, that's what we all need!"

"Moish'ele-shtois'ele, knock on the door. Old women are sleeping, hear them snore? Come over here, did you bring whisky? I love you, because who ever heard of a picnic without whisky?"

"Ovi-futter, Kalman-tutter, tutter-Kalman, Shnayur-Zalman, Zalman-Shnayur, say your prayers! Show us, show us, don't be ashamed! Only half an egg? A little piece of bread and honey? A rusty coin, too? All right, give it here, it doesn't matter! We're all partners in the Lag B'Omer picnic!"

"Topele Tootaritoo! What have you dot there? A topet and a roll and a piece of darlic? Why did your mother dive you so little?" Lipa Sholom-Isaac's mimicked Kopel's speech defect as the boys roared with laughter, and even Kopel laughed along with them.

"Yoylik-Baylik has brought the most, let's all give him a great big toast! You're a rich man's son, you must surely have a whole treasure of eggs and fat, wine and whisky and plenty of good things! So, was I right? Two rolls, a half of a roasted duck, oho! A score of eggs, and tea and sugar. Here we have nuts, carob, raisins and almonds, oranges and a lemon too—God bless your soul! Come here, let me at least thank you!"

Yoylik, the rich man's son, approached proudly, his hands in his pockets, and Lipa Sholom-Isaac's granted him a smart flick on the nose. Laughter broke out.

"Now, kids, spread yourselves out on these logs," said Lipa Sholom-Isaac's. "Let's get to work on the picnic! Eat and enjoy and 'be well,' as our rebbe says when he's whipping us. Who has a tumbler? Give it here, let's make a toast! *L'khayim, meylekh*! When you drink, you're happy! *L'khayim*, Noah! From whisky you get strength! Come here, Nissl, take a little whisky! *L'khayim*, Shepsl, take a swallow! *L'khayim*, Abraham-Moishe! Enjoy a large tumblerful! *L'khayim*, Topele! May it dive you health and luck and everything dood! Empty your dlass or I'll dive you what for!"

We all laughed, and Kopel himself laughed too.

"Kids! Tell me, where are we going this year?" said Lipa Sholom-Isaac's after the picnic.

There was a racket, a din. Everyone shouted out his preference.

"To the other side of the cemetery!" said Melekh, the widow's son.

"To the slaughterhouse!" said Noah, the ritual slaughterer's boy.

"To the brickyard!" cried Avraham-Moishe, the mason's son in a high voice.

"To the brickyard! To the brickyard!" several other voices joined in.

"What about the dogs, have you forgotten?" chimed in Nissl, a pale lad, with a terrified look.

"Who cares about them? Who's afraid of dogs?" said Yoylik, the rich man's son, boldly.

"You! You're scared to death of a dog!" broke in Dovidl-harelip.

"Not only of a dog, of a cat!" chimed in Shepsl, a boy with a strawberry mark on his cheek, and the gang broke into laughter.

Yoylik, the rich man's son, became furious, went over to Shepsl with the strawberry mark and waved his fist under his nose; for this he received a jab in the side from Dovidl-harelip; he jabbed back; in no time at all he was being hit from all sides. Any other time no one would have dared take it upon himself to stand up to a rich man's son, but on Lag B'Omer it didn't matter, on Lag B'Omer we were free.

"Quiet!" shouted Lipa Sholom-Isaac's. "Enough fighting! Do you know where we should go this Lag B'Omer?"

"Where? Where?"

"To Galaganovka!"

"To Galaganovka! To Galaganovka!" they all shouted in one voice, and even Kopel Kookarikoo added in his high-pitched voice, "Daladanovta! Daladanovta!"

And it was decided we would go to Galaganovka.

C

Galaganovka was a little village not far from Kasrilevka. If you were going to our Kasrilevka, you first had to drive through that little village; when you drove through that village, you usually came across a band of little gentile boys wearing large hats, who chased after your wagon throwing stones, turned their dogs loose on you, and grimaced wildly while chanting a nasty song:

> Zhid, zhid, scum of the earth!
> You've lost a shoe!
> So I went,
> And found it,
> Picked it up,
> And went my way!

And although those words made no sense whatsoever, nevertheless they made you very resentful; not so much the words themselves as their jeering laughter; and not so much their jeering as the stones they threw; and not so much the stones they threw as the dogs they turned loose on you.

"But what will we do," another of us asked, "if, God forbid, the gentile boys attack us?"

"What do we care about gentile boys," said Lipa Sholom-Isaac's, "when we are forty-four strong, armed with weapons, with bows and arrows and slingshots and with sticks as well? Let them dare attack *us*!"

"We'll show them who we are!" said Yoylik, the rich man's son, who had already forgotten that he had just been ridiculed and punched.

"We will be the 'Sons of Israel,' and they will be the 'Philistines'," said my brother, Mottel, coming up with a bright idea that pleased everyone.

"If you listen to *me*," suggested Chayim, a Gemorah student from Reb Efraim Talin's class, "we should divide into two armies: one army will be called 'Yehuda,' and the other, 'Efraim.' Let Lipa Sholom-Isaac's be the leader of the 'Yehuda' army, Yudel Angel of Death's class, and Mendl-Loshek will be the leader of the 'Efraim' army, Efraim Talin's class."

"Right, as I am a Jew!" agreed several others. "Our Patriarch, Jacob, when he went to war against Esau, also did it that way. He figured that if the enemy attacked and defeated one army, the other army could retreat."

"No one, no one will retreat!" declared Lipa Sholom-Isaac's. "We will destroy the 'Philistines,' drive them out! Gang, take your weapons and let's get the 'Philistines'!"

"Let's sing a song, kids!"

"A song, a song!"

"What song shall we sing?"

They sang an old Russian song:

Roz, dva, tri! Poydem, poydem na kvatiru!—One, two, three!
Akhter, bakhter, kolishka! Vasmum dyengi rabushka!—Split! Chop!

"Feh, feh! A Jewish song! A Jewish song!"

And Noah, the slaughterer's son, sang out in a sweet voice, a combination of Yiddish and Russian:

Skazal pan-bog do Yaakov—Said God to Yaakov
Al tirah, evdi Yaakov—Don't be afraid, my slave Yaakov!

Nye pugasya, barin Yaakov!—Don't be afraid, my faithful
 Yaakov!

And we all joined in cheerfully in Russian:

Nyet, nyet, nitshavo—No, no, nothing,
Nye boymsya nikavo—We aren't afraid of anyone
Tolko boga adnavo!—Only of God!

D

"Now where do we find some 'Philistines'?" called out
Yoylik, the rich man's boy, drawing his bow.
　"I will take revenge on them!" said Yenkl, and prepared his slingshot.
　"Make a shambles of them!" cried Chaim and raised
his stick.
　"Tear them in two!" added Avraham-Moishe, demon-
strating with his hands how he would tear a 'Philistine' in
two.
　"Quiet, kids!" one of us called out. "I see a 'Philistine'
riding towards us with a pair of oxen!"
　A peasant was driving from the village to town, sitting
calmly on his wagon, wearing a large felt hat and smoking
a pipe, waving his whip as he urged the oxen on, "*Hei, hei,
sub solovay!*"—Hey, my nightingale.
　"Children! Draw your bows!" commanded Lipa
Sholom-Isaac's to the 'Yehuda' army.
　"Children! Aim your slingshots at the 'Philistine'!"
commanded Mendl-Loshek to the 'Efraim' army.

We drew our bows and aimed our slingshots, and Noah, the slaughterer's boy, sang out, again in Yiddish and Russian:

Bukhur reb Yaakov—God chose Yaakov
Izbral pan-bog b'Yaakov—God chose Yaakov
Al tirah, ovdi Yaakov—Don't be afraid, my slave Yaakov.
Nye pugaysya, barin Yaakov!—Don't be afraid, my faithful
Yaakov.

And we all joined in cheerfully in Russian:

> *Nyet, nyet, nitshavo,*
> *Nye boymsya nikavo,*
> *Tolko boga adnavo!*

The 'Philistine' was apparently very frightened of our two armies; he removed his hat, crossed himself three times, spat, and called out to us in a deep voice:

"What are you doing here, unbaptized, accursed little Jews?" and with this blessing he was about to leap from the wagon with his whip and wage war with us.

"Listen to me. Let's leave this 'Philistine' alone!" said Yoylik, the rich man's son. "What has he done to us? We're supposed to wage war with the little 'Philistines' . . ."

"Right you are, as I am a Jew, right!" we all shouted out happily, girded our loins and ran off, like heroes, singing the same song:

Gal d' et Yaakov—God saved Yaakov
Spasal pan-bog et Yaakov—God saved Yaakov
Al tirah, evdi Yaakov—Don't be afraid, my slave, Yaakov.

Nye pugaysya, barin Yaakov!—Don't be afraid, my faithful Yaakov.

And we all sang along in Russian;

> *Nyet, nyet, nitshavo,*
> *Nye boymsya nikavo,*
> *Tolko boga adnavo*!

"Now, children, let's sit down and rest a bit!" ordered our two generals, Lipa Sholom-Isaac's and Mendl-Loshek. We rolled up the hems of our little kaftans and sat down in the field, on the green grass, stretching ourselves out. We lay there looking up at the clear blue sky where tufts of clouds were scudding by, white as silver and thin as smoke, where a long row of birds glided silently, dipped in the deep sky and vanished.

"Where do you think those birds vanished to?" one of the boys asked another, looking up at the sky.

"They've stopped off on top of Mount Ararat," the other boy answered him, as if he knew this for certain.

"How come Ararat?" the first boy asked with great curiosity.

"Because Ararat is the highest of all mountains!" the other one answered, like a person who knows everything there is to know in the world.

I lay and listened to the words of the two boys and I wondered how it was possible that Ararat could be nearby. Ararat was in Israel and we were far from Israel! But I quickly answered my own question with a new question: What about the 'Philistines'? The 'Philistines' were also over there but we were still going after the 'Philistines' here.

Those two talkative boys did not stop chatting to each other. One asked, the other answered.

"What will happen afterwards if we defeat the 'Philistines'?"

"What do you think should happen?"

"I mean, what will we do with their land?"

"What do you think we should do?"

"I mean, should we 'lay waste' to their land, 'scorch' their town and 'put to the sword' their women and little children?"

"Why should we scorch towns? And what do you have against those poor little children?"

"But, that's what's written in the Holy Book!"

"Some example! That was long ago, and this is now! It will be enough that we impose a tax on them and that they pay us."

The talk between the two lads, the soft, warm breeze, the blue sky, the green grass and the smell of the earth cast a spell over us of such sweetness that a delicious languor suffused our every limb. We would have lain there like that all day had not one of the boys leaped up with a cry:

"'Philistines'! Philistines'!"

E

We sprang to our feet and saw before us a flock of sheep and several young shepherds holding large staffs, standing next to us, looking us over, and discussing us in their language:

"What is this, Horitziu?"

"Looks like little devils."

"No, they're Kasrilevka Jewish kids."

"Jews—what do you know."

"And look, they've got sticks!"

"Come on, gang, let's get them!"

"Set the dogs loose on them!"

"Let's go, gang!"

"Hey, gang, gang!"

"Why don't you do something, kids?" called out our two generals, as we set our bows and arrows and aimed our slingshots, as Noah sang:

Derekh kokhav m'Yaakov—A star rose from Yaakov
Vzoshla zvyezda iz Yaakov—A star rose from Yaakov
Al tirah, ovdi Yaakov—Don't be afraid, my slave Yaakov.
Nye pugaysya, barin Yaakov!—Don't be afraid, my faithful
    Yaakov!

And we sang along out loud:

> *Nyet, nyet nitshavo,*
> *Nye boymsya nikavo,*
> *Tolko boga adnavo!*

The war between the "Sons of Israel" and the "Philistines" had begun.

* * *

Don't press me, Jewish children, to tell you how the war between the "Sons of Israel" and the "Philistines" came out! Don't ask me which side won. Why should you aggravate me? I can only assure you that the "Sons of Israel" fought like lions, ran like deer, and fought with devotion like true heroes, so that even Topele Tootaritoo sprang into the fire, as if possessed, crying out at the top of his little voice:

"Tids! Dive it to them! Till them! So they won't fordet us!"

But, oy vey, what could the lamentable "Sons of Israel" do when we were attacked by the dogs, the "Philistines'" dogs, who devastated us, destroyed our armies so that the "Sons of Israel" were forced to retreat in disgrace (the first to run was Yoylik the rich man's son, like a shot!), not so much from the "Philistines," but from their dogs, who chased after us till we reached the town. Alas, all that re-mained of our two armies was one tattered army! We no longer sang, "*Al tirah ovdi Yaakov, nye pugaysya barin Yaakov.*" No! We were now singing a different tune. We were screaming, "Help, God in heaven!! Save us! *Sh'ma Yisroel!!!*"

F

We arrived home late, about the time for evening prayer, and stole in, my brother, Mottel, and I, one at a time and sat down in a corner, quiet as doves so they would not, God forbid, see our wounds, our besmeared kaftans. But just our luck, who should be there visiting us but our Aunt Reyzl from Yampeli. Imagine that! We had seen neither hide nor hair of her for almost a year and a half!

"Yossel! Mottel!" Mother called us, "Aunt Reyzl's here!"

We didn't stir.

"Where are you?" cried Mother, "Why have you hid-den yourselves?"

We didn't make a sound.

Mother approached, saw us, and clapped her hands together:

"I am thunderstruck! I am shocked! Yerakhmiel, where are you? Come over here and you'll really see quite a sight!"

My father came over. He was a sickly man who as long as I could remember, always coughed. He stood there looking at us from head to toe and then the grilling began: Where had we been? What had we done? With whom had we been fighting? We stood there, my brother Mottel and I, looking down at the ground, wishing the earth would open and swallow us so we would be rid of all these troubles. And my father kept grilling us:

"So, tell me, where were you? What did you do? With whom were you fighting?"

And Mother stood to the side nagging him:

"Some father! Can't even say an angry word! In some families the father smacks and thrashes so a child will know for the next time! He should feel it! He should remember!"

But father didn't beat us. He never beat us. He only punished us with words. He didn't stop asking: What will become of you? He was eating his heart out. He began coughing and said we would shorten his days. We wept quietly, never speaking so much as a word.

"Wait! Wait!" my mother said to us, "Tomorrow, if we live so long, I'll report this to the rebbe!"

* * *

When we arrived at school the following morning after Lag B'Omer, my mother was already there with several other mothers who had come to give the rebbe a report. And the rebbe, Reb Yudel Angel of Death, did not have to be asked too long and executed a sentence on us all with a generous hand as he had promised, making sure not to overlook anyone. And when it was Lipa Sholom-Isaac's turn, he had to wrestle with him for a long time, forcing him to accept his punishment. Lipa, a *bar mitzvah* boy and a soon-to-be bridegroom with a pocketwatch and a silver watchcase, was under no circumstances going to lie down in front of the women—and Lipa got his way: the women left and the rebbe gave him over fifty lashes.

From then on we swore, and to you, children, I say the same, never, never wage war against the "Philistines"!

Greens for Shevuos

A

On the day before Shevuos I begged my mother, may she rest in peace, to let me go by myself beyond the edge of the town to gather greens for the festival. And she did! May God grant her eternal Paradise for that.

The best journey is one made without companions, without obligations. Free as a bird, I am the only one in the whole vast universe. Above me lifts the pure, blue canopy we call the sky; for my sake alone beams the radiant queen of day we call the sun; for my sake alone are assembled here in the open fields all sorts of creatures, those that sing and those that twitter and those that leap. Only for my sake does the fragrant rose bloom, does the golden sunflower spread out its petals, does a gentle nature spangle the countryside with her fresh delights. No one pesters me, no one keeps an eye on me except God. I can do whatever I please. Do I want to sing? Then I sing me a song. Do I want to shout at the top of my lungs? Then I scream like a banshee. Do I want to make a shofar out of my fist? Then I trumpet with a long, rousing sound on my shofar. Do I want to suddenly throw myself down on the green grass? Then I roll on all sides in the grass, cavorting and frisking like a colt. Who is there to stop me? Whom do I have to mind? I am free! I am free!!

The day was so balmy, the sun so glorious, the sky so clear, the fields so green, the grass so fresh, my mood so lighthearted, my soul so overflowing, that I forgot I was only a visitor who had come to gather greens for Shevuos. I found myself imagining I was a mighty ruler, a prince who was master over all he beheld as far as his eye could see—over the fields and all the things that grew in the fields and over the blue sky above as well. All belonged to me, I was their sole monarch and I made all the laws—no one else! And like a lord, I was determined to show my power and authority. I could and would do as I pleased!

First off, that tall giant with his yellow hat, the sunflower, displeased me. Suddenly it was transformed before my eyes into the shape of an enemy—Goliath, the Philistine. And all the other plants, with and without stalks, the string beans and the lima beans, they too became enemies who had taken possession of my land. Who had invited them? And those short ones, the cabbages, what were those round heads doing here? They might get drunk and cause trouble. To the devil with them—who needs them! Angry thoughts and fierce passions were stirring in me. A strange longing for revenge took hold of my being and I began to avenge myself on my enemies—and what a vengeance it was!

I had brought with me tools to cut the greens for Shevuos: a pocket knife with two blades and a sword that was sharp though it was made of wood. It was the very sword I had carried during the holiday of Lag B'Omer when my friends and I had fought pitched battles. Even though I had brandished it in battle at the edge of town, you can be sure it had not shed a drop of blood. My sword was the kind of weapon the army issued in peacetime only. Actually there wasn't a hint of war anywhere; it was calm and peaceful all over, but in order to maintain the peace, swords, guns, rifles, cannons, horses, and soldiers had to be kept in readiness, just in case. As my great-aunt Ettl used to say while putting up raspberries, "May we never need them . . ."

B

It is a well-known fact that during a battle, one attempts to bring down the field commander first. The general himself is better still; then the rank and file fall like so many dominoes. It shouldn't surprise you to hear that I attacked Goliath, the Philistine, first, giving him a sound thwack on his yellow hat with my sword along with a few slashes on the side for good measure. The villain was soon laid out full length at my feet. After him, I knocked down many other foes as I ripped the lances out of their hands and flung them to the winds. Those low-lying, stubby ones with the green heads were slain by other means: I tore off the green heads of those within my reach and the rest I trampled into the earth, crushing them to dust.

In the heat of battle, when the blood comes to a raging boil, a person can go berserk, annihilating everything in his path. When it comes to spilling blood, a person can take leave of his senses. He doesn't respect age or take pity on women and children. Blood gushes like water. My rage and my zeal increased after I delivered the initial blows to the enemy. The more I raged, the more I urged myself on and so vehemently did I enter into the work, so ecstatically, so violently, that any and all things in my way were soon destroyed. The young plants suffered the most at my hands: the little round watermelons, the squashes with their fat bellies, the tiny cucumbers still attached to their yellow flowers. They especially provoked me with their meek passivity and I gave them something to remember me by. I smashed heads, split bodies in two, chopped limbs to bits, beat, maimed, and slaughtered. I cannot begin to fathom the source of the fury that swept over me. Poor, innocent potatoes lying deep in the ground I tore from from the earth as a warning that from me there was no hiding place. Young garlic plants and green onions I tore out by the roots. Radishes went flying in all directions. May God punish me if I tasted so much as one radish because I remembered distinctly the words from the scripture, "Thou shàlt not plunder." Jews did not plunder. All the while, my evil impulse was urging me to taste an onion or enjoy a bit of garlic, but I could hear the prohibition from the scriptures sounding in my ear, even as it is chanted, complete with the proper intonation, "Thou shalt not plunder." Meanwhile I could not stop myself from battering, chopping, shredding, mutilating, and throttling young and old, big and small, rich and poor.

Utterly without mercy, I was untouched by their shrieking, their weeping, and their pleading. I was absolutely heartless. Unbelievable! I, who couldn't bear the sight of a chicken being slaughtered, a cat being thrashed, a dog being humiliated, a horse being whipped—how had I become such a brute, such a tyrant? "Vengeance!" I could not stop shouting, as if intoxicated, "Vengeance! I will make you pay for all the Jewish blood spilt. I will make you pay for Jerusalem and for Betar and for the Jews in Spain and Portugal and Morocco as well as our own. And for the Torahs that were defiled and for the . . . Oh! Oh! Oh! Help! Save me! My ear! My ear!"

Two sharp blows to the back of my head and two stinging slaps across my face brought me instantly back to reality and I saw before me a familiar figure, one I could have sworn was no other than Okhrim, a tenant farmer.

C

As far back as anyone could remember, Okhrim had rented some acreage at the edge of town. There he raised watermelons, pumpkins, cucumbers, potatoes, onions, garlic, radishes, and horseradish from which he made a decent living. How did I know Okhrim? He did business with us, borrowing money from my mother every year before Passover and paying it back a little at a time after Sukkos. My mother would enter his payments on the inside cover of her thick prayer book in which she kept all her accounts. There she reserved a space for Okhrim and had written in large letters, "OKHRIM'S ACCOUNT." Each payment was listed in a column:

From Okhrim—one ruble
From Okhrim—another ruble

From Okhrim—two rubles
From Okhrim—half a ruble
From Okhrim—a sack of potatoes

and so on. Although my mother was a poor widow with children, who managed to survive on the interest she earned from loans, she never charged Okhrim anything. He would repay us with produce from his garden, sometimes more, sometimes less—we never quibbled with him.

If the harvest was good, he would supply us with potatoes and cucumbers for the whole winter; and if it wasn't, he would apologize to my mother in Russian, "Don't be angry, madam, the harvest was poor." My mother would forgive him and tell him that perhaps next year he would be able to be more generous.

"Trust me, madam, trust me," Okhrim would say, and he always kept his promise. The first onions and garlic were always at our house before the rich folks'. I would overhear our neighbors grumbling that the widow wasn't as badly off as she would like people to believe. "Look at that, she gets the best of everything." Naturally, I immediately relayed this tidbit to my mother and she cursed them roundly.

"May they have salt in their eyes and stones in their hearts! May those who begrudge me what little I have, have nothing themselves!" Naturally, I immediately relayed to our neighbors what my mother had wished them and naturally, they were furious at her, calling her a name that made my ears burn. Naturally, I resented this and immediately told my mother about it. My mother rewarded me with two smacks and told me I had better stop carrying Purim treats from one to the other. I cried because the smacks hurt but the words "Purim treats" kept running through my mind.

I couldn't understand why she referred to my tales as "Purim treats."

It was a joyous occasion for me when I would see Okhrim coming from afar, wearing his thick, white, woolen jacket that he wore summer and winter. I knew he would be bringing a full sack of potatoes from his garden for us and I would run into the house to tell my mother the news that Okhrim had come.

D

I must confess that between Okhrim and myself there was an unspoken affection, a kind of sympathy that can't be expressed in words. We hardly ever spoke to one another because I understood only a few words of his language and he didn't understand mine at all. I was also shy. Such a big man was this Okhrim; how does one talk to him? I had to call on my mother to be my interpreter.

"Momma, ask Okhrim why he didn't bring me any sour cherries."

"Where should he get sour cherries? Sour cherries don't grow in a vegetable garden."

"But why don't sour cherries grow in a vegetable garden?"

"Because there aren't any cherry trees in a vegetable garden."

"Why aren't there any cherry trees in a vegetable garden?"

"Why! Why! Why! You are too curious for your own good," my mother would say, exasperated, giving me a smack.

"Madam, don't be harsh with the boy," Okhrim would say, trying to defend me.

Okhrim was that kind of peasant. His were the hands that now held me captive. How it had come to this was not difficult to figure out. When Okhrim arrived and saw his garden being demolished, he must have been stunned. Dumbfounded, he saw some creature devastating his property with a sword. Okhrim probably thought I was an imp or a demon and, most likely, he crossed himself several times. But once he came closer and saw that the demon was only a Jewish boy with a wooden sword, he grabbed me by the ear with such force that I fell to the ground and began to scream with all my might, "Oh! Oh! Oh! My ear! My ear! Let go of my ear!"

It wasn't till after the sharp blows and the stinging slaps delivered by Okhrim that our eyes met and we recognized one another. We were both stunned, unable to utter a sound.

"The widow's boy!" Okhrim cried and crossed himself. He surveyed the damage I had caused him, carefully examining each vegetable bed and each clod of earth, becoming so upset that the tears started in his eyes. He stood facing me, his hands folded across his broad belly and said but one word, "*Zashtcha*? Why?"

At that moment I fully realized what a terrible crime I had commited and to whom I had brought so much anguish. And I asked myself the same question, "Why? Why?"

"Come!" Okhrim commanded, yanking me by the arm as I cowered with fear. Soon, soon he would make mincemeat of me. But Okhrim didn't harm me; he just grasped my arm so tightly that my eyes almost popped as he led me home to my mother to tell her the whole story and to leave me in her hands.

E

Need I tell you what I received from my mother? Need I describe her shock and her fury, how she wrung her hands as Okhrim described the total destruction I had wreaked on his garden? Sparing no detail, he demonstrated to my mother, using his staff, how I had flailed away on every side, smashing and breaking, stabbing and trampling, how I had torn the young potatoes from the earth and ruined the little cucumbers. "Why did he do it? Why, madam?" Okhrim could speak no more. He was too choked with tears.

Children, I must tell you the honest truth. Better to have been punished right there and then by Okhrim than by my mother before Shevuos. To top it all, there was the humiliation I had to suffer from my classmates who tagged me with the nickname of "Yossel, the Gardener." This dandy nickname was to follow me right up to the time of my wedding.

And that's how I gathered greens for Shevuos.

Esther

Not a story about *cheder*, not a story about the rabbi nor the rebbitzin am I going to tell you now. I have told you those stories many times before. I hope you will permit me, in honor of Purim, to tell you a story about the rabbi's daughter, Esther.

A

If Esther in the Megillah was as beautiful as the Esther I am going to tell you about, then it was no wonder she turned King Ahashuerosh's head. The Esther I will tell you about turned everyone's head. Everyone was in love with her. Everyone, everyone, even I, and even my older brother, Mottel, although he had long been *bar mitzvah*ed and had long been considered eligible for a match and had long been wearing a pocketwatch and chain. (If I am not mistaken, he might even have begun sprouting a beard.) If you want to know whether my older brother, Mottel, was in love with her, ask me. I will tell you the honest truth. He thought I hadn't caught on to the real reason why he went to study a Mishna chapter with the rabbi every Sabbath morning. The rabbi would be snoring away, the rebbitzin would be out gossiping and we children would be playing a game of *Mem-shin-hay*. And Mottel and Esther would be making moon eyes at each other—he at her and she at him. Once in a while it would happen that we boys would be playing a game of *Kutzibaba*. Do you know how to play *Kutzibaba*? I'll tell you. Your eyes are covered with a handkerchief, you're placed in the middle of the room, everyone runs around you in a circle, calling out, "Hey, hey, catch me if you can!"

Mottel and Esther would also join our games. They especially liked *Kutzibaba*. I know why. Because when they played *Kutzibaba* with us, they kept chasing and catching each other. He her, and she him.

And I have a lot more goods on them. But I'm not that sort . . .

Once I caught them holding hands. He hers, and she his. And it wasn't even Sabbath but during the week. It was toward evening. Between the afternoon and evening prayers. He said he was going to *shul* but somehow he ended up in our *cheder*. "Where's the rabbi?" "The rabbi isn't here." Then he just went over and took her hand. Esther's, that is. I stood there and watched. She took her hand away. He offered me a groshen not to tell anyone. I said—two. He gave me two. I said—three. He gave me three. I bet if I had said four, he would have given me four. And five, and six. But I'm not that sort . . .

I could tell you quite a story about another time—but enough other stories. Better let me tell you the story I promised you.

B

My brother, Mottel, as I told you, was almost a grown-up. He didn't have to go to *cheder* any more. And he didn't want to study at home either. For that my father called him an ignoramus. He had no other name for him but "ignoramus." My mother would not tolerate this. "What sort of name is that to call a young man, almost a bridegroom?" Said my father, "Because he *is* an ignoramus!" And they began to quarrel. I don't know about other parents, but mine were always quarreling; night and day, day and night, always quarreling.

If I were to tell you about my parents and how they quarreled, you would hold your sides with laughter. But I'm not that sort . . .

As I was saying, my brother, Mottel, was no longer going to *cheder*. Still and all he never forgot to send the rabbi a Purim gift every year. Had he not once been a student of the rabbi's? This year he sent him a fine poem in Hebrew, decorated with a Star of David, along with two rubles as a gift. And who do you suppose he chose to deliver this Purim gift? Me! Obviously. My brother, Mottel, said to me, "Here, bring this Purim gift to the rabbi, and when you come back, I'll give you ten groshen." Ten groshen is nothing to sneeze at. You can't just shrug it off. Why did I hesitate? "I want the money in advance," I said. My brother called me a smart aleck. I said, "That may be true. I won't argue with you. But I want to see the money up front." Who do you think won out?

He paid me the ten groshen, handed me the rabbi's gift, a sealed letter, and as I was about to leave, he slipped into my hand another letter and whispered to me breathlessly, "And this you will deliver to Esther." "Esther?" "Esther." Another in my place would have asked to be paid double, but I'm not that sort . . .

C

"What in heaven's name could my brother be writing to my rabbi's daughter?" I thought on my way to deliver the gift. I simply had to have a look. Just a peek. It wouldn't hurt anyone. And I opened the letter to Esther and read a new version of the Megillah. Listen to this. I give it to you word for word:

FROM MORDEKHAI TO ESTHER.

"*Ish*—a man, *yehudi*—a young man, a bachelor, *haya*,—there was, *b'shushan haviri*—in our village, *u'shmo Mordekhai*—and his name was Mottel. *Va'yihi uman*—And he loved, *es Hadasa*—Hadassa, *hee Esther*—who was Esther. *V'hanara*—and the girl, *yefas*—she was pretty, *toar*—she was a beauty. *V'sitav hanara*—and the girl pleased him. *Lo hagida Esther*—Esther told no one, *ki Mordekhai*—because Mottel, *tzva eleyha*—bade her, *asher lo tagid*—not to tell. *U'vkhol yom v'yom*—and every day, *Mordekhai mishalekh*—

Mottel passed by, *l'das shalom Esther*—to catch sight of Esther. *U'v'hagiya tor Esther*—and when it would be Esther's time, *beys avikhayil*—to be married, *u'tlakeyakh Esther*—he would take Esther, *v'yimlikha*—and lead her, *takhas vashti*—under the *khupa*."

What do you say to my brother's interpretation of the Purim story? I would give anything to hear what the rabbi would have to say about a commentary like that! But how to make it happen? Wait! Where there's a will, there's a way! I could switch letters: give the poem intended for the rabbi to Esther and give Esther's Megillah to the rabbi. Let him enjoy it. So what if there's an uproar afterwards? Would it be my fault? Doesn't it happen that people make mistakes? Don't you think the mailman sometimes loses a letter? But I would never do anything like *that*. I'm not that sort . . .

D

"*Goot yontev*, Rabbi!" I burst into the classroom, startling the rabbi, "My brother has sent you a Purim gift and his best wishes."

I handed the rabbi the Megillah. My rabbi opened the Megillah, looked at it thoughtfully and turned the page over, apparently searching for something. "Keep on looking," I was thinking to myself, "You'll soon find something, alright."

And my rabbi donned his silver-framed spectacles, read through the Megillah and, I tell you, there wasn't so much as a hint of puzzlement on his face. Only a sigh, nothing more. Then he said to me, "Wait a minute, I want to

write a few words in response." In the meantime, I saun-
tered around the *cheder*, accepted a piece of honey cake and
a cookie from the rabbi's wife, and when no one was looking, slipped the poem with the Purim gift intended for the
rabbi into Esther's hand. She blushed, hid in a corner, carefully opened the letter and then flared up like a flame, her
eyes afire—it was a sight to see! "You don't seem to like the
Purim gift," I said to myself and went over to the rabbi. He
handed me the "few words" he had written.

"A very happy *yontev* to you, Rabbi!" I said in the same
high spirits as before. "May you have a long life!" And I was
off for home.

No sooner was I on the other side of the door than
Esther ran after me with red, teary eyes, "Here," she said
to me angrily, "I want you to give this back to your
brother!"

On the way home, I opened the rabbi's letter first—
the rabbi is more important. This is what it said, "My dear
and faithful student Mordekhai, may your light shine forever! I thank you heartily for the Purim gift you sent me.
Last year and the year before you sent me better Purim gifts.
This year you sent me a new commentary on the Megillah.
I thank you for the Megillah. But I must tell you, Mottel,
that your commentary doesn't please me at all. For one,
"*Shushan Haviri* is the capital city, not as you say, 'our village'. And second, I would like to know, where is it written that Mordekhai was unmarried? And why are you calling him Mottel? Where do you get Mottel? And whatever
made you think that the word *uman* is translated as 'loved'?
Uman means she was 'raised', from the word *oman v'peda-
gog*. And the way you interpret *v'yimlakha takhas vashti* to
mean 'he will lead her under the *khupa*,' well, that really is

astonishing, without any sense at all. First of all, this applies to Ahashuerosh, not Mordekhai. And second of all, nowhere in the Megillah is it mentioned that Ahashuerosh went under the *khupa* with Esther. What kind of nonsense is this, to take a verse from the Sacred Book and twist it so crazily? Every verse has to be interpreted properly. A year ago and the year before that you sent me something different. This year you got it into your head to send the rabbi an interpretation from the Megillah and a mad interpretation into the bargain. Well, there must be a reason for it. With these words and best wishes I send your Megillah back, and may God grant you a good year, from your rabbi."

That's what I call rubbing your face in it! Serves my brother right! You can bet he won't be writing Megillahs like that any more.

Having finished off the rabbi's letter, I had to see what the rabbi's daughter, Esther, had to say in her letter. I opened her envelope and out fell two rubles. What was going on here? I read what it said—just three lines:

"Mottel, I thank you for the two rubles. But you can take them back. I didn't expect that sort of Purim gift from you. Don't give me any gifts or charity either."

Ha-ha, what do you say to that? She doesn't want any charity! A fine story, as I am a Jewish child! So, what to do next? Another in my place would probably have torn up both letters and pocketed the money. He would have brought home two empty hands, not two rubles. But I'm not that sort . . . I did something much better. Wait till you hear. I figured I had already been paid for my troubles by my brother, Mottel. What more could I expect from him? I delivered both letters to my father. I was eager to hear what my father had to say. He would understand what the

Megillah was about much better than the rabbi even though my father was only a father while the rabbi was, after all, a rabbi.

E

Can you picture what happened when my father read both letters? He called my brother, Mottel, on the carpet demanding an explanation. If I wanted to show you how my brother, Mottel, reacted, I would have to chant the words of the Megillah:

"*V'ha'ir shushan n-vu-kha* . . . And the city of Shushan was in confusion."

But that's neither here nor there. I'm sure you want to know how it all turned out, what happened to the rabbi's daughter, Esther, and my brother, Mottel. What could have happened? Nothing much. Esther got married. She married a widower. My, how she wept! I was at her wedding. Exactly why she wept so much, I have no idea. Apparently her heart told her she would not reach old age with her spouse. And so it was. She lived with him altogether half a year and passed away. What she died of, I cannot tell you. I don't know. No one knows. The rabbi and the rebbitzin didn't know either. It was said she poisoned herself, just went and poisoned herself. But that's a lie. I heard the rebbitzin herself say that her enemies were spreading that rumor.

And my brother, Mottel? Aha! He was married before Esther became engaged and moved in with his father-in-law. But he soon returned home. And alone, too. What was the story? He wanted a divorce! My father exclaimed, "You're an ignoramus!" My mother wouldn't tolerate that and they quarreled. It was lively! But it didn't do any good. He divorced and married someone else. He already has two children, a little boy and a little girl. The little boy's name is Herzl, after Doctor Herzl. And the little girl is called Esther'l. My father said they should name her Gitl after his mother, my grandmother Gitl. And my mother wanted desperately for her to be named Leah'tzi, after her mother, my grandmother Leah. A huge argument broke out between my mother and father. A whole day and night they quarreled. It was decided the child would be called Leah-Gitl, after both mothers. Settled. But then my father decided he didn't want Leah-Gitl. What sense did that make? Why should *her* mother's name come first?

It was at this point that my brother, Mottel, returned from the synagogue and told us he had gone ahead and named her Esther. My father said, "Ignoramus! How did you come up with the name Esther?" And Mottel answered, "Have you forgotten that Purim is coming soon?" Well, what could anyone say to that? Settled. We no longer heard "ignoramus" from my father. But both of them, my father and my mother, exchanged queer looks and grew silent.

What did those looks and that silence mean? I don't know. Maybe *you* do?

The Penknife

Lo tiganuv—Thou shalt not steal!
(The Ten Commandments)

A

Listen, Jewish children, and I will tell you a story about a penknife. It's not a made-up story, but a true story that really happened to me. There was nothing on earth I yearned for as much as I yearned for a penknife; nothing on earth I desired as much as a penknife, my own penknife. It would nestle in my pocket, and whenever I felt like it, I would take it out and it would cut whatever I wished. Oh, how my friends would envy me! I had just started going to *cheder*, to Yosl Dardaki's, and I already owned a penknife, well, sort of a penknife. I had made it myself. I had pulled a goose feather from a feather duster, lopped off one end of it, flattened the other, and made believe it was a penknife that could cut.

"What's this about feathers, in heaven's name? What's this business with carrying feathers around?" demanded my father, a sickly man with a sallow, sunken face, beginning

75

to cough. "Just look at him—playing with feathers—khe-heh-heh-heh!"

"Why does it bother you that the child is playing?" interjected my mother, a tiny woman wearing a silk kerchief. "All you do is aggravate yourself, may my enemies suffer for it!"

Later on, when I was old enough to be studying the Pentateuch and the Commentaries, I almost had a real penknife, also home-made. I got hold of a metal stay from my mother's crinoline and set it very cunningly in a piece of wood. I carefully sharpened the metal on a pot, of course cutting all my fingers in the process.

"Will you just look how he's bloodied himself, that heir of yours!" exclaimed my father, grasping my fingers so tightly my knuckles cracked. "What an idiot, kheh-heh-heh!"

"God help me!" said my mother, taking the penknife away and throwing it into the oven, paying no heed to my tears. "Now that's an end to it, for pity's sake!"

But I soon acquired another penknife, this time a for-real penknife with a wooden handle. It was round and bulgy like a barrel, with a curved blade that opened and closed. Do you want to know how I came by it? I saved up enough from my lunch money and bought it from Shloime for seven groshens cash and three groshens on credit.

Oh, did I love it! Oh, how I loved it! I would come home from *cheder* slapped black and blue, starved, dead tired. Remember, I had just started studying *Gemara* with Moti "Angel of Death," the *Gemara* teacher. We were studying the part about how an ox gored a cow, which somehow led to my being slapped. Once home, the first thing I would do was to remove the penknife from beneath the black chest of drawers where it had lain all day long because I didn't dare take it to school, and at home certainly no one must know that I owned a penknife. Then I would stroke it, cut a sheet of paper, slice a straw in two and only then cut my portion of bread into tiny, tiny bits, spearing them on the point of my penknife and then putting them one by one into my mouth.

One time, before going to bed, I decided to clean my penknife, to scour it, shine it, take the whetstone that I had found in our attic, spit on it, and quietly go to work sharpening the blade, sharpening, sharpening . . .

My father, skullcap on his head, was poring over a prayer book, studying and coughing, coughing and studying.

My mother was in the kitchen, fussing over the challah while I continued sharpening, sharpening the penknife.

Suddenly my father jerked his head up, as if from sleep:

"What is that swishing sound I hear? What's going on there? What are you doing, you goo-good-for-nothing, kheh-heh-heh!"

He came over and looked down at my whetstone, grabbed me by the ear and fell into a fit of coughing.

"Ah-ah-ah? Knives?! Kheh-heh-heh!" my father coughed and took away my penknife and the whetstone. "What an idler, too tired to pick up a prayer book, kheh-heh-heh!"

I began to wail loudly; my father helped me along with a few slaps as my mother, sleeves rolled up, came running in from the kitchen, yelling,

"Sha, sha, what's happening here? Why are you hitting him? God be with you! What do you have against the child? Woe is me!"

"Knives?" cried my father and broke out coughing. "A little boy like that! . . . What a scoundrel! Khe-heh-heh-heh! . . . Too tired to pick up a prayer book? A boy of eight years! . . . I'll give you penknives, you loafer! . . . Out of the clear blue sky he wants knives, kheh-heh-heh-heh!"

God, what did he have against my penknife? What sin had it committed against him? Why was he so furious?

I remember my father as always sick, always pale and sallow, and always furious, always angry at the whole world. For the least little thing, he would fly into a rage and want to tear me limb from limb. It was lucky my mother was there to protect me, to save me from his wrath.

My penknife was thrown away, thrown so far away that even after eight days of searching and searching I couldn't find it anywhere! I deeply mourned that bulgy penknife, that wonderful penknife. How bitter and bleak were my schooldays when I would realize that I would be going home with swollen cheeks and red ears from having them painfully twisted by Moti "Angel of Death," only because an ox had gored a cow—and there would be no one to turn to. I was alone in the world without that bulgy little penknife, alone as an orphan, and no one, no one at all saw the tears I silently shed on my bed at night after coming home from *cheder*. I cried to myself quietly, dried my eyes, fell asleep, and the following morning was again off to *cheder*, again to learn how an ox had gored a cow, again to be slapped by Moti "Angel of Death," again home to my father's rage, coughing, curses—never a free moment, never a happy greeting, never a smile, not a single little smile from anyone, anyone. All by myself, alone, alone in the entire world!

B

A year, maybe a year and a half passed. I had just about forgotten the bulgy penknife; but it turned out I was fated by heaven to be bedevilled by penknives my entire childhood. Wouldn't you know, another penknife appeared in my life, a brand new penknife, a one-of-a-kind, extra-special, remarkable penknife with two blades, precious steel blades, sharp as slaughtering knives, with a white bone handle, a brass case with red rivets—I tell you, one-in-a-million, the finest made!

How was I able to get hold of this expensive penknife, one I would never have been able to afford? That's a long story, a sad one, but interesting, so I beg you, listen well.

How would you expect me to react to that "priest," that German Jew who was our boarder, a contractor, Herr Hertz Hertzenhertz, when he spoke bad Yiddish, wore no hat, no beard, no sidelocks and, please forgive me, wore a regular short suit jacket, not a long kaftan? I ask you, how could I keep from bursting out laughing when this Jewish gentile, or gentile Jew, insisted on speaking to me in Yiddish, but in some sort of strange Yiddish, with many drawled "ahh" sounds?

"Zo, my dearest young maahn, vaht iz di Toraah portion for zis veek?"

"Hee-hee-hee!" I giggled, hiding my face behind my hand.

"Pliz taal me, my dear kindkhen, vot iz di Toraah portion for zis veek?"

"Hee-hee-hee! *Ba-la-k*!!" I burst into laughter and fled.

But that was at the beginning, before I really knew him; afterwards, when I had become better acquainted with this German, Herr Hertz Hertzenhertz (he lived at our house for a year), I grew so fond of him that it no longer bothered me that he didn't say prayers and ate without having first ritually washed his hands. At first I didn't understand how he was still alive. Why had God allowed him to continue living? Why hadn't he choked to death while eating? Why hadn't his hair fallen out from his uncovered head? From the very mouth of my rebbe, Moti "Angel of Death," I heard that this Jewish German was really a *gilgl*, a reincarnated soul, which meant he was a Jew who had been reincarnated as a German but who could later come back as a wolf, a cow, a horse, or even a duck . . . a duck?!

"Ha-ha-ha! Wouldn't that be something!" I thought and truly felt sorry for the German. But one thing was a mystery to me: my father, who was an honest, God-fearing Jew, always deferred to him and paid him respect, as did all the others who came to our house,

"*Sholom aleykhem*, Reb Hertz Hertzenhertz, welcome to you, Reb Hertz Hertzenhertz, have a seat, Reb Hertz Hertzenhertz!"

I once asked my father about this, but he pushed me away, saying, "Be gone, it's none of your business! Why on earth are you hanging around here? Are you too sick to pick up a prayer book, kheh-heh-heh-heh!?"

Always about the same prayer book! God in heaven! I, *too*, wanted to see, I *too* wanted to hear what he was saying!

I went into the parlor, hid myself in a corner and listened to their talk, how Herr Hertzenhertz laughed out loud and smoked fat, black cigars that smelled so good. All of a sudden my father came over and slapped me.

"You here again? You loafer! What will become of you, you *goy* you? My God, what will become of you, keh-heh-heh-heh!"

Herr Hertz Hertzenhertz tried to take my part, "Ach, leef the boy be, leef him ahlone!"

But it did no good. My father chased me out. I finally picked up a prayer book but had not the least desire to pray. What could I do? I wandered from one room to the next until I came upon the nicest room in the house, the room in which Herr Hertz Hertzenhertz always slept. Ah, how lovely, how cheery it was! The lamps shone brightly and the mirrors gleamed; on a large table was a silver inkwell and fine pens; there were toy soldiers on horseback, knick-knacks, bones and stones and—a penknife! Oh, what a beautiful penknife! How lucky I would be if I had such a penknife! How many things I could carve with it! Yes, it had to be tried out. Was it sharp enough? Ah! It sliced a hair! Split it in two! Oh, my, what a penknife!!

In the twinkling of an eye the penknife was in my hand. I looked around and tried slipping it into my pocket for just a second . . . My hand trembled . . . My heart pounded so hard I could hear it going, "Tik-tik-tik!" I heard someone coming, someone's boots shuffling; it was he, Herr Hertz Hertzenhertz! Oh-oh, what to do? Let the penknife stay in my pocket for now, I would put it back later. In the meantime I had to get away, away from there, run! Run!

I could not eat supper. My mother felt my forehead. My father glared at me angrily and sent me off to sleep. Sleep? Do you think I could so much as shut my eyes? I was a goner! What was I to do with the penknife? How was I going to put it back?

C

"Come here, you little brat!" my father said to me in the morning. "Have you seen a penknife anywhere?"

At first I was terrified. I was positive he knew, that they all knew. I came ever so close to blurting out, "What? A penknife? Here it is!" But something seemed to choke back the words in my throat and I answered in a trembling voice, "What penknife?"

"What penknife!" my father mimicked me, "What penknife! The golden penknife! Our guest's penknife! You little brat, you good-for-nothing, kheh-heh-heh!"

"Why are you picking on the poor child?" my mother intervened. "The child doesn't have the slightest idea about it and you keep needling and needling him: Penknife! Penknife!"

"Penknife! Penknife! What do you mean he doesn't have the slightest idea about it?" my father said furiously. "All morning he hears us shouting, 'Penknife, penknife! Penknife, penknife!' We're turning the house upside down looking for the penknife and he asks: What penknife? Go, go wash, you empty-headed boy, you good-for-nothing, kheh-heh-heh!"

I thanked God they didn't search me! But what was I to do next? I had to hide the penknife in a safe place, but where? Aha, in the attic! I took the penknife from my pocket and shoved it into my boot. I ate, but had no idea what I was eating. I choked on my food.

"What's the rush, devil take it?" my father demanded.

"I'm rushing to go to *cheder*," I answered and felt myself turning red as a beet.

"A diligent student all of a sudden. What do you say to this scholar?" he growled and glared at me angrily. I barely finished eating and said my prayers.

"Well, why aren't you off to *cheder*, my little scholar?" my father asked.

"What are you rushing him for?" said my mother. "Let the child rest a minute!"

In a flash I was up in the attic. Way behind the rafters lay the little white penknife. It lay there in silence.

"What are you doing scrambling around in attics?" shouted my father. "You devil! You sniveler! Kheh-heh-heh-heh!"

"I'm looking for something," I answered and almost fainted from fright.

"Something? What 'something'? What do you mean, 'something'?"

"A p-p-prayer book . . . a . . . a . . . an old G-G-*Gemara* . . ."

"What? A G-*Gemara*? In the attic? You blockhead! Climb on down, come down, I'll give you a *Gemara*! You nincompoop, you moron, you rapscallion you, kheh-heh-heh!"

But my father's rage no longer worried me as much as my fear that someone might find the penknife. Who could tell? That might be the very day someone might go up to the attic to hang the laundry or paint the shutters. I had to take it down and hide it in a safer place! I was in constant terror! Every glance from my father's eyes convinced me he knew and would at any moment grab me and grill me about the boarder's penknife. I had already thought of a place for it, the perfect spot. In the ground, in a little hole near the wall was where I buried it and covered it nicely with straw as a marker. Returning from *cheder*, I immediately ran out to the courtyard, carefully removed the penknife and before I had time to admire it, I heard my father's voice in an uproar:

"Where the devil are you? Why aren't you saying your prayers, you ne'er-do-well, you lazy loafer! Khe-heh-heh!"

But no matter how much my father persecuted and harassed me, no matter how much the rebbe swatted me and rapped my knuckles, it was nothing compared to the pleasure I experienced when I returned from *cheder* and found my beloved, my only dear friend—my penknife! But the pleasure was—alas!—mixed with anguish, embittered with melancholy, with dread, with great, great fear!

D

Summer evening. The sun was setting, the air becoming a bit cooler, the grass sweet-smelling. Frogs croaked and wisps of rainless clouds wafted by past the moon as if trying to swallow it. The pale, silvery moon hid itself one minute and reappeared the next, seeming to be gliding yet remaining in the same place. My father sat down on the grass in his robe, half-naked but wearing his fringed undergarment. He held one hand to his chest and with the other he fingered the soil, gazed at the star-filled sky, and coughed. His face was as pale and deathly as the moon's. He was sitting on the very spot under which the penknife was buried, unaware what lay beneath him. Oh, if he only knew! What would he say? And what would happen to me?

"Aha," I thought in my heart, "you threw away my bulgy penknife and now I have a better one, a much more beautiful one! You're sitting on it and don't even know it. Oh, Father! Father!"

"Why are you staring at me like a tomcat?" my father said suddenly. "Why are you sitting there with idle hands like a lazy bigshot? Can't you find something to do with yourself? Are you through reading the *Krias-sh'ma*? Oh, to the devil with you, you do-nothing! May you not suffer for it, khe-heh-heh-heh!"

When he put the word not in his curses, it meant that he wasn't too angry. On the contrary, it meant he was feeling good. And surely, how could one not feel good on such a beautiful summer evening when everyone was sitting out-of-doors in the fresh air, in the gentle, fresh, delicious night air? Everyone, everyone was outside—my father, my mother, the younger children who were looking for little stones and playing in the sand. Herr Hertz Hertzenhertz was also strolling hatless about the courtyard, puffing away on a cigar and singing a German song. He looked at me and laughed, probably laughing because my father was torment-ing me. But I was laughing at them all. As soon as they would all go to bed I would sneak out to the courtyard (I slept in the front of the house, on the ground, because it was stiflingly hot inside), and take delight in my penknife!

Everyone was asleep. It was silent all over. Slowly I arose and on all fours and very quietly, like a cat, stole out into the courtyard. The night was still, the air fresh, delight-ing the soul. Carefully I made my way to the spot where the penknife lay buried. Carefully I dug it up and gazed at it by the light of the moon. It sparkled, it glittered like fine gold, like a jewel. I raised my eyes and saw the moon peering down on me, on my penknife. Why was it looking at me so intently? I turned around. It was still looking at me. I hid the penknife under my shirt—it was still looking at me. It knew for sure what kind of penknife this was and how I had gotten it. Gotten? I had *stolen* it!

For the first time since the penknife was mine, that dreadful word came to my mind. Stolen? That meant I was a thief! Just a thief! In the Torah it was written, in the Ten Commandments, in large letters:

THOU SHALT NOT STEAL!

And I had stolen! And I had stolen! What would they do to me for that in Gehenim? Oh my! They would chop off my hand, the hand that had stolen. They would beat me with iron rods. They would roast me and broil me on hot coals. Forever and ever I would roast. I had to return the penknife, I had to put back the penknife, I didn't want a stolen penknife! Tomorrow I would put the penknife back.

With these tormenting thoughts, I put the penknife back in my bosom pocket and felt as if it were burning me, scalding me. No, it had to be kept hidden, buried in the earth till tomorrow. And the moon above gazed down on me. What was it looking at? The moon saw, it was a witness. I crept slowly back into the house, into my bed, but could not fall asleep. I tossed and turned and could not sleep. Finally I fell asleep as day was breaking and I dreamt of a moon and I dreamt of iron rods and I dreamt of penknives. I awoke very early, said my prayers with great fervor, bolted my breakfast, and went hurrying off to *cheder*.

"What's your big rush to get to *cheder*?" my father called after me. "What's the hurry? That Torah of yours won't run away! Better say your prayers the way you're supposed to. And don't skip any words! There'll be time enough for you to be lazy, you rascal, you dimwit, you pig-eater, khe-heh-heh-heh-heh!"

E

"Why so late!" my rebbe scolded me, adding, "Look here!" and pointed to my friend, Berl the Redhead's son, who was standing in a corner with his head bowed. "Do you see, you good-for-nothing? Know that from this day on his name will no longer be Berele the Redhead's son, as he's been called till now. No! Now he has an even finer name; now his name is Berl the Thief! Say out loud after me, children: Berele the Thi-e-e-f! Berele the Thi-e-e-f!"

The rebbe drew out the words in a sing-song and all the students echoed after him, like choir boys:

"Berele the Thi-e-ef! Berele the Thi-e-ef!"

I stood frozen to the spot and a chill spread over my body. I didn't know what was going on.

"Why don't you say something, simpleton!" the rebbe called to me, granting me an unearned slap, "Why are you silent, pagan? You hear everybody singing. Help them sing along. Chime in with them, 'Berele the Thi-e-e-f! Berele the Thi-e-ef!'"

My hands and feet were trembling. My teeth were chattering. But I chimed in, "Berele the Thi-e-ef!"

"Louder, you no-good!" the rebbe egged me on, "Louder! Louder!"

And I and the rest of the choir sang out at the top of our lungs, "Berele the Thi-e-ef! Berele the Thi-e-ef!"

"Sh-sh-sh-sh-sh-a-a-a-a!" the rebbe suddenly cried out, slapping the table hard, "Sha! Now we will proceed with the trial." And in a sing-song, he continued, "So, Berele the Thi-e-e-f, come over he-ere, my child, fa-aster now, a little faster! Te-ell us, my boy, wh-at is your na-ame?"

"Berl."

"What e-else?"

"Berl . . . Berl . . . the . . . Thief!"

"That's the way, my dear child, now you're a good boy. No-ow, Berele, ma-ay you be healthy and stro-ong in every li-imb, please be so ki-ind, Berele, and remo-ove your nice little clo-othes. That's the way! Speed it u-up, speed it u-up! I beg of you, hurry up and go fa-aster—that's the wa-ay, Bere'shi, my de-ear!"

Berl stood naked as the day he was born. The blood drained from his face. Not a muscle moved. His eyes were downcast. He looked like death itself, a corpse!

The rebbe called to one of the older students, still chanting,

"So-o, Big Hershele, get up from the ta-able, come here to m-ee, quickly, that's the wa-ay; tell us the story exa-actly, from beginning to e-end, how our Berele became a thie-e-f. Listen carefully, boys!"

And Big Hershele began relating the story; how Berl had gotten hold of the charity box for Reb Meir the Miracle Worker into which Berl's mother would throw in a coin or two every Friday before candle-lighting; how Berl had gotten into the charity box which had a lock on it; how Berl had, with a straw dipped in tar, drawn out every single coin one at a time; how his mother, Hoarse Zlate, had become suspicious, had opened the charity box and had found nothing but a straw dipped in tar; how Hoarse Zlate had turned him in; how Berl, soon after the rebbe's beating, had confessed that all year, that entire year, he had been swiping coins from the charity box; how every Sunday he had bought two little honey cakes and a stick of carob for himself! How . . . and so on and so forth.

"Now, children, sentence him! You know what to do. This isn't the first time. Let each of you decide what a thief deserves who steals coins from a charity box. Little Hershele, speak up first, what is the punishment for a thief who steals coins from a charity box with a straw?"

The rebbe bent his head to the side, shut his eyes and put his ear close to Little Hershele. Little Hershele answered loud and clear,

"A thief who steals coins from a charity box deserves to be flogged till the blood flows."

"Moishl, what does a thief deserve who steals coins from a charity box?"

"A thief," said Moishl in a whiny voice, "a thief who steals coins from a charity box deserves to be streched out, two holding his head, two holding his feet and two beating him with salted rods."

"Topele Tootaritoo! What does a thief deserve who steals coins from a charity box?"

Kopel Kookarikoo, a youngster who could not pronounce his k's and g's, wiped his nose and sang out his sentence in a squeaky voice,

"A thief who steals toins from a charity bots deserves to have all the tids det tlose to him and say to him right in his face three times in a row, 'Thief! Thief! Thief!'"

The *cheder* filled with laughter. The rebbe placed his thumb on his Adam's apple, like a cantor, and called me up in the sing-song with which a bridegroom is called to the bima:

"*Yamod ha-kha-san Sha-lom b'Reb Nakhum maf-tir!*— Ri-ise, O bridegroom Reb Sholom ben Reb Nakhum for the *Maftir* prayer! Speak out, now, Shloime'li, my darling, what is your opinion on what a thief deserves who steals coins from a charity box?"

I wanted to reply—but my tongue would not obey. I shivered as if in a a high fever and my throat tightened. I broke out in a cold sweat from head to toe. There was a whistling in my ears. I saw standing before me neither the rebbe, nor the naked Berele the Thief, nor the students; I saw before me only penknives, endless penknives, white, opened penknives with many blades and there, by the door, hung the moon, smiling and gazing at me like a human being. My head was spinning, as were the whole room and the table and the books and all the boys and the moon that hung on the door and all the penknives . . . I felt my legs buckling under me. In a moment I would fall in a faint. But I pulled myself together with all my strength so as not to fall down.

That evening I came home feeling as if my face were on fire, my cheeks burning and my ears buzzing. I knew people were talking to me but what they said, I didn't know. My father was saying something angrily, wanting to hit me; my mother was interceding, using her apron like a hen spreading her wings to protect her chicks from harm. I heard nothing and wished to hear nothing. I only wanted night to come soon so I could finally get rid of that penknife. But what to do with it? Confess and give it back? Then I would suffer Berele's fate. Try to sneak it back? What if I were caught? Toss it away and get rid of it once and for all? Where could I toss it so no one would find it? On the roof? They would hear a bang. In the garden? They would find it. Aha! I knew, I had an idea: throw it in the well! A great idea, no? In the well, right there in our very own courtyard!

That idea pleased me so, I didn't want to waste more time thinking about it. I grabbed the penknife and ran right to the well and felt I was holding in my hand, not a penknife but something vile and hateful that I wanted to rid myself of as soon as possible. But I had feelings of regret— such a wonderful penknife. I stood deep in thought for a moment and I imagined I was holding in my hand a living thing. My heart was aching; after all, it had cost me so dear, it was like killing a living soul! I took courage and let it drop from my fingers—plop! A splash and then nothing more was heard . . . no more penknife! I stayed a moment longer at the well and listened—nothing. Thank God, I was rid of it! But my heart ached and was heavy: "After all, what a penknife, what an extraordinary penknife!"

I went back to my bed and saw the moon's gaze following me and I imagined it had seen everything I had done and I heard like a cry from afar, "But you're still a thief! Grab him! Beat him! He's a thief! A thi-e-e-f!!!" I stole back into the house and went to sleep and I dreamt I was running, I was floating, I was flying in the air with the penknife, and the moon gazed at me and said, "Grab him! Beat him! He's a thief! He's a thi-e-e-f!!!"

F

A deep, deep sleep! A painful, a very painful dream! A fire burned in me. My head was buzzing. Everything I saw was red as blood. Burning rods of fire were lashing my body and I was rolling in blood. Around me snakes and scorpions were writhing and crawling, their gaping mouths eager to swallow me. I heard a sharp blast right in my ear, sounding like a shofar on the High Holidays. Someone was standing over me, shouting in a sing-song in rhythm, "Beat him! Beat him! Beat him! He is a thi-e-e-f!!!" And I was screaming, "Help! Take the moon away from me! Give back the penknife! What have you got against poor Berl? He isn't guilty—it is I who am a thi-e-e-f! A thi-e-e-f!"

And that is all I remember.

* * *

I opened one eye, then the other. Where was I? It seemed on a bed. What was I doing there? Who was that sitting on a chair next to the bed? Ah! "Is that you, Mama? Mama!" She didn't hear me! ... "Mama! Mama! Ma-aamma!!!" What was this? I thought I was shouting out loud. Sha! I could hear her—was she weeping? Yes, she was weeping silently. I could also see my father with his sallow, sickly face. He was bent over a prayer book, muttering softly, coughing, sighing, groaning. Apparently I had died ... died? Suddenly my eyes could see more clearly, my head felt better, as did all my limbs. I could hear a ringing in one ear, in the other ear: Rinnnng!!! I sneezed: "Katchoo!"

"God bless you! Long life to you! A good sign! *Mazel tov*! Praised be God!"

"A real sneeze! Praise the One Above!"

"We have a great God! He will get well, God willing, blessed be His name!"

"Quick, call Mintzi the ritual slaughterer's wife. She knows how to chase away the Evil Eye."

"We'd better call the doctor!"

"The doctor? What for? Nonsense! *He* is the doctor! The One Above is the best doctor! God, Blessed be He and blessed be His name!"

"Please, people, don't crowd around him so! It's terribly hot! For pity's sake, give him some air!"

"You see? I told you they had to make a waxen image of him for a cure. Who was right?"

"Praise God! Praise His blessed name! Oy, God! God! Blessed be He and blessed be His name! . . ."

People were crowding around me, examining me, feeling my head. They intoned magical incantations over me, they patted me, they licked my forehead testing for fever, and spat to ward off the Evil Eye and cossetted me. They poured hot chicken soup in my mouth and fed me spoonfuls of jam. They all hovered over me, nursing me like a spoiled child and fed me egg yolks and ducklings like a baby and never left me alone. My mother was always sitting next to me, constantly repeating the whole story: how they had picked me up from the ground almost dead; how I had lain for two weeks in a delirious fever and just croaked like a frog and ranted about beatings and penknives. They thought I was more dead than alive. And then, suddenly I had sneezed seven times and had come back to life.

"Now we see what a God we have, blessed be He and His name!" my mother exclaimed through her tears. "Now we see that when we cry out to Him, He heeds our sinful prayers and our guilty tears. Many, many tears have we shed, I and your father, until God took pity on us. We almost lost a child, God forbid, may we suffer your sufferings, and for whose sake? For what reason? Because of a boy, a thief, some Berele that the rebbe beat till the blood ran. When you came back from *cheder*, you were half-dead, may I suffer for you! He's a devil, he's a demon, that rebbe, may God repay him! No, my child, if God gives us life and you will be well, may it happen soon, we will send you to another teacher, not that executioner, that fiend, that Angel of Death, may his name and memory be cursed and obliterated!"

This news thrilled me! I hugged and kissed my mother. "Dearest, dearest Mama! . . ."

My father approached slowly, laid his pale, cold hand on my forehead and said to me gently, without any anger, "Ay, did you give us a scare, you scamp you, kheh-heh-heh-heh!"

Also the Jewish German, or the German Jew, Herr Hertz Hertzenhertz, with a cigar between his teeth, with his shaven face, bent down over my bed and patted my cheek and said in German, "*Gut, gut! Gezundt, gezundt!*"

* * *

A few weeks after I got out of bed my father said to me, "So, my son, now go to *cheder* and forget all about pen-knives and other such nonsense. It's high time you behaved yourself; God willing, in three years time you'll be a *bar mitzvah*, may you live till a hundred and twenty, kheh-heh-heh-heh!"

With those endearing words my father sent me off to *cheder*, to the new teacher, Reb Khayim Koter. That was the first time I had ever heard sweet and loving words from my father and I immediately forgot his persecutions, his curses, and his smacks, as if they had never occurred. Had I not been embarrassed, I would have hugged and kissed him too. But, hee-hee-hee—how do you kiss a father?

My mother gave me an apple and two groshen to take to *cheder*, and the German gave me a few kopeks along with a pinch on the cheek, saying in German, "*Hiebsher knabe! Gut, gut!*"

I put my *Gemara* under my arm, kissed the *mezuzah*, and was off to *cheder* like a newborn child, with a pure heart, at peace, with a clear head, with fresh, honest, pious thoughts. The sun peered down and greeted me with its warm rays. A little breeze stole under an earlock, and little birds tweeted, "Tiff-tiff-tiff-tiff!" I was lifted, wafted in the air. I wanted to run, to leap, to dance. Ah, how lovely, how sweet it was to be alive and to be honest, not a thief, not a liar!

I pressed my *Gemara* to my heart very hard and ran to *cheder* with great joy, vowing by that *Gemara* that I would never, never take anything that wasn't mine, never, never steal, never, never lie, be honest always, yes, honest always.

Playing the Violin

A

Today, children, I will play something on the violin for you. To my mind, there is nothing more beautiful, nothing better than to be able to play the violin. Do you think I am wrong? I don't know how it is for you, but as for me, from the time I can remember, I longed for a violin and simply worshiped all musicians! If there were a wedding anywhere in the village I would be the first to run and greet the musicians. I would sneak up behind the bass fiddle, pluck the fattest string— boom!—and run off. Boom!—and run off. For this "booming," I once got into trouble with Berl the bass player, a sullen Jew with a flattened nose and a piercing look. He pretended not to see me sneaking up behind the string bass, but as I stretched out my hand towards the fattest string, he grabbed me by the ear and led me unceremoniously straight to the door:

"There, you rascal, kiss the *mezuzah* and out with you!"

But that hardly deterred me. I still kept on shadowing the musicians. I loved them all, from Shyke the violinist, with his beautiful black beard and slender white fingers, to Getzi the drummer, with his fine humpback and bald patches behind his ears. Many was the time I would hide under a bench listening to the musicians play because otherwise they would chase me out. From under the bench I would watch Shyke's slender fingers dancing over the strings and listen to the sweet sounds he so expertly drew from his violin.

For several days afterwards I would go around in a state of ecstasy, Shyke and his violin always before my eyes. By night he was in my dreams and by day he was in my thoughts—he was never far from my mind. I would pretend I was Shyke the violinist, crook my left arm, wiggle my fingers and make bowing motions with my right arm while tossing my head to the side, eyes half-shut—just like Shyke, down to the last detail!

When my rebbe, Noteh-Leib, saw me making all these motions with my arms, tossing my head and half-shutting my eyes—it was right in the middle of class—he favored me with a ringing slap:

"Look at that scoundrel! We're studying the alphabet and he's making faces, catching flies!"

B

I promised myself that even if the world were to turn upside down, I had to have a violin, no matter what it would cost me! But how could I make myself a violin? Naturally, out of cedar. Oh, it's easy to say, "cedar," but where could I get hold of cedar wood when it only grew, they said, in Israel? But leave it to God—He put an idea into my head. In our house we had an old sofa, one inherited from my grandfather, Reb Anshel, over which my two uncles and my father, blessed be his memory, had feuded continuously. Uncle Benny argued that since he was the eldest son, *he* deserved the sofa; and Uncle Sender argued that since he was the youngest, *he* deserved the sofa; and my father argued that although he was no more than a son-in-law and had no claim to the sofa, his wife, my mother, deserved the sofa because she was an only daughter. That was one point. Secondly, since the sofa was in our house, it was *already* our sofa. But then the two aunts, Aunt Itke and Aunt Zlatke, got into it and carried on so scandalously about the sofa that the whole town was rocking with gossip about the sofa! To make a long story short, the sofa remained *our* sofa.

It was an ordinary sofa with a wooden frame; the thin veneer had become unglued and was warped in egg-shaped blisters in several places. But the veneer coming unglued was real cedar violin wood. That's what I had heard in school. The sofa had one fault that turned to my advantage, namely, when you sat down on it, you couldn't get up because it stood sort of down-hill, on a slope, with a sagging middle. No one wanted to sit on it, so it was stuck away in a corner, "pensioned off," which was a good thing for me.

I had my eye on this sofa. I had long ago acquired a bow. A friend of mine, Shimeli, the son of Yudel the coachman, had promised me a few hairs from the tail of his father's horse. I already possessed resin to smear the bow. I hated relying on miracles, so I traded a metal stay from my mother's crinoline, which had been knocking about the attic, for the resin from my friend, Meir-Lippa, Sara's son. From that bit of metal, Meir-Lippa, Sara's son, fashioned for himself a knife with a double-edged sharp blade. I also had my eye on that knife and wanted him to trade it back but he wouldn't have it. He began shouting:

"Smart aleck! What do you say to that wiseguy? I work my fingers to the bone for three nights, I sharpen and sharpen and cut my fingers into the bargain and he comes along and wants me to trade it back!"

"Just look who's complaining!" I said, "Who needs it! Some bargain, a bit of metal! As if there isn't plenty of metal rolling around our attic! There's enough for generations to come!"

In any case, I had everything I needed. One task remained: to strip the cedar from the sofa. I chose a very good time to do it. While my mother was tending the shop and my father was taking a nap after lunch, I hid in a corner with a nail and then went diligently to work. Somehow in his sleep, my father must have heard the scraping. At first he must have thought it was mice in the house and began shouting from his bed, "Kish! Kish!" I was frightened half to death. My father turned over on his other side and when I heard him snoring, I resumed my work. Suddenly, I looked up—my father was standing there and looking at me strangely. At first, it seems, he could not figure out what I was doing. Then, when he saw the ruined sofa, he dragged me out by the ear and beat me within an inch of my life. I had to be revived with cold water. "God be with you! What have you done to the child?" my mother wept, tears in her eyes.

"Your son and heir will be the death of me!" exclaimed my father, white as a sheet, clutching his heart and falling into a coughing fit for several minutes.

"Why do you have to eat yourself up alive?" my mother said to him, "You're a sick man as it is! Look at your face, may it happen to my enemies!"

C

My desire to play the violin grew as I grew, and to make matters worse, I heard musicians playing daily. Exactly midway between my house and *cheder* stood a little sod-covered shack from which emanated the sounds of many instruments, and above all, the strains of a violin. In the house lived a musician, Naftaltzi the Beardless, a Jew who wore a shortened kaftan, his earlocks tucked behind his ears and a starched collar. He had a substantial nose that looked as if it had been pasted on, thick lips and black teeth, a pock-marked face without a trace of a beard, and that's why they called him "beardless." His wife was a baby machine, nick-named, "Mother Eve." They had a dozen and a half children, if not more, all ill-kempt, half-naked, and barefoot, and every one of them, from the eldest to the youngest, played an in-strument, be it a violin, a cello, a string bass, a trumpet, a flute, a bassoon, a harp, a cymbal, a balalaika, a triangle, or a drum. Several could whistle the best tunes with their lips and with their teeth, or create music by beating on glasses or pots or pieces of wood or even with their cheeks—demons they were, no more, no less!

It was quite by accident that I came to know this fam-ily. I was once standing under their window listening to them play, when one of the older children, Pinni the flut-ist, a lad of fifteen, barefoot, saw me standing there, came out and asked me whether I liked their playing.

"How I wish in ten years I could play like that!" I said.

"You can do it," he said to me and told me that for two rubles a month his father would teach me how to play.

"Which instrument," he asked, "would you like to play? The violin?"

"The violin."

"The violin?" he said. "Can you pay two and a half rubles a month? Or are you a pauper, like me?"

"I can do it," I said, "but there's one thing. No one must know about it, not my father, not my mother, not the rebbe."

"God forbid!" he said. "Who's going to trumpet that around? Maybe you have a cigar butt on you, or a cigarette? No? You don't smoke? Then lend me a little money to buy my own cigarettes. But don't tell anyone because my father mustn't know I smoke and if my mother finds out I have money, she'll take it away and buy bagels for supper. Come into the house. Why stand around out here?"

D

With great fear, a pounding heart, and unsteady legs I crossed the threshhold into this little Garden of Eden.

My new friend, Pinni, introduced me to his father:

"This is Sholom Nakhum Vevik's, a rich man's son. He would very much like to take violin lessons."

Naftaltzi the Beardless tucked his earlocks behind his ears, straightened his collar, buttoned his kaftan and proceeded to deliver a long lecture on playing music in general and on the violin in particular, giving me to understand that the violin was the best and most beautiful of all instruments, the oldest and most respected instrument in the entire world. To prove his point, he noted that the violin was always the solo, not the trumpet or the flute. Always the violin—it was the mother of all instruments.

As Naftaltzi the beardless delivered this lecture on music, he gesticulated so broadly that his nose twitched in accompaniment. I stood gaping at his mouth with its black teeth, taking in his every word.

"The violin, you must understand," said Naftaltzi the beardless, apparently pleased with his lecture, "is an instrument older than all other instruments. The first violinist in the world was Tuval-Cain, or was it Methusaleh, I don't remember exactly. You probably know better than I, you must study this in *cheder*. Another violinist was King David. Another, a third, was Paganini, also a Jew. All the greatest violinists in the world were Jews. For example, Stempenyu and Podhotzur. Of myself I mustn't speak. They say I don't play badly, but how can I compare myself to Paganini? Paganini, they say, sold his soul to Ashmodei for the violin. Paganini hated to play for great people, royalty and popes, even though they paid him handsomely. He preferred to play for poor people in all the little inns, in villages or just in the woods for beasts and birds. That's the kind of violinist Paganini was. All right, kids, to your instruments!"

So Naftaltzi the Beardless commanded his crew of children who assembled in a split second, each picking up his instrument. Naftaltzi himself stood up, tapped his bow on the table, cast a sharp glance at each player and at the group as a whole, and they proceeded to give a concert on their instruments of such power that it almost knocked me off my feet. Each strove to make more noise than the other, and louder than anyone else, screaming in my ear, was a small fellow named Khemele, a skinny boy with a damp nose and bare, swollen feet. Khemele played the oddest instrument, sort of a bag that once inflated, let out the most peculiar sound, a strange screech like a cat whose tail has been stepped on. With his bare foot, Khemele tapped the beat, looking at me all the while with his mischievous little eyes and winked, as if to say: "Don't you think I blow well?" But more than anyone else, Naftaltzi worked the hardest: he played, he conducted, kept the beat with his hands, his feet, with his nose and eyes and with his entire body. And if, God forbid, anyone made a mistake, he gnashed his teeth and said angrily:

"Forte, idiot! Forte, fortissimo! The beat, moron, the beat! . . . One, two, three! One, two, three! . . ."

E

I arranged with Naftaltzi the Beardless to take three lessons a week, an hour and a half each for two rubles a month and implored him to keep it an absolute secret or else I would be a goner. He gave me his word that not a soul would know of it.

"We are the sort of people," he said to me with pride as he straightened his collar, "who never have any money, but honesty and integrity we have more than the wealthiest man! Maybe you have a few groshen on you?"

I took out a ruble and handed it to him. Naftaltzi removed the money delicately from my hand with two fingers, like a physician accepting his fee, called over Mother Eve, turned to her and said:

"Here, go buy something for lunch!"

Mother Eve grabbed the ruble from him with both hands and all her fingers, examined it, and asked her husband what she was to buy.

"Whatever you wish," he answered, affecting indifference. "Buy a few rolls, two or three herring and a little kishka, and don't forget an onion, vinegar and oil, yes, and a bit of whisky while you're at it . . ."

When all these items appeared on the table, the band of children fell to it with enormous appetite as if after a fast. I too was tempted and when I was invited to the table I couldn't refuse. I cannot remember when I have so enjoyed a meal as I enjoyed that feast.

After the feast, Naftaltzi winked to his crew to take up their instruments and this time he honored me with one of his own compositions. It was played so loudly that my ears were deafened and my mind numbed. I left reeling from Naftaltzi the Beardless's composition. All the following day in *cheder*, the rebbe, students, and books were spinning before my eyes, and in my ears all I heard was the din of that composition. At night in my dreams Paganini came riding on Ashmodei and hit me on the head with his violin. I awoke with a shout and a headache and words came pouring out of me as from a faucet. What I said I don't know, but my older sister, Pessl, told me afterwards that I spoke feverishly. The words didn't make sense—crazy words like "composition," and "Paganini." My sister also told me that during the time I was ill, I was visited several times by Naftaltzi the musician's son, a barefoot boy asking after my health, but he was chased off and told never to come back again.

"What's that musician's son doing here?" my sister kept after me to tell her but I held it in, "I don't know, I don't know. How should I know?"

"How does it look?" said my mother to me. "*Kayn eyn horeh*, you're a respectable boy, they're beginning to talk of making a match for you, and you hang out with such fine friends, barefoot little musicians! What can you have in common with musicians? What was Naftaltzi the musician's son doing here?"

"Which Naftaltzi?" I said, pretending ignorance, "What musician?"

"Look at him, that saint," my father put in, "he doesn't know what we're talking about! Innocent as a lamb! When I was your age I was already engaged, and you're still playing with kids! Get dressed and go to *cheder*! If you run into Hershl the tax collector and he asks you what was wrong with you, you are to tell him—nothing was wrong! Do you hear what I'm saying to you? Nothing!"

I hadn't the vaguest idea what Hershl the tax collector had to do with all this. And why did I have to tell him nothing was wrong? In a few weeks my question would be answered.

F

Hershl the tax collector was called by that name because he and his father and his grandfather before him had always held the right to collect taxes. He was a young man with a round belly, a red beard, moist eyes, and a broad white brow—the sign of an intellectual. He did, in fact, have the reputation in the village of being a fine young man who was enlightened, accomplished, educated in Torah, and who wrote well, meaning he had a fine hand. His handwritten documents found their way to all parts of the world. In addition to money, he had an only daughter with red hair and moist eyes, the spitting image of Hershl the tax collector. Her name was Esther, but her nickname was Flester'l. She was timid and refined and was as afraid of us schoolboys as of the Angel of Death. We used to pester her, tease her, making up songs about her:

> Esther'l!
> Flester'l!
> Why don't you have
> A—sister'l?

What could be the harm in those words? Really nothing. Nevertheless when Flester'l heard them, she would cover her ears and run off crying, hide inside her house and be afraid to come out for days.

But that was long ago, when she was a child. Now she was a respectable young lady who braided her red hair in a long plait and dressed like an eligible bride in the latest fashion. My mother thought highly of her, couldn't praise her enough, called her "a gentle dove." On occasional Sabbaths, Esther'l would come visit my sister Pessl and when she saw me, she would turn even redder than she was and would lower her eyes. My sister Pessl would make it a point to call me over to ask me something and would look us both in the eyes.

One day it happened that my father came to my *cheder* with Hershl the tax collector followed by Reb Sholem-Shachneh, the matchmaker, a Jew with six fingers, a curly black beard, a great pauper. Upon seeing such fine guests,

Rebbe Reb Zorach quickly threw on his kaftan and hat. Out of great excitement, one earlock got all tangled up behind his ear, his hat crumpled up exposing most of his yarmulke as his cheeks grew crimson. It was evident something was going on, especially since Sholem-Shachneh the match-maker had for some time now started visiting our *cheder* a bit too frequently. He would call the rebbe out and stand there talking with him for awhile, whispering in hushed tones while gesticulating with his hands, shrugging, and letting out a sigh:

"Well, what is there to say, it's the same old story! If it was meant to be, it will be, but who knows what will happen?"

When the guests came in, our Rebbe Reb Zorach was at a loss to know where he could seat them. He grabbed a kitchen stool on which the rebbitzin salted the meat, spun around a few times, paced back and forth across the room with the stool, then finally set it down and sat down on it himself. But he soon sprang up as if he had been singed, terribly confused, and slapped the back pocket of his kaftan as if he were missing some money.

"Here's a stool, sit down!" he motioned to the guests.

"It's all right, sit, sit!" my father said to him. "We've come here for only a minute or two, Reb Zorach. They want to hear my son read the *Tanakh*."

And my father indicated Hershl the tax collector.

"Ah, with pleasure, why not?" said Rebbe Reb Zorach, grabbing a small *Tanakh* and handed it to Hershl the tax collector, his facial expression seeming to say, "Here, do with it what you will!"

Hershl the tax collector took the small *Tanakh* in his hand like a person who was an expert in the matter, bent his head to the side, shut one eye, shuffled the pages, and placed before me the first chapter of "Song of Songs."

"The 'Song of Songs'?" said the rebbe with a little smile on his lips, as if to say, "You couldn't find anything harder?"

"'Song of Songs'," Hershl the tax collector answered, "'Song of Songs' is not as easy as you think; you have to appreciate the 'Song of Songs'."

"Absolutely!" chimed in Sholem-Shachneh with a little laugh.

The rebbe winked at me. I went to the table, swayed back and forth in prayer and began chanting the lovely melody:

"'Song of Songs'—a song above all songs! Other songs were sung by a prophet, but this song was sung by a prophet who was the son of a prophet! Other songs were sung by a sage but this song was sung by a sage who was the son of a sage! Other songs were sung by a king but this song was sung by a king who was the son of a king!"

As I was chanting I looked at my examiners and noted a different expression on each one's face. My father's face exhibited pride and pleasure. The rebbe's face showed fear and dread lest I make a mistake and fail; his lips silently said each word along with me. Hershl the tax collector sat with his head bent slightly to the side nibbling the tip of his red beard, one eye shut, the other looking up at the ceiling, taking it in like a true connoisseur. Reb Sholem-Shachne the matchmaker never took his eyes off him for so much as a moment. Half of his body leaned forward helping me sway to and fro as I chanted and, not being able to contain himself any longer, he exclaimed, laughing and coughing at the same time as he pointed his index finger at me:

"When people say he knows—he really knows!"

In a few days the engagement platters were broken and I became the lucky fiancé of Hershl the tax collector's only daughter, Flester'l.

G

It sometimes happens that a person grows up more in one day than another does in ten years. When I became engaged I suddenly felt as if I were an adult, seemingly the same person as before, but not really. From my youngest friend to Rebbe Reb Zorach, they began looking at me with more respect—after all, I was engaged and owned a pocketwatch. Even my father stopped scolding me, never mind hitting— how can you treat a bridegroom wearing a gold watch with blows? It would be a disgrace in the eyes of others and a shame for oneself! True, they once hit a bridegroom named Eli in our *cheder* because he was caught skating with the gentile peasants on the ice. The whole village gossiped about it. When his future bride found out about the scandal, she cried so hard they had to break the marriage contract, and the groom, Eli, out of heartbreak and disgrace, wanted to jump into the lake, but it was frozen over.

A calamity like that befell me, not over beatings and not over skating on the ice, but over a violin.

This is how it happened.

In our tavern we had a frequent visitor, Chechek the bandleader, whom we used to call, "The Colonel." He was a hearty young man, tall, with a full, round beard and enormous eyebrows. His speech was a strange mixture of several languages. While speaking, his eyebrows would rise and fall; when he lowered his brows, his face would turn dark as night, and when he would raise them, it became bright as day because under those thick eyebrows were a pair of bright blue, kindly, smiling eyes. He wore a uniform with gold buttons and that is why we called him "The Colonel." He was a steady customer in our tavern, not because he was, God forbid, a drunkard, but for the simple reason that my father was very good at making the best, most delicious Hungarian raisin wine that Chechek adored, could not praise enough. He would lay his huge hand on my father's shoulder and say to him in his strange mixture of languages:

"Herr winemaster! You serve the best Hungarian wine! There is no wine like it even in Budapest, by God!"

Chechek was always very friendly to me, praised me because I was studying hard, would often listen to me, ask me questions and test me. He would ask me about Adam, about Isaac, about Joseph.

"Yoisef?" I asked him in Yiddish, "You mean Yoisef the Righteous?"

"Joseph," he said.

"Yoisef," I corrected him again.

"To us he is Joseph, to you he is Yoisef," he said, pinching my cheek, "Joseph—Yoisef, Yoisef—Joseph, they're both the same."

"Hee-hee-hee!"

I covered my face with my hands and had a good laugh.

But ever since I became engaged, Chechek stopped treating me like a child and started talking to me more as an equal, telling me stories about his regiment and about musicians (this "Colonel" had no end of talk in him but no one had time to listen to him except me). Once when he started to tell me all about playing music, I asked him:

"What instrument does the Colonel play?"

"Every instrument," he answered, raising his eyebrows at me.

"The violin too?" I asked and suddenly his face looked like an angel's to me.

"Come to visit me sometime," he said, "and I'll play for you."

"The only time I can visit you," I said, "is on Saturdays. But only on the condition that no one knows. Do you promise?"

"By God!" he said to me and raised his eyebrows at me.

H

Chechek lived far beyond the town in a little white cottage with small windows, painted shutters, and a flower garden from which peered many tall, proud sunflowers. They inclined their heads slightly to the side, swayed a little and seemed to announce to me: "Come here to us, young man! Here there is space, here there is freedom, here it is light, here it is fresh, here it is warm, here it is pleasant!" And after the stench and the heat and the dust of the town and after the racket and din of the crowded *cheder*, I was drawn there because indeed, there *was* space, there *was* freedom, there *was* light, there it *was*, fresh, warm, pleasant! One longed to run, jump, shout, sing, or throw oneself on the ground and bury one's face in the green, fragrant grass. But, alas, not for us Jewish children!

Yellow sunflowers, green cabbage, fresh air, clean earth, a clear sky, I am sorry to say, are not to be found in our refuse heaps!

I was greeted by a black, shaggy dog with red, fiery eyes. He fell upon me with such force that the wind was almost knocked out of me. Luckily he was tied up. Hearing my cries, Chechek ran out without his uniform and began scolding the dog to be quiet, and the dog quieted down. Then he took me by the hand, led me straight to the black dog and told me not to be afraid of him, he would not harm me. To prove it, he told me to stroke the dog's fur. Without thinking too long, he took my hand and passed it across the dog's back while uttering the dog's name and saying tender words to him. The black fellow dropped his tail, lowered his head, licked himself and gave me a sidelong glanced as if to say: "You're lucky that the master is near or you would be leaving without a hand."

Having gotten over my terror of the dog and gone in the house with "The Colonel," I was astounded to see all the walls hung from top to bottom with guns. On the floor lay an animal fur with the head of a lion or a leopard with terrifyingly sharp teeth. Well, the lion wasn't too worrisome—after all, it was dead; but the guns, the guns! I could hardly enjoy the fresh plums and ripe apples my host served me from his own garden; my eyes kept leaping nervously from one wall to the next. But later, when Chechek removed a violin from a red case, a small, round violin with an odd belly, and laid on it his large spreading beard and his ample, strong hand gave the first few sweeps of the bow, and there poured out the first few melodies, I forgot, in the wink of an eye, the black dog, the fierce lion, and the guns. I saw only Chechek's large, spreading beard and his thick, lowered eyebrows, I saw only a round violin with an odd belly and fingers that danced over the strings with such dexterity that no human mind could be capable of fathoming where he could have gotten so many fingers.

Then Chechek vanished along with his spreading beard and his thick eyebrows and his remarkable fingers and I saw nothing at all before me. There was only a singing, a groaning, a weeping, a sobbing, a murmuring, a roaring—weird, strange sounds that I had never in my life heard before! Sweet sounds like honey, smooth as oil poured forth—poured right into my heart ceaselessly and my soul soared far, far to another sphere, to a paradise of voices only, of pure song.

"Would you like some tea?" Chechek called to me, laying down the violin and slapping me on the back.

I felt as if I had fallen from seventh heaven down to earth.

From that day on I started going every Sabbath to hear Chechek play the violin. I would go directly to the house, not fearing anyone, and I even became so friendly with the black dog that when he saw me, he would wag his tail and try to jump on me, to lick my hand. But I wouldn't let him, "Let's be good friends from afar!"

At home not a soul knew how I was spending my Sabbaths—after all, I was a bridegroom!—and they would never have known about it to this day had not a new calamity befallen me, a great misfortune that I will now tell you about.

I

Why should anyone care, I ask you, if a young Jewish fellow takes a Sabbath afternoon stroll a little further outside the town? Is there really nothing better to do than keep track of others and watch their every step? But of what use are these complaints when human nature dictates, especially Jewish human nature, that Jews must keep an eye on each other, intrude in each others' affairs, find fault and give unsolicited advice? For example, why go over to an utter stranger during prayers and straighten out the front piece of his phylacteries; or stop someone as he is rushing somewhere because it bothers you that one of his trouser legs is turned up; or point a finger at someone so that he can't figure out what is being pointed at: his nose, his beard, or what the devil; or take something from someone's hands as he is struggling to open it and tell him: "You can't do it, let me!" Or stop someone as he is building a house and point out a fault—the ceiling is too high, the rooms too big and the windows too wide, as if he could just take the house apart and start building all over again! That trait is built into us, do you hear, from time immemorial, from the day the world was created. We can't change the world, it isn't our responsibility.

After this introduction, you will not be surprised to learn that Efraim Klutz, a total stranger who had very little to do with us, had been keeping an eagle eye on me, sniffing out where I was going and had exposed me to my father, swearing he himself had seen me eating *treyf* at "The Colonel's" and smoking a cigarette on the Sabbath. He swore an oath, "May I see only good things happen to me, and if I am lying, may I not live to see another day, and if I am speaking so much as one false word, may my mouth be twisted to the side and my eyes fall out!"

"Amen! May it be so!" I said and received a slap from my father for my impertinence. But I am serving the noodles before the fish. I forgot to tell you who Efraim Klutz was, what he was, and what happened.

At the edge of town, on the other side of the bridge, lived this Jew named Efraim Klutz. Why did they call him Klutz? He used to deal in lumber, but no longer. It was a complicated story involving a frame-up. They had discovered in his possession lumber with someone else's trademark and this led to a great deal of trouble, a drawn-out lawsuit; he barely avoided prison. From that time on he gave up his business and became involved in community affairs, public matters, guilds, taxes, synagogues. At first he wasn't successful at all, there were humiliations; but the more he became involved, working his way into people's confidence, letting them know he knew "how to open the right doors," the more Efraim in time became a useful person, so essential they couldn't do without him. That's the way a worm crawls into an apple, makes himself at home, beds himself down comfortably, and soon takes over.

Efraim was short, with stumpy legs, small hands, red cheeks, a quick, bird-like, hopping gait accompanied by a toss of the head. He spoke rapidly in a squeaky voice and his staccato laugh sounded like the scattering of dried beans. I could barely stand to look at him; I don't know why. Every Sabbath when I was going to Chechek's or coming from Chechek's, I would meet him on the bridge strolling along wearing a full-length, patched, sleeveless Sabbath coat. He walked with his arms folded behind him, humming in a thin, high-pitched voice as his long coat flapped against the heels of his shoes.

"Good *Shabbos*!" I said to him.

"Good *Shabbos*!" he said. "Where is the young man going?"

"Just strolling," I said.

"Just strolling? All by yourself?" he said and looked straight into my eyes with the kind of smile whose meaning was hard to guess: was it clever of me to be strolling alone, was it a joke or plain stupidity?

J

Once, on my way to Chechek's, I noticed Efraim Klutz's eyes following me closely. When I stopped on the bridge and gazed down into the water, Efraim also stopped and gazed down into the water. When I started back, he also started back. When I turned the other way, so did he. Then I managed to lose him. Later, when I was sitting at Chechek's table drinking tea, we heard the black dog barking loudly at someone and straining at his rope. Looking out the window, I imagined I saw a short, dark person with stumpy legs scurrying off. By his gait I could have sworn it was Efraim Klutz.

And so it was. I came home on the Sabbath at dusk, after the *Havdalah* service, my face aflame, and found Efraim sitting at the table. He was talking rapidly and laughing his curious little laugh. When he saw me, he fell silent and tapped his short fingers on the table. Across from him sat my father, pale as a ghost, twisting his beard nervously, pulling out the hairs one by one, a sign he was very angry.

"Where are you coming from?" my father asked and looked at Efraim.

"Where should I be coming from?" I said.

"How do I know from where?" he said. "You tell me from where. You know better."

"From the study house," I said.

"And where were you all day?" he said.

"Where should I have been?" I said.

"How do I know where?" he said. "You tell me where, you know better."

"In the study house," I said.

"What did you do in the study house?" he said.

"What should I have done in the study house?" I said.

"How should I know what you should have done?" he said.

"I studied," I said.

"What did you study?" he said.

"What should I have studied?" I said.

"How do I know what you should have studied?" he said.

"*Gemara* is what I studied." I said.

"Which *Gemara* did you study?" he said.

"Which *Gemara* should I have studied?" I said.

"How do I know which *Gemara* you should have studied?" he said.

"The *Gemara* on the Sabbath is what I studied." I said.

At this point Efraim Klutz burst out laughing in his staccato little laugh and here my father could stand it no longer. He sprang up from his chair and bestowed on me two resounding, fiery slaps that made me see stars. My mother heard this from the other room and ran in screaming:

"Nakhum! God be with you! What are you doing? He's engaged to be married, and this before the wedding? Just think, what if his future father-in-law finds out, God forbid?"

My mother was right. My future father-in-law did find out about the whole episode—Efraim himself told him and in this way got back at him because the two of them had always been at swords' point.

* * *

On the following day the marriage contracts and presents were returned and I was no longer a bridegroom-to-be. My father fell ill from grief and was bedridden for some time, refusing to look upon my face no matter how much my mother pleaded with him on my behalf.

"The shame!" he said, "The shame is worse for me than anything!"

"It's no great matter!" my mother tried to comfort him, "God will send us another match. What can we do? Take our own lives? Maybe it wasn't meant to be."

Among those who came to call on my father was Chechek the bandmaster. When my father saw him, he removed his yarmulke, sat up in bed, and extended an emaciated hand, looked him right in the eyes and said:

"Oy, Colonel! Colonel!"

That was all he could manage to utter as he choked back the tears and the coughs.

That was the very first time in my life I had ever seen my father cry. My heart ached and my soul grieved. I stood looking out the window, swallowing my tears. At that moment I truly regretted the pain I had caused. I repented with all my heart and solemnly vowed I would never, never arouse my father's anger again, never, never cause him to suffer on my account.

No more violins!

Robchik

(*A Jewish Dog*)

A

Robchik was a white spotted dog, not large but medium-sized, shy, not a grabber. Unlike other dogs, he loathed attacking people from behind, ripping a trouser leg or biting them on the calf. He was content to be left alone. And as luck would have it, everyone tormented him, anyone at all. To swat Robchik on the rump with a stick or to kick him in the flank with one's heel, to fling a rock at his head, or to pour slops on him was almost an obligation, a great sport.

When Robchik received a blow, he didn't hold his ground like other dogs, didn't argue, bark or show his teeth; no, at every blow Robchik would cower almost to the ground, yowl: "Ai—ai!" and run off with his tail between his legs, hide in a corner and lose himself in his thoughts and catch flies.

B

Who was Robchik? Where did he come from? That's hard to say. It could be that he was left behind by the old landowner. It's possible he was a stray, had lost his master, found a new master and remained on.

Have you ever found a woebegone dog following at your heels as you are out walking? "Where did this pest come from?" you might wonder as you raise your hand to shoo the dog away, "Scat! Get out of here!" The dog stops, cowers like a person expecting a blow, but keeps following you. You lean over close and make as if to throw something at him. It does no good. Finally you stop and look at the dog; the dog stops and looks at you; you look at one another wordlessly. You spit in disgust and go on your way—the dog still trails behind you. You lose your composure, pick up a stick and go at him angrily. The dog suddenly rolls over on the ground, legs in the air, trembling and staring you in the face, as if to say: "Here! You want to beat me? Go ahead and beat me!"

That's the kind of dog our Robchik was.

C

Robchik was not a greedy dog. Even if good food were left about, he would not touch it. Robchik knew that whatever lay under the table belonged to him, and anything else was not his business.

When he was younger, they say, he was a rather bold rascal. He once unthinkingly grabbed a goose foot from the salting board. He was caught by Brayne, the cook, a woman with a dark mustache, who began to shout: "Isaac! Isaac!" Isaac came running at the very moment Robchik was running through the door with the goose foot, and Isaac trapped him so that half of his body was on one side of the door and the other half on the other side. They really taught him a lesson: on one side Isaac beat him on the head with a stick while on the other side Brayne did the same with a slab of firewood, all the while screaming, "Isaac! Isaac!"

From that time the memory of it remained indelible: when anyone approached him and merely shouted at him, "Isaac!" he would take to his heels.

D

More than anyone he was tormented by Paraske, the peasant woman who did our laundry, whitewashed the walls, and milked the cow.

What grudge she had against Robchik is hard to say; he seemed always to be underfoot and when she would see him, she would become enraged, "May the plague take you, you miserable cur!" And as if to spite her, Robchik was always underfoot.

At work Paraske would have her revenge on him, as we did on Haman. When she did the laundry, she would pour a cold tub of water on him. Robchick hated this kind of bath and would take a long time shaking himself off. When she whitewashed the walls, she would splatter white lime on his face that took him an hour to lick off. When she milked the cow, she would honor him with a whack on the legs with a chunk of firewood. Robchik learned how to jump skillfully so that when he saw the chunk of wood coming at him, he would avoid it with an agile leap.

Once he was severely punished for this trick. Paraske threw a chunk of firewood at him and this time struck his foreleg. Robchik yelped, not in a dog's voice but in a strange high-pitched screech: "Ai-ai-ai-ai-ai-ai!" People came running from all around. When Robchik saw all the people, he began to feel sorry for himself, showing everyone his injured leg, as if to say: "Just look at what Paraske has done to me!" Robchik thought they would all come to his defense and Paraske would surely be beheaded for this deed.

Instead the crowd broke out in laughter; Brayne with the mustache flew out of the kitchen with a ladle in hand, wiping her nose with her bare arm: "Broke the *shlimazel*'s leg? Good for him!" Also the street urchins, those mischief-makers, came running and began shouting and whistling at Robchik. Along came Paraske and delivered the final blow: she poured a pail of boiling water on him. Robchik began howling and yelping, "Ai-ai-ai! Ai-ai-ai!" as he leaped in the air, spun in circles, bit his own tail and kept yowling with such intense pain that the laughter among the young scamps redoubled. When they saw Robchik dancing on three legs, they cursed him out and gave him a few extra good blows. Robchik limped off with a whimper, rolled over and over on the ground as the boys chased after him with sticks and stones, whooping, whistling, driving, and shooing him away further and further out of town, to the far side of the mills.

E

Robchik ran with the conviction that he could never return to the town as long as he lived! He ran aimlessly, wherever his legs took him. He ran and ran until he arrived at the next village, where he encountered the village dogs. The village dogs sniffed him over.

"Welcome, dog! Where are you coming from and what's wrong with your back? Looks like a chunk of fur is burned right off there."

"Ach! Don't ask!" said Robchik to them with a sad expression, "It's a long story, not worth hearing. Is it possible to stay the night here?"

"With the greatest pleasure!" said the village dogs, "The out-of-doors is big enough and under the sky it's even bigger."

"How is the eating situation here?" asked Robchik. "How do you satisfy your hunger when the stomach craves food?"

"Oh! One can't complain!" said the village dogs, "There's garbage everywhere, and God created bones when He created meat. Let them eat meat, the masters, so long as we have the bones. Anything, as they say, just to fill the gut."

"So, and what are your masters like?" Robchik went on and wagged his tail like someone who wants to thoroughly assess the situation.

"Masters are masters," said the village dogs and ended the discussion.

"And Paraske?" said Robchik.

"Who's Paraske?" asked the village dogs.

"Paraske," said Robchik, "the one who does the laundry, whitewashes the walls, and milks the cow. You don't know Paraske?"

The village dogs looked at Robchik as if he were out of his mind, "Who is this Paraske?" They sniffed him over a second time and went off one at a time, each to his own refuse heap.

F

"What lucky dogs!" Robchik thought and stretched himself out on God's earth, under God's sky, preparing to catch a little nap. But he couldn't fall asleep. First, there was the scalded hide; it smarted and itched terribly! And the flies pestered him awfully, there was no escape from them! Second, his stomach was grumbling; he would love to be able to chew something, but there wasn't anything to eat; he would have to wait till morning. And third, keeping him from sleeping were the thoughts he had about what he had heard from the village dogs; they didn't have any Isaacs who squashed them in a door and beat them with slabs of firewood; they didn't have any Paraskes who poured boiling water over them; they didn't have any street urchins who threw stones, whistled, and chased them away. "There are lucky dogs in this world! And I thought mine was the only world. A worm lies in horseradish and thinks there is nowhere sweeter."

Robchik fell asleep and he dreamed of a slop pile, large and full of chunks of bread, chicken innards, beefy blood vessels, buckwheat kasha mixed with millet and beans, and bones, bones—a veritable treasure of bones!

Knuckle bones, rib bones, marrow bones, fish bones, whole herring heads, not yet sucked out. Robchik didn't know where to begin.

"Welcome!" said the village dogs, looking at him from a distance as he prepared to dig into the feast.

"Come eat!" Robchik said generously.

"Eat your fill!" said the village dogs in a friendly manner.

Suddenly he heard a voice right in his ear: "Isaac!" Robchik woke with a start—it was just a dream! . . .

In the morning Robchik set out through the alleyways searching for a garbage heap, a dry crust of bread, a little bone. But wherever he went, all the places were taken.

"Is there any room to join you for a meal?" asked Robchik.

"Here? No! Maybe in the next alley."

Robchik ran from one alley to the next. Everywhere it was the same story. Then he decided—why wait to be invited? No, he would go over and grab whatever he could. But at the first grab he received an ignominious rebuff from the village dogs. First they looked at him angrily, growling and baring their teeth, and then a few of them suddenly attacked him, tearing and biting his flesh, tattering his tail and escorted him to the other side of the city gate.

G

With his tail between his legs, Robchik headed for the next village. When he arrived, it was again the same story: at first polite words, a hearty welcome, "our pleasure." But afterwards, when it came to the garbage heap, they began glaring at him angrily, growling, baring their teeth, tearing and biting him—and away with you!

Robchik was getting tired of this exile, this wandering from one place to the next and he came to this conclusion: people are bad; dogs are no better. He might as well set out for the woods and live among the wild animals.

And Robchik headed for the woods.

For three days he walked aimlessly, a lonely dog going in circles as he felt his belly shrink and his intestines shrivel. He was virtually dying of hunger and thirst! He might as well stretch out on the ground in the middle of the woods and expire! But for some reason, he yearned to live on.

Robchik lay down under a tree, extended his tail behind him, stretched out his front paws, stuck out his tongue, and pondered a canine question: "Where to get a crust of bread? Where to get a bit of meat? At least a bone? A drop of water?" And out of great anguish he became a deep thinker, a philosopher: why was he, a dog, being punished more than all the other beasts and birds and all the creatures in the world? "Look, there a bird is flying straight to its nest . . . there a lizard is running home to its hole . . . there a little worm is crawling, a beetle, an ant—all of them have what they need; all I can do is howl and howl!"

"Who's that howling in the woods?" called out a wolf running past, his tongue hanging out in hunger.

Robchik had never seen a wolf. He thought it was a dog and so he got up slowly, unhurried, stretched, and approached the wolf.

"Who are you?" the wolf said to him haughtily. "What's your name? Where are you coming from? And what are you doing here?"

Robchik was delighted to have found a kindred spirit; at least he would have someone to share his troubles with. And he poured out his bitter heart to the wolf.

"To tell the truth," Robchik ended his sad account, "I would be happy to encounter a lion, a bear, or even a wolf."

"What do you think would happen?" said the wolf with a nasty smile.

"Who knows? Who cares?" said Robchik, "If I'm fated to die, I'd rather be devoured by a wolf rather than perish from hunger among my own, among dogs . . ."

"So!" the wolf said, drawing himself up to his full height and gnashing his teeth, "Know that I am a wolf! And I am most eager to tear you to bits and make a meal of you because I am very hungry. I haven't had anything in my mouth for eight days!"

Hearing those words, our Robchik became so frightened that his ragged hide began to quiver.

"My lord, my king! Dear Reb Wolf!" Robchik said with a piteous face and a weeping voice, "Let God send you a better meal. How much will you get to eat of me, more's the pity? Fur and bones? Take my advice, let me go, have pity on my dog's life!"

Saying this, Robchik hung his tail, bent his back, groveled on his belly and made such revolting, subservient movements that he made the wolf sick to his stomach.

"Lift that disgusting tail of yours," said the wolf, "and get the devil out of here, you mongrel, so I don't have to look at your ugly mug any more!"

Half dead, half alive, Robchik began to run, not feeling the ground beneath him, afraid even to look back. He made tracks, fleeing far, far from the woods, back to his own town!

H

When he returned to the town, Robchik discovered how much he missed the courtyard where he had grown up. His heart tugged, pulled him back to the very courtyard where he had been beaten and attacked, the very courtyard where they had broken his leg and scalded his back. He headed for the marketplace, to the butcher shops, to join the butcher's dogs, that is to say, his *own* kind.

"Look who's here! Where has a dog been?" the butcher's dogs greeted him with a yawn as they prepared for a night's sleep.

"I'm really from around here," said Robchik, "You don't recognize me? I'm Robchik!"

"Robchik? Robchik? A familiar name!" said the butcher's dogs and pretended not to remember who he was.

"What's that big scar on your rump?" asked Tzutzik, a little dog, jumping right in his face with great impertinence.

"It's an identification mark. It's a beauty mark, don't you understand?" added Rudek mockingly. He was a red dog with mottled fur.

"Listen to him!" responded Sirko, a gray dog, an old fellow with one eye and a torn ear. "When it comes to scars, ask me; *I'll* tell you what it means. It's a sign of fights with packs of dogs."

"Everyone has something to say!" cried Zhuk, a black dog without a tail, "Better let Robchik talk, he'll tell us himself."

And Robchik stretched out on the ground and began to tell his entire story, not omitting a detail. They all lay there listening, but Rudek, the red dog who liked to mock, kept interrupting him with snide comments.

"Rudek, will you be quiet?" said Zhuk, the black tailless dog, and gave a great yawn, "Tell us, tell us, Robchik! We love to hear stories after supper."

And Robchik went on telling his woeful tale in a sorrowful voice, but no one was really listening. Tzutzik was talking quietly to Sirko, Rudek made snide comments, and Zhuk kept snoring like ten sleeping soldiers, jerking awake, yawning and saying, "Tell us, tell us, Robchik! We love to hear stories after supper."

I

Robchik was on his feet first thing in the morning. He stood at a distance observing the butchers with their cleavers hacking up the meat. In one direction he saw a whole forequarter hanging, blood running from its neck; in another direction he saw a hindquarter lying, a beautiful side of beef, marbled with fat. Robchik looked and swallowed hard. The butchers hacked the meat into chops, occasionally tossing a piece of skin, some gristle, or a bone to the dogs who quickly snapped up whatever they could in mid-air. Robchik was amazed at how the dogs could know exactly how high to leap, not letting the smallest bone get by, and each dog, after snagging his share, would move to the side and lie down proudly to devour his feast, all the while looking balefully at the other dogs as if to say:

"See this bone? This is my bone, and only *I* am going eat it."

The other dogs pretended not to be impressed but inwardly they were thinking:

"Choke on it! Get sick on it! All he does is gobble up his food and we have to watch him eat. May worms eat *him*!"

One dog was carrying off a piece of hide looking for a spot where he could eat it without being seen—he didn't trust his good luck.

And another dog stood in front of an angry butcher who was lashing out, shouting and cursing everyone in sight. The dog was wagging his tail obsequiously and called out to the other dogs smugly:

"Do you see that butcher? He looks angry to you, doesn't he? I assure you he is a wonderful person! A gem of a man! A golden character! He really has pity on dogs; he loves dogs. You'll soon see a bone and a piece of meat come flying—grab!"

And he leaped into the air and snapped his teeth so the others would think he had really snared a tasty morsel.

One of the dogs said contemptuously, "Either he is a lying flatterer or a braggart, may the devil take him!"

Another dog stood near a wooden chopping block. When the butcher turned away for a moment, the dog leaped up to the cutting block and began licking it with his tongue. A loud barking ensued as the other dogs denounced him to the butcher and swore up and down that this thief of a dog had stolen a huge piece of meat. Would that they had a chunk of gold as big! May what they had just seen with their own eyes be theirs! If it were not so, may they drop dead on the spot, may they choke on the first bone they ate, may they never enjoy the horns or the hooves of slaughtered sheep!

"Feh, repulsive! It makes you sick to your stomach!" cried an old dog who would himself have been eager to steal a lick. And Robchik thought to himself: "What's the use of standing about and just looking on?" These other dogs were all jumping and grabbing; he would do the same. But barely had he made a move when several dogs at a time had him by the throat and were biting him. They bit him hardest on the very spot where he was already hurt.

Robchik lowered his tail, crawled off into a corner, drew in his chin and began to whimper.

"Why are you crying?" said Zhuk, licking his chops after eating.

"Why shouldn't I cry?" said Robchik, "I am the most unfortunate dog in the world! I thought that here, among my own, I would at least be able to get something to eat. Believe me, I wouldn't come begging but I'm starving to death, dying of hunger!"

"I believe you," said Zhuk with a sigh. "I know what hunger means. I feel for you. But I can't help you at all. Here the custom is that each butcher has his own dog and each dog has his own butcher."

"Is that right?" asked Robchik, "Where is justice? Where is humanity? After all, how can a dog be shunned by dogs? Why should a hungry dog among the well-fed be allowed to die of hunger?"

"I can only help you with a sigh," said Zhuk, who yawned broadly and eased into his after-meal snooze.

"If that's the case," said Robchik, steeling himself, "I'll go straight to the butchers. Maybe I can get myself a butcher."

"With pleasure!" said Zhuk sleepily, "So long as you don't go to *my* butcher, because if you do, I'll see to it that you'll be without a tail, like me. Do you understand?"

J

And Robchik ran off straight to the butchers, bypassing and avoiding the other dogs and began to ingratiate himself to the choppers, jumping in their faces and wagging his tail. But a *shlimazel* never has any luck. One of the butchers, a healthy youth with broad shoulders, in jest apparently, threw a cleaver at him. Luckily Robchik could jump, otherwise he would have been cut in half.

"You're a pretty good dancer!" said Rudek to him mockingly, "Much better than our Tzutzik. Tzutzik! Come here and you'll see dancing!"

Tzutzik came running and jumped right in Robchik's face. Robchik could bear it no longer. He gripped Tzutzik with his teeth, threw him down and bit him in the belly. He let out all his bitterness on Tzutzik and then turned tail and took off.

Robchik found himself alone on the outskirts of town, stretched himself out in the middle of a path, and out of dismay and shame he buried his chin between his paws and hid from the bright pitiless sun. He no longer noticed the swarming flies biting him. "Let them bite me, let them torment me, what difference does it make!"

"It's the end of the world!" thought Robchik, "If a dog can't survive so much as one day among his *own*—well, it's the end of the world!"

Methuselah

(*A Jewish Horse*)

A

ethuselah—that was what he was called in Kasrilevka because he was so old. He didn't have any teeth in his head except for two or three stumps with which he barely managed to chew whatever food came his way. He was tall, emaciated, with a mangy hide, a sway back, bad eyes—one had a cataract, the other was bloodshot—spindly legs, protruding hipbones, sunken flanks, a mournfully sagging lower lip, and a threadbare tail—such is his portrait. In his old age he worked for Kasriel the water-carrier, pulling a water cart.

By nature Methuselah was obedient and stoic and had long been overworked. After a full day of slogging through the Kasrilevka muck and providing the town with water, he was content to be unhitched from the water cart, thrown some straw and fed some slops that Kasriel's wife served him as if he were a special guest dining on a platter of fish or a bowl of holiday dumplings. Methuselah would look forward to the slops as if it were a treat, because he could always find in it a piece of soaked bread, some kasha, and other soft food that didn't require chewing. Kasriel's wife collected food for Methuselah all day, throwing into the slop pail anything she could spare—let the poor horse have something to eat. And when Methuselah was finished eating, he would turn his head toward the water cart and his back toward Kasriel's wife as if to say: "Thank you very much for this meager fare," his sagging lower lip sagging a bit more, his seeing eye shut, he would sink into equine thoughts.

B

But do not be misled into believing that life was always this way for Methuselah. There was a time in his youth when he was still a colt running behind his mother's wagon, when he showed promise of becoming a top-notch horse. Connoisseurs predicted great things for him. "Someday," they said, "you will see him harnessed to a carriage among the finest and most excellent of horses!"

When the colt became a full-grown horse, they threw a bridle on him and led him to the fair where, along with many other horses, he was run back and forth some fifty times for prospective buyers who carefully examined his teeth and raised his legs to check his hoofs. He was eventually sold.

That was the beginning of his long diaspora, his wandering from one place to the next, from one master to another, perpetually hauling large, heavy wagonloads, slogging through belly-high mud, accompanied by no end of whippings, floggings, and blows to the flanks, the head, the legs, and other parts.

C

For a long time he was part of a mail-wagon team, with the postal bell announcing their arrival ringing constantly in his ear: ding-ding-dong! At top speed he flew back and forth daily along the very same route. Then he was sold to an ordinary farmer whom he helped with his back-breaking labors: plowing, planting, hauling enormous wagonloads of grain, kegs of water, loads of manure, performing tasks more suitable for oxen than for horses. From there he fell into the hands of a gypsy who abused him cruelly to make him run faster, something he would never forget the rest of his life!

From the gypsy he went to a horsefarm and shortly thereafter he was sent to a Mazepevka coachman who drove a heavy wagon reinforced with iron, hung with many bells and covered with a strange thatched canopy. There, at this coachman's with the covered wagon, he was constantly on the receiving end of whippings and floggings, as if a horse's hide were made of leather, not flesh and blood, as if a horse's flanks were made of iron, not of bones. Poor horse, how often did it happen that he barely managed to stagger home, feeling the harness straps cutting into his flesh and a heavy weight in his stomach like a knot while the brutish coachman kept crying, "Giddyap!" lashing and poking him with the whip for no earthly reason.

But luckily for him, the coachman made it a rule that one day a week they remained in one spot and then he could simply stand still and chew and do nothing at all. More than once Methuselah would wonder about this pause but his horse's mind could not figure it out. What was the reason for this day off on which no one budged from his spot? And why couldn't it be like this every day? He thought about this as he pricked up his ears, shut one eye, and looked at his two comrades who were harnessed to the same covered wagon.

D

After leaving the coachman with the covered wagon, Methuselah was hitched to a threshing machine. He did back-breaking labor, trudging all day long around a wheel in a circle, inhaling more than his share of dust and chaff that invaded his nose, his mouth, and his eyes, while he was deafened by the constant din of the threshing machine. "What can be the purpose of this going round and round in one place?" he would often think and wish he could stop and rest for a moment. But they didn't let him ponder for long. Behind him stood a man goading him on with a whip. "Imbecile!" thought Methuselah stealing a sidelong glance at his tormentor, "I'd like to see them hitch *you* to this wheel and whip *you* to go round and round without any rhyme or reason!"

Understandably enough, this revolving in ever-present dust ruined his health, one eye developed a cataract, the other became bloodshot, and his legs stiffened. These serious defects made him of no use to anyone. Again he was led to the fair with the thought of palming him off on someone. They combed him down nicely, tried to make him presentable by tying his tail under and polishing his hoofs with grease. But it was useless; no one was fooled. No matter how hard they tried to make him look younger, to hold his head with pride, he remained what he always was: his head lowered meekly, his bony legs splayed out, his lower lip drooping to the side, and a tear slipping from one eye. No, there were no buyers for Methuselah! The few men who approached didn't bother to look into his mouth but merely ran a hand over his chin, spat, and left. One showed some interest but not so much in Methuselah as in his hide. But they couldn't settle on a price; the hide dealer figured it didn't pay: transporting, slaughtering, and skinning him would cost more than the hide was worth.

But it was apparently Methuselah's destiny to have a comfortable old age. Kasriel the water carrier appeared and brought him to Kasrilevka.

E

Up until that time, Kasriel the water-carrier, a broadboned Jew with a flat nose and a hairy face, was his own horse, lugging the water himself. He harnessed himself to the water cart and pulled it all over town. As much as Kasriel suffered all his life, he never envied anyone, but when he would see someone riding a horse, he would stop and look longingly after him. His one wish in the world was that God would help him obtain a horse. But no matter how hard he scrimped he was never able to come up with enough capital to buy a horse. Yet whenever the fair was in town, he never failed to stroll among the horses, just looking, as they say. One day, seeing a miserable, mangy, dejected horse at the fair, without a bridle and not hitched up, Kasriel stopped. His heart told him this horse would suit his purse.

And so it was. He didn't need to bargain very long; Kasriel took the horse and ran home with a happy heart. He knocked at the door and his wife ran out, frightened.

"What is this? God be with you."

"I bought it, as I am a Jew, I bought it!"

Kasriel and his wife didn't know where to put the horse. Had they not been embarrassed for their neighbors, they would have taken him into the house. They soon gathered some straw and hay and the couple stood admiring their new horse, unable to look their fill.

The neighbors came around to check out the bargain that Kasriel had picked up at the fair. They laughed at the horse, ridiculed it, made snide comments about him, as was their way. One joked that this was no horse at all but a mule. Another said, "What mule? It's really a cat!" A third said it was no more than a wraith that a strong wind could carry off.

"How old could he be?" someone asked.

"Older than Kasriel and his wife put together."

"He's as old as Methuselah."

"Methuselah!"

And from that day on the name of Methuselah stuck.

F

Life with Kasriel the water-carrier and his wife was better than ever before, even in his best years. First of all, his labor was ludicrously easy. Pulling a water cart and stopping at every house was hardly what you would call work! And his master was an absolute gem of a man. He never touched him, never raised his voice, carried a whip only for appearances! And the food. True, he never laid eyes on oats, but what good were oats when he had no teeth to chew them? Weren't the slops and the soft bread chunks that Kasriel's wife served him every day far better? And not so much the slops as the manner in which it was served. You had to see Kasriel's wife, her arms clasped over her heart, thoroughly enjoying watching Methuselah eat, *kayn eyn horeh*. At night they would prepare a bed of straw for him in the back of the house and take turns checking to make sure no one had run off with him. Early in the morning, when even God Himself was still asleep, Kasriel was already tending the horse. He would harness him gently to the water cart, seat himself and ride to the lake to fetch water while singing a strange song:

Ashrei ha'ish asher lo halakh . . .

"Happy is the man who does not go by foot . . ." And when he had filled the barrel with water, he would walk back, now without a song, plodding through the mud alongside Methuselah, waving his whip: "Come on now, Methuselah, get a move on, get a move on!"

Methuselah pulled his legs from the mud, shook his head, and peered with his good eye at his master, thinking: "In all my days as a horse I've never worked for such a strange creature!" And the horse decided there and then to plant his rear legs deep in the mud as a prank, as if to say: "All right, let's see what happens now?" When he realized the horse had suddenly halted, Kasriel began poking around the water cart, checking the wheels, the axles, the reins; and Methuselah turned his head to Kasriel and moved his lips in a horselike smile, thinking: "What a fool this water-carrier is! An idiot, a simpleton!"

G

But no happiness is ever complete. As happy as Methuselah was in his old age with Kasriel and his wife, that's how wretched, abused, miserable, and humiliated he was made to feel by their children, by their neighbors' children, and all the other children.

From the moment they brought him home and the children laid eyes on him, they immediately felt—not hatred, God forbid—but on the contrary, great love for him; but this love was for Methuselah his undoing. Would that they had loved him less and pitied him more.

When no one was looking, Kasriel's sons, barefoot Talmud Torah students, tried to test whether he had the same feelings as a human being. They lightly jabbed his hide with a stick—nothing; they tickled his legs—nothing; a flick on the ear—barely a reaction. Only when they poked a little straw into his wall eye did they realize he had the same feelings as a human being because he blinked his eye and jerked his head back and forth as if he were saying: "No, don't do that, I don't like it." If that were the case, they found a twig from a broom and shoved it way up his nose. Methuselah sprang back, pranced and snorted until Kasriel came running, shouting at the top of his lungs:

"Misfits, monsters, why are you torturing the horse? Get to *cheder*, you good-for-nothings!"

The boys took to their heels and ran off to school.

H

In the Talmud Torah there was a boy named Reuve'le, a spirited lad, an imp, may God protect us from that sort! His own mother used to say of him, "Such children are sown thickly but should be weeded out quickly." His purpose in life was to get under everyone's skin. Wherever there was a roof, he was on it, wherever there was a cellar, he was down it. The greatest fun for him was chasing chickens, geese, and ducks, frightening goats, tormenting cats, and beating dogs. We won't even speak of pigs! The spankings he received from his mother, the lashings from the Talmud Torah teacher, and the slaps from total strangers were wasted, and the curses that were cast on him were like spitting into the wind. It seemed he shed tears when he was spanked, but the minute you turned away—aha! Reuve'le had stuck out his tongue, thrust his lower lip out or puffed up his cheeks at you. And he had a pair of cheeks like dumplings. He was always healthy and always cheerful. The fact that his mother was a destitute widow and worked herself to death to pay a ruble a month for his tuition was not his concern.

When Reuve'le found out from Kasriel's children that their father had brought home a horse named Methuselah from the fair, he jumped up on a stool, wiped his nose with both hands, and roared:

"Kids, we have our 'violin bow'!"

It must be noted that from childhood on, Reuve'le had loved musicians, longed for a violin, went out of his mind when he heard a violin playing. He also had quite a nice singing voice and could sing songs by heart. He had no other ambition than to grow up, God willing, buy a violin, and play it night and day. In the meantime he had made for himself a little violin out of a piece of wood, using thread instead of strings, thereby earning a good spanking from his mother.

"A violinist is what you want to be? May I never live to see the day!"

In the evening, after Chaim-Khone, the Talmud Torah teacher, had dismissed the students, they all went to welcome Kasriel the water-carrier's horse. The first to speak up was Reuve'le, saying he thought this horse was an excellent horse who would donate as many violin strings from his tail as they would need. To prove it, he would show them!

And Reuve'le stole up behind Methuselah and began plucking hairs from his tail. So long as Reuve'le plucked the hairs one at a time, Methuselah tolerated it, as if to say: "A hair from my tail? What harm can that do me? My life will be the same if I have one less hair!" But when Reuve'le became more enthusiastic and began tearing out whole tufts, Methuselah was not pleased at all, thinking: "Let a pig in your house, he climbs up on your table." And without thinking too long about it, he kicked Reuve'le right in the teeth with his hind leg, splitting his lip.

"Serves you right! He'll be the death of me! You deserved it! He'll give me a stroke! Don't go where you don't belong!" lamented his mother, Yente the busybody, as she applied cold water to his split lip, crying and wringing her hands, then ran to Khyene, the healer's wife, complaining furiously all the way.

I

Reuve'le was, thank God, the kind of child who healed as quickly as an animal. Before you knew it, his lip was as good as new, as if nothing had happened and he came up with a new idea: it would be great to take a ride on Methuselah, all the Talmud Torah students at one time. But when and how could this be pulled off so that no one would know? Reuve'le decided the only time would be Sabbath afternoon after everyone had eaten and laid down for a nap. At that time you could walk off with the whole town. But one Talmud Torah boy challenged this plan: "How can a Jew ride on the Sabbath?" Reuve'le had an answer: "Dolt! It's not riding! It's playing!"

Sabbath afternoon, after everyone had finished eating and had laid down for a nap, Kasriel and his wife among them, the boys carefully stole into the water-carrier's yard and Reuve'le began dressing Methuselah up for the occasion. First he braided his mane, weaving in bits of straw; then he put a tall white paper hat on his head and tied it under his chin; and finally, he tied an old broom to his rump so that his tail would look fuller and handsomer. The boys clambered over each other and onto Methuselah's back; whoever got a seat first sat on the horse's back; the others would have a turn later but in the meantime they followed behind, urging Methuselah to go faster as they sang:

"This is how we honor the horse as Reuve'le commands!"

But Methuselah was in no mood to run and simply walked at his own pace, step by slow step. First of all, what was the rush? And second of all, wasn't this a day of rest? But Reuve'le kept urging the horse on, prodding and jabbing and screaming with all his might at the other boys:

"To the devil with it, why don't you all say something too?!"

And Methuselah kept to his own leisurely pace, thinking: "The kids are playing, let them have fun."

But when the boys began pushing him too hard, teasing him and waving their hands in his face, Methuselah started to go faster and when he did this, the broom banged against his legs; he quickened his pace and the broom banged against him even harder; when he began to rear and buck, the boys were delighted and Reuve'le encouraged him: "Hup-hup-hup!" He reared and bucked until the boys began to fall off one by one. And only when Methuselah had thrown them all off and felt he was free did he begin to run wildly, running easily past the mills, far, far beyond the town limits.

Seeing this utterly ridiculous creature wearing a tall paper hat come galloping past, the gentile shepherds started to chase him. They teased him, threw their staffs at him, and set the dogs on him. The dogs didn't need to be asked twice and chased after Methuselah, biting and snapping at him. Several caught him by the calfs of his leg, a few attacked him at the throat. Methuselah began snorting, and in a short time they brought about his death.

J

The following morning the boys received their just deserts. In addition to banged noses and bruised foreheads from the fall, they received punishments at home and lashings from Chaim-Khone, the teacher. But more than the rest, it was Reuve'le who was punished the most because all the other boys, when they were spanked, at least wept. But instead, Reuve'le laughed. So he was punished all the more; but the more he was spanked, the more he laughed, and the more he laughed, the more he was spanked, until Chaim-Khone, the teacher, also began laughing, and seeing this, so did the students. Such laughter broke out that all the neighbors and men, women, boys, and girls from the street, came running, "What is this? What's all the laughter about?" No one could utter a word, so hard were they laughing. Then the fresh arrivals began laughing. Those who started the laughter laughed all the harder and the newcomers, looking at them, redoubled their laughter. In the end, they were all rolling on the floor, holding their sides from laughter.

Only two people didn't laugh. They were Kasriel, the water-carrier, and his wife. When a child dies, God forbid, I am not sure his parents mourn him as much as Kasriel and his wife mourned their terrible loss, their poor beloved horse, Methuselah.

No More Kapores

or

The Sacrificial Chicken Revolt

Kapores is the pre-Yom Kippur atonement ceremony performed by Jews in which a scapegoat, usually a fowl, is sacrificed, usually symbolically, to atone for one's sins.

A

O n the first day of Rosh Hashanah, when the townspeople were all going down to the river to cast away their sins, one could have observed an army of barnyard fowl—old hens, young chickens and chicks and cockerels—running through the back streets, their necks stretched out, thighs and legs churning, hopping along at full speed, all of them headed far beyond the town limits. It was a surprising sight but no one thought of stopping to watch this spectacle and wondering where all these silly birds were heading.

Only later, during the ten days of repentence between Rosh Hashanah and Yom Kippur, did people begin to realize that the cages were open and wherever you would expect to see a bird, it had now flown away, God knows where! A hue and cry arose: "What should we do? What will we use for *kapores*?" The most upset of all were the women; for a good white sacrificial hen a housewife would almost sacrifice herself, even though she were a wealthy aristocrat with a hat and a piano. In a frenzy they tore off to the marketplace, ready to pay top prices in order to obtain a chicken; if not a white hen, let it be a speckled black one, let it be red—so long as it was a sacrificial chicken! And just for spite, there was not one chicken to be had even if your life depended on it. Oh, there was poultry at the marketplace, but not the kind that would serve the purpose. There were ducks with fat navels, geese with ample bellies, and beautiful puffed-out turkeys with drooping beaks. On display for sale were pure white, innocent doves recently captured. But none of these fit the bill. This ritual required chickens and there were no chickens, even if you were ready to die for one!

Where had all the barnyard fowl gone?

Read on, I beg you, and you'll hear an interesting story.

B

Far beyond the town limits, on the other side of the mills, chaos reigned. Entire fields were filled with hens, roosters, old chickens, and little chicks. The clucking of the hens, the crowing of the roosters, and the peeping of the chicks was so loud it was deafening. They were all shoving and crowding towards an old hollowed-out tree, upon which had flown a very young rooster, flapping his wings. He began to crow:

"Kookarikoo, fellow fowl! Hear what I have to say to you! You are all aware of the disgraceful ritual practiced by our masters. Every year at this time our masters and mistresses go on a rampage, the devil take them! They pull us from our roosts, drag us out one at a time from the cages, bind our legs together and twirl us around their heads while muttering some mumbo-jumbo from a *siddur*, and then fling us under the table and finally cart us away to the slaughterer where he finishes us off. They call it *kapores*. How does that kind of carrying on strike you? How do you feel about an indignity like that? Brethren! How much longer will we remain silent? It's high time we made an end to that disgraceful ritual! Let's stand up once and for all! Do whatever you want with us—but we will not be sacrifices for you! No more *kapores*!"

"Cluck-cluck-cluck!" all the fowl joined in, "No more *kapores*!"

"Kookarikoo! Remember now, devoted brothers and dear sisters, are you sure you will be ready to resist temptation? You will not let yourselves be seduced? They will surely come and offer you corn and millet. I know you gluttons, for a little corn and millet you'll give away three dozen eggs."

"Cluck-cluck-cluck! God forbid! Even if they give us gold! Cluck-cluck-cluck!"

"Kookarikoo! Remember now and don't forget. Be of iron and steel! And if they try to catch you, don't let them. Peck out their eyes! Don't let them, do you hear? No more! An end to it! No more *kapores*!"

"Cluck-cluck-cluck! Cluck-cluck-cluck! No more *kapores*!"

C

And in the town it was bedlam—a great din, a hullaballoo, a commotion. The world was shaken to its foundation. Men stopped one another in the street, exchanged words, shrugged shoulders, gesticulated.

"What do you say to this?"

"Yes, a fine how-do-you-do!"

"Something like this happens once in a thousand years!"

That is all they talked about in the town. It was decided that the women should undertake to lure the barnyard fowl back to their cages. That's what women do best! And the women obeyed the will of their husbands. One brought along some corn, one some millet, this one a sieve, that one a sack, and they headed for the outskirts of town prepared, by trickery, to capture the fowl and toss them back into their cages.

"Tzip-tzip-tzip-tzip-tzip!" the women called, creeping towards the fowl, squatting low to the ground and pouring out small amounts of corn and millet for them. "Tyu-tyu-tyu-tyu . . . sila-sila-sila-sila . . . " and other such enticing sounds in order to lure the fowl.

Spying the corn and millet, the hungry fowl descended on the grain which vanished in a moment. Not a kernel was left, but they didn't allow themselves to be caught.

A few women were clever enough to trap a few chicks under a sieve, but some of the ducks and hens came to the rescue, falling upon the women and flying right in their faces, almost pecking out their eyes. The women barely escaped with their lives.

When they came home and told their husbands what had happened, great laughter broke out among the men. They were rolling on the floor, holding their sides.

"Ha-ha-ha, silly women! You're worse than the chickens, really! Have you ever heard of a chicken being stronger than a person? Fools, ha-ha-ha!"

"Do you know what?" their wives said, "If you're such experts, why don't you go wage war with the chickens! Show us how good you are at it!"

And the men took their staves in hand and went out beyond the town limits to see for themselves what the barnyard fowl were up to.

D

But men are men, after all, not women. Men are possessed by an altogether different instinct!

When they saw from a distance the horde of barnyard fowl, they decided upon a strategem and cleverly snuck around from behind, raised their staves all at the same time and began shooing them home:

"Kish-kish! Kish-kish! Kish-kish-kish-kish-kish!"

This "kish-kish" had no effect whatsoever. The army of birds headed straight towards the men, flying in their faces, pecking at their calves, tearing at their long gaberdines, plucking their beards, all the time crowing and clucking and peeping. Feathers flew in the air, darkening the sky—a veritable war!

Many fowl actually fell dead in the battle, trampled by their own brothers and sisters and beaten by the staves. And many of the men were maimed and wounded as well, their hands and faces bloodied. The birds pecked out one man's eye, part of another's nose, someone's cheek was perforated, exposing his back teeth. Much blood ran on both sides. Who knows what the end would have been had not the men thrown aside their staves, pulled up their long coats, and run pell-mell back to town!

When they saw the beaten, bloodied men in their bedraggled kaftans, the women were triumphant:

"So, why aren't you laughing now? Experts! Men! Males! The masculine sex!"

E

"If you can't go through, you go around." So said those experts, the men, and were happy that God had provided them with a suitable proverb. They gathered at the rabbi's for a meeting, debated a long time, prating and babbling. It was decided they would send a delegation to the barnyard fowl to ask them in a friendly spirit what they wanted. As you might expect, they elected the most prominent, wealthy elders of the town, the rabbis, judges, cantors, and ritual slaughterers. The delegation went out beyond the town limits, this time without weapons. The rabbi came forward and called out to the fowl in these words:

"Listen, gentle birds, hear us out! Tell us what you want. Tell us, we will take it seriously, and if your request is reasonable, we will certainly grant it, God willing."

There arose such a squawking among the fowl, a crowing and cackling and peeping that one couldn't hear a word. The rabbi then said to them:

"Hear me out, birds. Your shouting all at the same time will get us nowhere. Listen to me, our community has elected us as deputies. Why don't you also elect a delegation of fine, upstanding fowl with whom we can negotiate. Aren't there among you some turkeys, geese, or ducks?"

"Gobble-gobble! Gobble-gobble!" announced the one and only turkey who had somehow been caught up in this exodus with the rest of the fowl, and puffed himself up like a rich relation and lowered his beak to show he was there and was ready to be a deputy for the community.

"Gaw-gaw-gaw!" was heard from an old gander, supported by a whole gaggle of geese, his concubines.

"Qua! Qua! Qua!" jumped in some of the ducks, loud quackers, to show they were also present among the fowl. But one insolent red rooster sprang forward and shouted out:

"Kookarikoo! Chickens! If you want to be sold for a bushel of oats, put yourselves in the hands of these puffed-up relations, the turkeys, or those aristocrats, the geese, whose ancestors once saved the city of Rome, or those gluttons, the gossiping ducks. They are not the ones who are sacrificed so they mustn't butt in! We are the chickens, it is *us* they sacrifice and so *we* must be the delegates!

"Kaw-kaw-kaw-kaw! True, true, as we are chickens!" all the chickens backed him up as one and an even louder din arose; the chickens clucked all at the same time, sprang at one another, pecked at each other's heads until at last a delegation emerged: two or three purebred roosters with ample wattles, a pair of fine chickens, and a few young cockerels, loud crowers with strong young voices. And negotiations began between both delegations that will now be described.

F

THE ELDERS: What is it you want, chickens? Speak up!

THE CHICKENS: What do you think we want? We don't want to be your sacrificial birds. We give you our flesh, our feathers, whatever you want, but you shouldn't use us as sacrifices!

THE ELDERS: But after all, we are Jews, we have to do that!

THE CHICKENS: Is that so? Where is it written?

THE ELDERS: Where is it written? What's the difference? What business is it of yours where it is written? It's an old custom of ours from way back. What strange fowl you are! If we slaughter you and roast you and eat you, is that any better? What do you care if you help Jews earn a *mitzvah*?

THE CHICKENS: You have six hundred thirteen *mitzvos*.

THE ELDERS: And doesn't the one that requires that we twirl you around our heads and say *"B'nai Adam"* three times mean anything to you?

THE CHICKENS: May you know what it's like to be roasted as much as we know about your *"B'nai Adam."*

THE ELDERS: And the prayer that the slaughterer recites over you?

THE CHICKENS: Better let him recite a prayer on his own head!

THE ELDERS: And how about the fact that Jews eat you as their last meal before a holy fast like Yom Kippur and end their fast with you?

THE CHICKENS: Why has this fate befallen us poor chickens? Aren't there enough lazy geese, fat ducks with round bellies, and aristocratic turkeys who do nothing except eat and slurp and paddle around in all the puddles?

THE ELDERS: Geese we slaughter Chanukah time and we render their fat for Passover, ducks we roast all year round, turkeys we raise for the holidays, but *you* we need for the sacrificial ritual. So don't be so impudent, we are not children talking to you, we are elders, rabbis, judges, slaughterers!

THE CHICKENS: Slaughterers? Killers! Kaw-kaw-kaw! May all slaughterers suffer a miserable death wherever they are! Just hand over a few slaughterers!

THE ELDERS: You reject this age-old custom of the people? You want to make a revolution? You are rebels! You are traitors! You will have us to answer to!

THE CHICKENS: Is that so? Ay-ay-ay! What will you do to us? Will you denounce us? Report us to the Heavenly Court? Go! Kaw-kaw-kaw! Kaw-kaw-kaw!

And a clucking arose from among the hens. The roosters began to crow so loudly at the top of their lungs that they could be heard for ten miles around.

G

The elders withdrew to the side, whispered and muttered to one another, wondering what to do next. It was decided they would try once again to speak with the troublemakers, to offer them something that will make it possible for them to strike a bargain: use one chicken for two families, or three families, so long as it was a *kapora*. And the rabbi stepped forward and again called out to the fowl:

"Listen, gentle birds, hear us out, listen to what we have to tell you. Here's the situation. Normally we wouldn't be discussing this with you. We aren't accustomed to doing this. Surely you must know we have the means with which to take you by force. As time is short, it's almost Yom Kippur, and we might be left without sacrificial chickens, may it not happen, we are therefore ready to offer you concessions."

"Kookarikoo! Concessions!" one rooster, a troublemaker, drew out the words and among the hens was heard, "Kaw-kaw-kaw! Concessions, concessions!" And the rabbi explained, in the name of the elders, the concessions the fowl were being offered:

CONCESSION NUMBER ONE: On the day of the sacrificial ritual, the fowl is to be given food and drink as if nothing unusual is going to happen.

CONCESSION NUMBER TWO: While performing the ritual and reciting "*B'nai Adam*," they would not twirl the fowl roughly and not rush the "*Zeh-kaparti-zeh-khalifti-zeh-tamorti*," but would calmly, slowly recite, "*Zeh-kaparti—zeh—khalifti—zeh—tamorti*."

CONCESSION NUMBER THREE: After the sacrificial ritual, the chickens would not be flung under the table as before but they would gently be laid down and carried to the slaughterer.

CONCESSION NUMBER FOUR: The chickens would not be tied together in pairs as before, but singly, each chicken separately, because not all chickens get along—it happens sometimes that they peck each other and bloody one another when bound together.

CONCESSION NUMBER FIVE: The chickens would be plucked *after* being slaughtered, not before, which is done in many places.

CONCESSION NUMBER SIX: When the ritual slaughterer placed the chicken between his legs and drew back its head . . .

"Kookarikoo! How do you like those concessions?" crowed a young, arrogant rooster, and he was echoed by the rest of the fowl, clucking loudly: "Kaw-kaw-kaw! Enough with these concessions! The devil take your elders and their concessions!"

And the fowl began attacking the elders. The elders, may no shame come to them, apparently realized what was in store for them. They took to their heels and ran all the way back home, each to his own place.

* * *

That is how the remarkable revolt of the barnyard fowl ended.

Since that time the fowl are still slaughtered the same way as before—yes indeed. They pluck them and cut them up and roast them and broil them and fry them and serve them to the table with all kinds of sauces and side-dishes— just as before. But they don't perform the sacrificial ritual with them and they don't recite "*B'nai Adam*," with them . . . Feh! No more *kapores*! The custom, you see, is no longer practiced.

Does anything in this world last forever? Everything has its time, everything has its own time!

Pesseli the Rebbe's Daughter

A

Short Friday and Tall Sabbath

That's what they were called.

He, because he was short and fat, and she, because she was tall and thin.

She was tall, thin, scrawny, dried-out as a Sukkos *lulav*! When she needed to whisper a secret in his ear ("What a bother you are with those short legs!") she would have to stoop over, *lower* herself several inches to his level. He hated that and would stoop lower still. She would then have to stoop still lower. Then he would stoop still lower and she would have to stoop lower still and so on:

"What a bother you are with those short legs!"

In a word, she made his life miserable and he took it. And we schoolboys, good-for-nothing scamps, enjoyed the greatest revenge.

Why?

Because he made *our* lives miserable, tormented us with the *Gemara*, broke our bones, whipped us again and again. Whatever she did to him, he did to us. But now I return to Short Friday and Tall Sabbath.

He was, as you've probably figured out by now, our rebbe and his name was Reb Zorakhl and she was his wife, the rebbitzin.

He taught us from early morning till late at night, hammering the lessons into our heads, ruining his health for a few rubles a month, while she baked blini and pancakes for us and made buckwheat dumplings, babkas, and other items to sell.

Whether or not she made any money I cannot tell you, but that we schoolboys, good-for-nothing scamps, cheated her—of that I can assure you. Each of us bought on credit, racking up a considerable debt, and she trusted us all implicitly. You had to have a heart of stone to cheat the rebbitzin! And who knew her as well as I did?

I had taken room and board with them because I came from a distant village. I observed how hard she toiled, waking early when God Himself is still asleep, setting to work at the bread board or the flour trough, rolling up her sleeves and kneading the dough energetically with her long, thin, scrawny arms. The kneaded dough went "slap-slap," the bread board groaned and she herself groaned, pausing occasionally to rest and wipe the sweat from her forehead with her sleeve, uttering an exhausted: "*Oy, Reboynu-shel-oylem-mama-zisse-hartzige-getraye!*"

Take note of that. Literally that "*Reboynu-shel-oylem-mama-zisse-hartzige-getraye!*" meant "God-in-heaven-sweet-kind-devoted-mother!" But I knew what that really meant:

The flour was obtained from Gnessi the wholesaler on credit till Thursday, the baked goods would be distributed on credit and only God knew if the money would be paid by Thursday, and Gnessi the wholesaler would not wait, Gnessi the wholesaler had also gotten the flour till Thursday, and if you said Thursday, it had to be Thursday, because a promise is a promise and Thursday is not just any old day, Thursday is almost Sabbath eve, the day you had to ask your husband for money and woe unto Tall Sabbath when she has to stoop down to Short Friday to ask for money for the Sabbath and woe unto Short Friday when Tall Sabbath came to ask him for money—woe unto both of them!

That was the meaning of the rebbitzin's: "*Reboynu-shel-oylem-mama-zisse-hartzige-getraye.*"

And perhaps her "*Reboynu-shel-oylem-mama-zisse-hartzige-getraye*" had another meaning. Perhaps it included other woes. And of woes she had plenty, more than enough!

First of all, may it not happen to you, she herself was sickly, would cough quietly off to the side so that no one would hear. And second of all, she worried about Pesseli, her elder daughter, a grown girl with flaming red hair and a freckled face whom no one wanted to marry—what would their children look like? And then there was Creature, her real tragedy! Creature was hunchbacked, a freak with crippled arms, legs, mute, helpless—woe unto her who was born like that and had to live in this world!

But we will meet Creature later on and soon we will become acquainted with Pesseli. In the meantime we return to Short Friday and Tall Sabbath.

The rebbitzin deserved all one's sympathy, for she alone had to mix, knead, punch, and bake, sweltering at the oven; she alone had to lug the water, bring in the wood, do everything alone with no help from anyone. Who could help her? Zorakhl was teaching, Pesseli was studying along with the other children, as she was a good student with a man's head on her shoulders, and Creature sat alongside the oven in a corner, her legs under her, waiting till a morsel of food was shoved into her hand with a "Here, Creature, choke on it!"

That was apparently the meaning of her "*Oy, reboynu-shel-oylem-mama-zisse-hartzige-getraye. . . .*" Or might it have been because Pesseli always sided with her father and both father and daughter were always at odds with her?

"Like father, like daughter! May you both be buried in one grave!"

Pesseli loved her father and her father loved Pesseli. Between them was a strange, unspoken love.

None of us ever heard them say a kind word to one another. On the contrary, he would deal with her not as a daughter, but as a servant, "Do as I say!"

But it was in his eyes one could see how he loved her, loved her deeply and could not do without her.

Was it because he had such a miserable life with his wife? Was it because Pesseli was a capable girl, had a man's head on her shoulders, and was a good student? Or was it because Pesseli knew her father's every way, always sensed what he needed, handed him his yarmulke at the right time, the classroom whip, his tobacco pouch, or a drink of water?

"Like father, like daughter!" the rebbitzin would exclaim, "He would do better to think of a match for her, find her a husband!"

The rebbe just responded with a sigh, as if to say: "Find a husband? Go find one when there's none to be found!"

But for every thing there is a time. Every kind of merchandise sooner or later finds its buyer. The girl who cannot find her intended does not exist in the world. As you well know, there are no Jewish convents.

Pesseli's time came. Suddenly she was in demand. That's what the rebbitzin said. But in truth it was fated. If you have to know, it was a romance, a real romance—don't be embarrassed, it was a true romance with "love at first sight," with passion, a romance with all the trimmings.

But that's another story.

B

Gone

Tall but stooped, a pock-marked face with kind gray eyes, a young man but gray-haired—there you have a portrait of Feivel Kolboinik, or, as we called him in Kasrilevka, "Feivel Jack-of-all-Trades."

He wasn't called "Jack-of-all-Trades" for nothing: in his wooden chest you could find all sorts of things: big buttons, little buttons, needles and needle cases, thread and silk and ribbons and tapes and yarn and cotton, yarmulkes and dresses, pieces of soap of all sorts, in addition to all kinds of wares impossible to enumerate or remember.

It was a holiday for the wives and young girls when they heard that Feivel Jack-of-all-Trades had arrived, and for us schoolboys, good-for-nothing scamps, it was a double holiday. First of all, Feivel Jack-of-all-Trades with his marvelous chest was itself a holiday, and second of all, when Feivel Jack-of-all-Trades was in town, we would be spared a few hours of study, we would be free. Why? Because Rebbe Reb Zorakhl loved hearing news of what was doing in the world, and who knew more about what was going on in the world than Feivel Jack-of-all-Trades, whose business took him into every nook and cranny?

Feivel Jack-of-all-Trades brought with him news by the wagonload, a treasure trove of news, and it wasn't only the news but his way of telling it as well. Do you know what I will tell you? You have to know *how* to tell news—and Feivel Jack-of-all-Trades could do that. He had a talent for describing things, an eloquence that drew you in; he could go on endlessly, and I could listen to him forever, never tiring of his stories.

"What's the news, you ask? Oy, it's doesn't look good!" Feivel Jack-of-all-Trades would begin, while unpacking his chest and laying out his wares, "It doesn't look good for our little Jews, our brethren of Israel! I'm just now coming from Zhitomir, I mean not from Zhitomir itself, but not far from Zhitomir where there's a village called Tchidnev. Have you ever heard of Tchidnev? Well, there's a rabbi in Tchidnev and this rabbi is actually from this town, one of ours, a Little Russian from Ukraine. The Ukraine is not Lithuania, they don't have as many poor people as in Lithuania. When we happen to have a poor man, he's poor and that's it, but in Lithuania, please forgive me, he's *really* a poor man, the poorest of the poor. I have never met such poor people as I have met in Lithuania and I've been everywhere, traveled all over the world, in Lithuania, in Poland, deep into Poland, in Radom, in Lodz, and in Warsaw. Oy, Warsaw! Long live Warsaw! A wonderful, a golden city, that's what Warsaw is! And cheap, dirt cheap! You can get a meal for eleven groshens and what a meal it is, with rolls made of sifted flour that melt in your mouth like butter. I could live in Warsaw forever if not for their language, which is difficult to understand because they talk funny and fast, most of the time with a lot of ah's and with a drawl: "Ayy! Vayy! Yay should live so long!" And they're all called "Itchemeir," all have the same name after a good Jew called Itzi-Meir, just like in Berdichev they're all called Levi-Yitzkhak after Reb Levi-Yitzkhak, the Berdichever rabbi who was famous, whom they tell fine stories about to this day; for example, they tell about . . ."

"Maybe that's enough stories?" the rebbitzin cut him off right in the middle. "How much do half a dozen white buttons cost?"

Feivel Jack-of-all-Trades was not deterred by this interruption. He showed the rebbitzin an assortment of buttons and went on talking, words pouring forth as from a sack, or faucet, without pause, without end, like that magician who pulls all those ribbons from his mouth—red, green, yellow, blue—and no one knows when the red leaves off and the green begins, when yellow leaves off and blue begins—the ribbons just go on and on, ribbons flash before your eyes, a mountain of ribbons, endless ribbons and ribbons and ribbons . . .

And one day, something happened: Feivel Jack-of-all-Trades called the rebbe aside and conferred with him for almost two hours, wiping his brow with a large red handkerchief as the sweat poured from him. And Rebbe Reb Zorakhl was oddly upset, quite agitated and distracted, almost not hearing what was being said to him. And when the rebbitzin returned from the market, the rebbe called her over to where he had been conferring with Feivel and before long there was heard a cry: "It can't be!" Soon the rebbitzin's cheeks reddened as if with a strange fire, glowing like we had not seen for a long time.

"I'm letting you off today, today we're not having school!" the rebbe announced to us and let out the whole school. Only I, the rebbe's boarder, remained and all the students envied me because I would be a witness.

Witness to what, no one knew, but it was understood that something was happening, a celebration or something worth witnessing.

And there was something to witness . . .

First the rebbitzin gasped: "Oy, a curse on me, no honeycake!"

And the rebbe answered: "And no whisky either?"

Feivel Jack-of-all-trades interjected with, "I'll take that upon myself."

In short, honeycake, whisky, and food appeared, and soon after evening prayers a quorum of Jews gathered from our synagogue, among them Reb Moishe-Shmuel the cantor, Reb Henikh the scribe and Reb Ozer the sexton, and they drew up the betrothal agreement.

A wordless scene took place: the scribe looking at the rebbe; the rebbe looking at the rebbitzin; the rebbitzin, at the bridegroom; the bridegroom, at the bride; the bride, at the scribe; the scribe, at the rebbe; the rebbe, again at the rebbitzin, and so on. If one could put into words what they were thinking, it would come out like this:

THE SCRIBE TO THE REBBE: So? Why don't you say something? *You're* the father-in-law.

THE REBBE TO THE REBBITZIN: How should I know? Ask *her*.

THE REBBITZIN TO THE BRIDEGROOM: Bridegroom, why don't you say something? You're the one paying for this.

THE BRIDEGROOM TO THE BRIDE: It would be fine with me if we married tomorrow. What do you think, Pesseli?

THE BRIDE TO THE SCRIBE: Ask my father, though I know he'll say to postpone it.

In short, it remained that as it was Rosh Chodesh, the first day of the month, the wedding would take place in the middle of the month, in a few weeks, because a few things had to be sewn up, a few things had to be prepared. When the betrothal platter was broken ("*Mazel tov! Mazel tov!*"), I noticed Rebbe Reb Zorakhl's face went dead; like the platter that had just been shattered, his heart had been shattered. I heard him say to Reb Moishe-Shmuel, the cantor, as they lifted the first glass of whisky, the mere sight of which had made the rebbe tipsy:

"Along comes a stranger and steals the Sabbath challah. . . . Out of nowhere. Ach-ach-ach!"

"No matter!" answered Reb Moishe-Shmuel, the cantor, who had already drunk more than half a glass of whisky and whose tongue was loosening: "No matter, well, there you have it! God will provide blessings from afar, we should live and be well, salvation and consolation for all, for all of Israel!"

"Ay, it's high time, high time! Long overdue!" Reb Henikh the scribe tried to help, gazing at the glass and the bottle very diplomatically, obviously eager for a refill.

"Amen!" chimed in Reb Ozer the sexton and, not one for tact, emptied his glass unceremoniously.

The bridal couple sat at the head of the table, close together, so close, so cozily that I could in no way have pushed myself between them, but don't worry, I am not nearsighted, I could see very well from a distance how *her* hand was in *his* hand. Her face was flushed, her eyes were bright. She had suddenly become charming, pretty, beautiful! What had happened to her awful red hair? Where were the freckles on her face hiding? She had become, I tell you, a beauty!

And not just for that evening—the entire time they were preparing for the wedding, Pesseli shone like the summer sun, grew prettier and prettier from day to day. But on the day of the wedding things changed because she wept hard, her tears gushing from her eyes. Perhaps her heart told her she would not be too happy with her chosen one, her intended? And perhaps she was feeling bad for leaving her father who would now be lonesome as a stone?

But if it was difficult for Pesseli to separate from her father, it was a thousand times more difficult for the father to separate from the daughter! Rebbe Reb Zorakhl did not weep. Was he a woman that he should weep? Rebbe Reb Zorakhl languished silently, flickering like a candle.

When people were taking their leave, this scene took place: After the bundles of belongings—her bed linens and clothing and his chest of wares were already packed together and in the coach; Feivel Jack-of-all-Trades waited for Pesseli to climb in. The rebbitzin stood nearby, drawing herself up to her full height with one hand across her heart, two fingers of her other hand to her chin, while giving the rebbe a strange look, as if to say: "What a pain you are with those short legs. Will you get on with it and say good-bye to her?"

Rebbe Reb Zorakhl understood that look and said to his son-in-law in a hesitant voice:

"Hmm . . . so . . . hmm . . . should we, what do you think, begin to say good-bye?"

"Be well, father-in-law! Be well, mother-in-law!"

"Go in good health! Go in good health!"

"Be well, Mama. . . . Be well, Papa!"

At this point Pesseli, dressed for travel, wrapped in two shawls, suddenly leaped from the coach and threw herself on her father's neck, sobbing and weeping:

"Pa-pa! Sweet, beloved Papa!"

Everyone who was there in the street wept: Pesseli and the rebbe and the rebbitzin, Feivel Jack-of-all-Trades, and I, and Reb Lazer, the coachman, who was sitting up front with his whip, and all his other passengers, those sitting inside and those sitting up front with him; Dvossi, the sexton's wife, the rebbitzin's neighbor, a sickly woman, and Dvossi's older daughter, Zlatke, a blond, elflike girl with darkened teeth, who was holding a baby in her arms, and Akulina, the gentile woman who understood every word of Yiddish, and Khlavne, the shoemaker, who had come to pick up payment for repairing boots but there was no money, and an ordinary Jew, a stranger who happened to be passing by and seeing people leaving and hearing weeping, stopped, sniffled quietly and also began wiping his eyes.

Lazer cracked his whip, "Giddyap!" the horses bolted forward and the coach was off in a cloud of dust.

All of us stood there in the street for a long, long time looking after them until the coach could no longer be seen and nothing remained but some dust hovering in the air and the smell of the horses and the greased wheels.

"Gone!" said the stranger who had been passing by, as if he were telling us some news that we wouldn't have known without him.

"Gone!" Rebbe Reb Zorakhl replied as if the man were waiting for that reply.

"Gone!" we all said, as if we were all telling one another some remarkable news.

Pity for Living Things

A

Be a good boy and help us grate the horseradish while we prepare the fish for the holidays."

That is what my mother said to me on the day before Shevous. It was just after noon as she and the cook were scaling the fish, still alive and thrashing, for the dairy meal. When the fish were placed in a large, glazed ceramic bowl of water, they were still thrashing about.

Liveliest of all was a poor little fat-bellied fish with a round mouth and little red eyes. It apparently wanted desperately to be back in the lake and so it thrashed and flopped around in the bowl, opened its mouth, slapped its tail, and splashed water right in my face:

"Little boy, save me! Save me!"

I wiped my face and set to work grating the horseradish for the holidays, thinking: "Poor little fish! I can do nothing for you. Soon they'll get to work on you. After they scale you, they'll slit your little belly and take your insides out. Then they'll cut you into little pieces, put you into the pot, salt and pepper you, place you on the fire, and cook and fry and roast and roast and roast you."

"A pity," I said to my mother, "a pity for this living thing."

"A pity for which living thing?"

"For this little fish."

"Who put that idea in your head?"

"The rebbe."

"The rebbe?"

She exchanged glances with the cook who was helping her scale the fish and they both began laughing.

"You're a fool and your rebbe is an even bigger one! Grate the horseradish, grate it!"

I knew that *I* was a fool. My mother had told me that many times. And my father too. And my brothers too. And my sisters too. But that the rebbe was an even bigger fool than I—that was news to me.

B

I have a friend, Pinnele, the slaughterer's son. Once when I visited him I saw a little girl carrying a large, purebred rooster, its legs bound with rope. My friend's father, the slaughterer, was asleep and the girl sat by the door and waited. The rooster, a feisty rascal, struggled to free himself from the girl's arms, kicked her in the stomach with his strong feet and gave her hand a good peck while loudly crowing, "Kaw-kaw-kaw," protesting as hard as he could.

But the girl was no pushover. She tucked the rooster's head under her arm and kept jabbing him with her elbow while saying:

"Keep still and take what's coming to you."

And he obeyed and kept still.

After the slaughterer awoke, he washed his hands and got out his slaughtering knife. With a wink he asked the rooster to be brought to him. I could see a ray of hope in the rooster's eyes as he mistakenly thought they were about to untie his bound legs and let him go free, back to his hens, to the corn and the water trough. Instead the slaughterer placed him between his knees, pulled his head back with one hand, plucked a few feathers with the other, obliged him with a prayer and khik!—with the slaughtering knife across his throat, drained a bit of blood onto the ashes and flung the rooster away with such force I thought it would break apart.

"Pinni! Your father is no Jew!" I said to my friend.

"Why is he no Jew?"

"Because he has no pity for living things."

"I had no idea you were such a softy," said my friend and stuck his tongue out at me right under my nose.

C

Our cook was called "Fruma One Eye" because she was blind in one eye. The girl was completely heartless. Once she beat the cat with nettles because she imagined it had run off with a chicken liver from the salting board. In the end, when she counted the chickens and the livers again, it turned out she had made a mistake. She reckoned they had slaughtered seven chickens and so there had to be seven livers, but there had only been six chickens. And if there were six chickens, there should not be more than six livers—God's wonders! In vain had the cat been beaten.

Do you think Fruma felt guilty about it or asked the cat's pardon? Not a chance—forgotten instantly! She and the cat both forgot. Within a few hours the cat was sitting quite placidly on the hearth, licking herself as if nothing had happened. No wonder they say of some people that they have the brains of a cat.

But I didn't forget. No. I didn't forget. I said to our cook: "You beat up a cat for no reason. For no reason you committed a sin—you didn't have pity for living things. God will punish you."

"Get away from here before I slap you in the face with this dishtowel!" said Fruma One Eye, and added:

"God in heaven! Where in the world do such foolish children come from?"

D

Then there was the incident with a dog who was scalded with boiling water. Yes, she, the same Fruma One Eye. Oh, was that dog in agony! At first he yowled, screetched and bellowed terribly, complaining pitifully. The whole village came running to see what the noise was all about and they ended up laughing and laughing. All the village dogs of the town showed up, some from their garbage heap, each in his own manner, as if their advice had been asked. When the scalded dog had finished shrieking, he began whining, whimpering, and licking his singed hide, crying quietly. It broke my heart. I went over to him, trying to pet him.

"There, there, Sirko!"

The dog saw me raise my hand and started up as though about to be scalded once more. He lifted his tail and scurried off.

"Stop, Sirko!" I tried to calm him with soothing words, "Why are you running away, silly? I won't hurt you."

But a dog remains a dog. A dumb animal. He didn't know about having pity for living things.

When my father saw me fussing over the dog, he gave me what for:

"Get to school, you dog beater!"

Now *I* was the dog beater.

E

This next is about two birds, two ordinary little birds that two gentile boys killed. When the two birds fell to the ground they were still alive, their feathers ruffled, poor things, their entire bodies trembling and wings fluttering.

"Grab 'em, you idiot!" the older of the two boys said to the younger one and they picked up the fallen birds and beat their heads against a tree the way we beat willow twigs against the synagogue lectern during Sukkos, until the birds were dead.

"What are you doing!" I could not contain myself any longer and ran over to the gentile boys.

"What's it to you?" they answered calmly. "They're just birds, nothing more, ordinary birds."

"And if they're birds, what of it? Don't you have pity on a bird, pity for a living thing?"

The gentile boys looked at each other strangely. As if they had agreed ahead of time, they took off after me.

When I came home, my torn jacket told the whole story and my father gave me my just desserts.

"Idiot!" my father shouted at me.

Well, I can forgive him his "idiot." But why did I deserve to be spanked?

F

Why did I deserve to be spanked? Didn't the rebbe himself say that all living things were precious to the One Above? Even a fly on the wall mustn't be touched, he said, because we must have pity for living things. Even a poisonous spider mustn't be killed. And he said it cleverly, "When it's the spider's time to die," he said, "God Himself will kill it."

But there remains the question: If that is so, why do we slaughter oxen, calves, sheep, and barnyard fowl every day?

And not just cattle, beasts, and birds—don't people kill one another? During the pogrom, didn't they toss tiny children, babies, from the rooftops?

Didn't they murder our neighbor's daughter—Perele was her name—and *how* they murdered her!!

Oh, how I loved that child! And how that child loved me! "Uncle Beh-beh-beh," she used to call me—my name is Velvele—and pull my nose with her small, slender little fingers.

Because of her, because of Perele, everyone called me "Uncle Beh-beh-beh."

"Here comes 'Uncle Beh-beh-beh,' he'll lift you in his arms."

G

Perele was a sickly child. There was nothing really wrong with her except she couldn't walk or stand. Just sit. She had to be carried outside and seated on the ground in the warm sun. She loved the sun more than anything. When I carried her she would hug my neck with her thin, sweet little fingers and press herself to me with her whole body and lay her little head on my shoulder and say: "Love Uncle Beh-beh-beh."

Her mother, our neighbor, Kreni, said that to this day she couldn't forget her calling "Uncle Beh-beh-beh," and when she looked at me, she was reminded of her Perele.

My mother scolded her for crying. "You mustn't cry," said my mother. "It's a sin. You must forget, forget . . ."

So said my mother and tried to distract her. I was chased away and told not to be underfoot to remind people of what they didn't need to be reminded of.

Hah! How was it possible not to remember? Whenever I thought of that child, tears would come to my eyes of their own will.

"Look, he's crying again, the genius!" Fruma One Eye announced to my mother and my mother threw me a quick glance and began laughing:

"Did the horseradish get into your eyes? Curse it! It's very strong horseradish! I forgot to tell him to shut his eyes, my fault! Here's my apron. Wipe your eyes, silly boy, and while you're at it, your nose too. Your nose! Your nose!"

Creature

A

Once, on a summer Friday, a few of us boys were walking home together. We were walking quickly, almost running, first because we had been let out early for the Sabbath and second, because we were hungry and awaiting us were hot pot roasts with freshly baked, delicious-smelling challahs.

Suddenly one of our gang shouted: "Look, a little bird!" and we stopped.

In a little ball, sitting on the ground, head twisted to the side, lay a small, young bird with a yellow beak. The poor bird was shivering, its feathers ruffled; it was trembling, fluttering, beating its wings weakly and repeatedly opening its little yellow mouth like a baby when it wants to eat, and emitting in a pitiful, hoarse little voice, "Pi!" This sight awakened in us a feeling of great pity and we began to wonder what we should do with the little bird.

One suggested we let it lie on the ground until the mother bird came. Another suggested we toss it in the air and it would fly away. And yet another concluded we ought to take it home. But that it was deserving of pity, that one had to feel compassion for all living creatures, we all agreed.

We brought the bird home, forgetting we were hungry, and began giving it water to drink. The little bird shivered, blinked its eyes, trembled and fluttered in our hands and finally threw its little head to the side, its eyes glazed over and—it was dead.

"Why was the little bird ever born? For what purpose and for whom was it created? For what purpose was it needed on earth?" Those were the questions that went through my mind and for which there were no answers.

In a half hour, with all due honors, we dug a deep grave in the garden, wrapped the bird in a shroud (a white piece of handkerchief), buried it and erected a marker—a board with the inscription:

HERE LIES THE LITTLE BIRD, TZIPUR BEN BALAK

and all of us who had participated in the burial signed our names: Berl, Yossi, Dovid, Mottl, Kalman, Getzl.

The happy, warm summer flew by. The damp autumn arrived with its dreary cold days. The rain washed away the "gravestone," along with the grave and the incident with the bird was forgotten like everything that the earth covers. But once in a while, when I remember the little bird, "Tzipur Ben Balak," Creature comes to mind.

B

Creature was Rebbe Reb Zorakhl's child, a crippled little girl, a hunchback, poor thing. What age she was I do not know, but she had an old, wrinkled little face, two long, emaciated arms, sparse hair, and tiny, black, shiny, mouse-like eyes. She always kept her legs under her, always sat in one spot, unable to walk, alas.

Creature's spot was alongside the oven, in a corner, on the bare ground. There she sat for days on end; one never heard a peep out of her so that it was easy to forget that Creature existed.

If she were handed a piece of bread, she would stretch out a long, shriveled arm with thin, strangely twisted, wrinkled, monkeylike fingers and would grab the piece of bread and bring it straight to her mouth. The mouth was so large that a whole apple could disappear into it.

"Creature! Do you want a piece of spongecake?"

"Creature! Will you eat potato with shmaltz?"

"Creature! Do you want to crack nuts?"

"Creature! Do you want to play some checkers?"

That's how we schoolboys, scamps, imps, trouble-makers, teased Creature. But Creature never answered, just stretched out her slender little arm with its thin fingers and looked us in the eyes like a hungry dog when it thinks that any minute now a bone would be thrown its way.

"A mute!" explained Yaakov-Eli, the oldest of our group, who was the rebbe's son, a foolish boy with swollen cheeks. "A mute, can't talk, only eats, always hungry, a bottomless stomach."

Only rarely was Creature heard from, emitting a strange mixture of laugh, cry, and cough. Then the rebbitzin would scream at her:

"Creature! Shut up, Creature!"

Creature knew that when they called her "Creature," things were not going well and that a beating would soon follow.

And beatings Creature received often, almost every day, mostly from her mother. When her heart was heavy, the rebbitzin would let out her bitterness on Creature.

"Oy, Creature, may I live to bury you! God in heaven, why does such a thing live on this earth?!"

C

Love was not anything people felt for Creature, only pity, and more than anyone, Rebbe Reb Zorakhl pitied her.

"A pity for a living thing!" he would say, looking at her from a distance with great compassion, sighing quietly, and when the rebbitzin wasn't looking, he would bring her a piece of bread, a little potato, or a drink of water. And when he saw us sucking a candy or cracking nuts he would tell us that if we wished to earn a *mitzvah*, we should give Creature some too. The rebbitzin would also give her food and water, but she did it without pity, without heart, shoving everything in her hand as if to say, "Here, choke on it!"

At first we schoolboys were simply afraid of Creature, hated to look at the hunchback, hated to hear her weird laugh. But in time we became accustomed to her and she became "friends" with us, knew each one by name. In the evening, between the *minkha* and *maariv* prayers when the rebbe was at the synagogue and the rebbitzin was in town, we would play games with her in which girls could join in. We included Creature in our games by surrounding her as she sat in the center. Oh, Creature really enjoyed that! She would open her frightfully large mouth a mile wide and laugh her little sob-like laugh. As soon as the rebbe or the rebbitzin came in, she would again turn silent, look sober, sad, and worried, trying to appear as if she had not been doing anything wrong.

Creature had her own peculiar language that not everyone could understand. For bread, she said, "ded," for water—"tarberli," for buttons—"pendelis," for apples and potatoes—"topetzis," and for a boy—"metzutzeli." Why a boy became "metzutzeli" I will never know.

"Metzutzeli! Metzutzeli! Here's a pendeli, dive me a topetzi, a tiece of ded . . ."

That meant: "Little boy! Little boy! Here's a button, give me an apple, a piece of bread."

Creature would also sing, her voice high-pitched and piercing like a bat's call. When no one was around, she would open her mouth wide, stretch out her thin neck and sing something that no person could understand, ending with a chant that the High Priests must have intoned on Yom Kippur:

> "Tudeli hoo-hoo!
> "Tudeli hoo-hoo!"

When the rebbitzin would arrive and hear her singing she would scream:

"Creature, may I bury you, why are you singing again?"

Hearing her mother scream at her, Creature would draw her head into her shoulders, like a turtle, and become mute.

D

In the village, Creature was well-known. People spoke about her. When someone suffered a loss—a young woman died in childbirth, a bride passed away before the wedding, or a father of children died—Creature would come to mind:

"What can you expect? Someone like Creature lives on! I suppose God knows what He is doing!"

People did not begrudge her her existence—God forbid! They said this more out of pity and only because God was truly a great God and ruled His little world wisely and with much mercy. But, may we not be punished for these words, it sometimes does happen that He does not behave justly. For example, Reb Zorakhl himself once had a little boy, Levi-Yitzkhak, named after the Berdichev rebbe. This boy was so gifted that who knows what he could have grown up to be! At the age of eleven the whole town was talking about him. The town? The whole world! Well, of course he died suddenly in a matter of three or four days.

Do you know what he died of? The doctor said it was an inflammation of the brain, Reb Zorakhl maintained it was because he had studied too much, and the rebbitzin argued that both of them knew as much as a corpse. She said the child died of an evil eye. He died because people resented her having a bit of good fortune. Since when are poor people permitted a good thing? A poor person isn't even allowed a gifted child!

From that time on Creature became even more widely known in town and even more wretched at home. Her mother could not abide her, grew to hate her as one hates a spider, "set apart as a leper," and more than once she cursed her husband with deadly oaths for coming to her defense, for feeling sorry for her.

"After all, pity for a living creature!" Zorakhl would try to reason with her, "After all, she has a soul!"

"A soul?" his wife would say, "A freak, a cripple, a monster, an affliction, a retribution for the sins of others!"

E

"Guess what!" said the rebbe's son, Yaakov-Eli, the foolish boy with the swollen cheeks, a happy smile on his face as if he were about to tell us some happy news. "Guess what? Creature is as good as dead. Basya the healer was there and she said it's bad. No more Creature, she's finished!" he said, gesturing like someone who had just completed a business deal.

All of us felt sick at heart at this news. While Creature was alive, we hardly even thought of her, but now that we heard she was dying, we all realized we had not treated her right and we were filled with a strange feeling one could call regret. Regret over what I don't know, but nonetheless, regret! We rushed over and saw the rebbitzin seated near Creature with eyes red from crying. We felt ashamed and quickly retreated.

"Come over here, why are you running away?" the rebbitzin called us back and spoke softly. "Don't be afraid,

Creature isn't dead yet. Creature is still alive, although if God, blessed be He, wishes it, He could . . . He is a great God, He can, He can, if only He wishes it. He is a reviver of the dead. The rebbe is not here, the rebbe went to buy a *poltshina*, an orange. Will you eat a *poltshina*, Creature, a *poltshina*?"

And the rebbitzin wrung her hands and bent over the invalid. We had never seen the rebbitzin so devoted.

Creature lay curled up in a ball, her eyes shut, her fearful mouth open, moving her dry lips and letting out a hoarse little cry, like a stricken bird: "Ee! . . . Ee! . . . Ee! . . ."

Looking at Creature, I was reminded of the little bird with the yellow beak that we had found on the ground, and my heart ached. I was choked with tears and I saw my comrades blinking back their own tears, too embarrassed to look at one another. We took to our books and when the rebbe returned with the *poltshina* he found us on our best behavior. He praised us, telling us we were fine boys to be so quiet. He sat down and continued with our lessons, burying himself in the *Gemara* with us, rubbing his forehead and singing with us, "*Omar Reb Pipa*," with spirit. But we could easily tell his mind was not on the *Gemara*, not with Reb Pipa, but alongside the oven. He kept turning his head around, forgive the comparison, like a cow looking for its lost calf, letting out a deep, deep sigh and a heavy, heavy groan, and each sigh and each groan tore a piece from my heart.

F

"Alright! Alright! Alright! You can turn around and go home now!" Yaakov-Eli, the rebbe's son, the foolish boy

with the swollen cheeks, announced the news early the following morning, hopping toward us on one leg.

"Home? What's going on?"

"What's going on? My father, my mother and all of us
have to sit *shiva*, can't teach all week because Creature died."

"Died?"

"Died, died last night. I'm off now to tell the members
of the Burial Society."

We were stunned.

On the one extreme the terrible news that poor Creature had died! And on the other extreme the good news
that we would be free from school all week! It was sum-
mertime. The sky was washed clean, clear as a mirror. Not
a speck of cloud, not a breeze. The hot sun smiled and
baked. We would be able to go swimming in the pond all
day and catch fish. We began dancing for joy, bleating and
mooing like calves and making crazy grimaces. One of us
made a funny face like a monkey and meowed like a cat.
Another responded with a "bow-wow," like a dog. And a
third quacked like a duck. A fourth spun around on one
leg like a top while singing a song:

> One-two-three,
> Yoder-lieder-lee,
> Oken-boken
> With the glocken . . .

and a fifth smacked his cheeks three times wordlessly and
began to run wildly in every direction, soon followed by the
rest of us rascals. But I, the one who knew Creature the best
because I used to eat a meal at the rebbe's occasionally,
remained standing as if glued to the spot.

"Died?" I pondered. "What does that mean, 'died'? For what reason had she lived? And why did she die?"

And I went into the rebbe's room, at least to see from a distance how one dies. What was it like to die?

I moved to the door and heard a strange crying and heart-rending keening like the drawn-out wailing accompanying women's prayers:

"Woe is me, alas, why did I give birth to you, may I be cur-sed? What was your life here on earth, wretched soul? What did God have against your innocent soul that he brought it down from His holy seat only to torment it here below, to be a retribution for the sins of others, may lightning str-ike me? Would that you had miscarried in your mother's womb before I delivered you to such wo-es! Would that I had not lived to bury you, so great is my punish-ment! May you merit a bright paradise, may you be a good advocate there for your parents, for the other children and for all our near and de-ar!"

I was suddenly overcome by a terrible melancholy. I wanted to run away, but I also wanted to see what was happening in that room. I opened the door and saw something lying on the ground, covered in black, a lit candle at the head, the rebbitzin sitting near, her legs folded under her, swaying back and forth, weeping and wailing in that same keening chant. Opposite her stood three women, close neighbors, Basya, Pessi, and Sossi, their hands clasped to their hearts, looking at the rebbitzin with such contorted faces that had it not been Creature lying there on the ground, one would have burst out laughing. The three neighbors had come to help keen over Creature but they were crying instead for the living, for her poor parents who had raised a cripple, alas, who had been born a cripple and had died a cripple.

I also saw the rebbe's other children sitting on the ground weeping silently, except for Yaakov-Levi (he had hopped off with such glee on one leg to the synagogue officials to have them bring the burial stretcher, you would have thought he had been sent to bring back musicians), and off to the side, in a corner on a stool, sat the rebbe, his head bowed, hands on his knees. I was curious to know whether or not he was crying—*how would a rebbe cry*? The door squeaked and I gave a little cough. The rebbe slowly raised his head so that I saw his brows, and then his red eyes. I could have sworn he had been crying.

"Go home, you impudent boy!" the rebbe shouted out at me, scaring me to death. I ran out of there as fast as my legs would carry me.

G

Lying in my bed at night I saw Creature before my eyes, her body covered in black, and still resounding in my ears were the rebbitzin's weeping and wailing. I recited my evening prayers.

When the lights were out I again saw Creature before my eyes, her body covered in black, and still resounding in my ears, the rebbitzin's weeping and wailing. I shut my eyes tight in order not to see; I covered my ears hard in order not to hear—it did no good. I saw Creature, her body covered in black, and heard the rebbitzin's weeping and wailing.

I tried hard to think of something else, deliberately choosing things that made me laugh, like the three neighbors with their contorted faces—it did no good, it didn't

make me laugh! All kinds of thoughts and images pene-
trated my mind: "Died . . . what does living mean, what
does dying mean? Why did Creature live? Why did she die?
For what reason . . . ?"

I pulled the blanket over me tightly, recited the night
prayer, and fell asleep.

I fell asleep and saw before me a black *khupa*. I was
standing with Creature under the *khupa*. All the classmates
were clapping their hands, singing:

> One-two-three,
> Yoder-lieder-lee,
> Oken-boken
> With the glocken . . .

Yaakov-Eli, the foolish boy with the swollen cheeks, was
hopping on one leg and shouting: "Metzutzeli! Metzutzeli!", and the rebbe and rebbitzin were weeping and wailing. Creature looked at me pitifully, imploringly, stretched
out to me her emaciated little hand with its twisted, dry
little fingers. I was drawn to her, my heart aching. My soul
was deeply moved.

"What do you want, Creature?" I said, "What do you
want? Perhaps a *poltshina*?"

I took a closer look—it wasn't Creature at all. It was a
young little bird with a yellow beak, Tzipur ben Balak. The
little bird was shivering, fluttering, trying to move its wings,
opening its mouth like a hungry baby while chanting
the way ancient High Priests must have intoned on Yom
Kippur:

Toodeli hoo-hoo!
Toodeli hoo-hoo!

* * *

I suddenly awakened. It was a warm, beautiful, bright summer day. All the windows were open. The tweeting of the birds and the droning of the locusts were grating in my ears. Standing by my bed were my two sisters, Zlatke and Blyumke, pretty girls with pink cheeks like peaches, wearing green and white aprons with blue polka dots. Their hair was braided with red ribbons. Their faces shone like the sun, they blossomed, like roses.

"Wake up now!" they said to me, "Finish your prayers and go outside. Your friends are waiting for you. They were already here twice. You're free from school today, free all week! Lucky you!"

Those sweet words, "free from school, free all week," delighted my heart, warmed my soul, lifted my spirits and made me desire to run out to my friends. But together with this sense of freedom I still remembered Creature and I felt a stab, like a dagger in my heart:

"Creature is gone! Creature is dead!"

And I ran out to my friends.

H

Summer outdoors. The sky washed clean, clear as a mirror. Not a speck of cloud, not a breeze. The sun smiling, the sun baking, the sun broiling. We all ran down to the pond to swim and to catch fish. And even while I was swimming and fishing, one thought never left my mind:

"Creature is gone! Creature is dead!"

All of us were undressed, as naked as Adam. We would swim, come out of the pond, roll around in the mud like swine and again jump into the water, staying in so long we turned blue and began to shiver, our teeth chattering. Then we lay stretched out on the sparkling sand under the hot, burning sun, under the blue canopy of sky. But two of our crowd, Big Chayim and Little Chayim, were still in the water. They had cleverly tied two shirts together by the sleeves and made a net to catch fish. If there *were* fish at all, they would catch them. The problem was, there were no fish. There *were* fish, but they wouldn't swim into Big Chayim and Little Chayim's net. The fish were not interested.

"Deeper, Chayim, deeper! Bend down, Chayim, bend down! Deeper, Chayim, deeper, but don't scare the fish!" Big Chayim was ordering Little Chayim around and both fishermen waded out till the water reached their necks, slowly dragging the net to the edge of the pond and continually checking the shirts—no fish!

"Let me, me and Mottel, we'll catch them!" said Mottel the redhead and jumped into the water with black haired Mottel, and the two new fishermen weren't too bad, made good progress, step by step, properly bent down, almost to the surface of the water.

And the pond shimmered with little waves, reflecting the blue canopy of sky that trembled in the water, rocking back and forth. The air was quiet. Not a living being was visible. Not so much as a peep was heard. Later Dovid-Leib, the water-carrier, came by with his water cart to fill his barrel to water his horse, wash his handsome red face with its plush, dusty beard, dry it off with the greasy hem of his coat—and off he was for town. The two or three washerwomen kneeling at the pond, who till that time had been slapping the clothes against a washboard, gathered their laundry on their backs and returned to town. It was still and serene. The water was still, the sky was still, a stillness reigned throughout. Even the frogs, who had been croaking all the while with their "kurr-kurr" and their "bul-bul-bul," had fallen asleep. It wouldn't be long before everything would have died down. Eyelids were becoming heavy and all one wanted to do was to lie there with one's wet body on the hot dry sand, lie, eyes half-shut, and look and think and doze. . . . Suddenly a cry was heard:

"We've got one! We've got one!"

That cry was so joyous it was like the cry of someone who had sailed on Columbus's ship when they discovered America.

We all sprang up and flew downhill to the edge of the pond, to the two new fishermen, peered into the net and saw a shirtsleeve thrashing in the water.

"Fish! Fish! Fish!" we all sang out, dancing up and down. And as we were singing and dancing, a huge, gray, ugly, disgusting frog with two foolish-looking, watery eyes jumped right out at us! We all ran pell-mell uphill, over the hot sand, screaming:

"Help, Jews, *sh'ma Yisroel*, save us!!!"

* * *

The fright, naturally, ended in laughter and the gang became even more cheerful, more lively. We lay around in the sand, rolled in the mud, splashed in the pond. It was pure pleasure—endless delight. No small thing—we were free, free all week! But only I was still plagued by that thought, that same thought:

"Creature is gone! Creature is dead! Dead! Dead! Dead!"

Flowers

(*Ten Little Stories*)

A

From Mount Sinai

In our Kasrilevka, on the other side of the synagogue, stood a mountain, a high mountain, high as the clouds, reaching the sky.

That's how it seemed to me when we were going to school, and we called it "Mount Sinai."

Very early one lovely summer day, ten of us boys, still young, were going to school with our holy books under our arms and our lunches in our hands.

The sun was just beginning to rise out of its "butter barrel" and was pouring its mild, golden rays over the peak of the mountain.

The mountain was covered with dew glistening like diamonds; the drops hung like pearls. The air was clean, delightfully pure, unimaginably pure.

We were excited, enchanted by this divine morning.

"You know what, boys?" one of us suggested, "Let's climb Mount Sinai!"

"Good idea," said another, "Let's climb Mount Sinai. We've never been there."

And we all started clambering up Mount Sinai, climbing eagerly on all fours.

When we reached the top and looked down, all the way down, we started to tremble.

We were so high up that the ground below appeared very small.

"Where are we, kids, where are we?"

"Where are we, you say? Under the clouds."

"Higher! Higher! UNDER THE SKY!"

"Do you see the synagogue, kids? Do you see the synagogue?"

"Yes, barely, like a little tiny house."

"Like a little tiny house, you say? Like a little table, like a little chair."

"Like a little chair, you say? Like a *Gemara*, like my Siddur."

"Like your little Siddur, you say? Like an egg, like a little nut."

"Like a nut, you say? Like a bean, like a pea."

"Like a pea? Like a poppy seed, like a mite, like a . . . a . . . a . . ."

And we all agreed to stretch out on the mountain top, face up.

I looked intently into the blue sky and my eyes brought the sky closer and closer to me till I had drawn it quite close to me, so close that I could stretch out my hand and with my fingertips touch the sky, the cold sky, touch it, stroke it, feel it, hold it, hold it, hold it.

Not only did my eyes bring me close to the sky, but my soul, my heart, my body, my entire being—all of me was up there high above, in the sky.

I was in heaven and I saw angels. With their broad white wings the angels were floating under the wide blue sky. They soared and glided, hovered and floated—and remained in one spot. I could hear voices singing, quiet, beautiful, sweet singing, like that of the High Priests and the Levites, like the Holy Organ in the Temple of old, as it is written in the Holy Book.

And a gentle, cool breeze passed over me and barely, barely grazed my forehead. A delicious perfume, a perfume from the Garden of Eden, wafted by me and my eyes closed, closed . . .

"Get to school, good-for-nothings, troublemakers, rowdies! Get to school, scoundrels! Better listen, you rascals, or I'll tell the rebbe on you! Get to school, lazy idlers, loafers!"

That was the sexton of the synagogue, Reb Yekusiel, an angry Jew with a flat nose who always had a pipe between his teeth.

And we suddenly fell from the sky to earth.

B

The Western Wall
(The Remaining Wall of the Temple)

"Tell me exactly, I beg you. Did you see the Western Wall with your own eyes? Really? Did you get a good look at it? Tell me all about it."

So said my rebbe to a Jew who had just come back from Jerusalem.

"Tell me, I beg you, describe it exactly, every last detail."

The Jerusalem Jew described it exactly, in great detail, and my rebbe drank in every word, beamed with joy, was filled with pleasure like a person receiving regards from a close friend in a far-off land.

The rebbe was concentrating so intensely on the Jerusalem Jew that he didn't notice how we boys had each moved away from the table and had snuck outside to get in a little sliding on the ice.

When we came back into the classroom, we found them still sitting together.

"The Western Wall!" the rebbe said to the Jerusalem Jew, "The Western Wall! That is all that is left for us from our Holy Temple, from our whole state! The Western Wall! The Western Wall!"

And the rebbe burst into tears.

C

Avreml

When I met them, their two ages added up to almost two hundred years.

"Avreml! We have a guest."

"Who is it?"

And the two hundred year old couple welcomed me with pleasure, with joy.

And I visited with the two hundred year old couple with pleasure, with joy.

Both were small, with hair as white as snow, toothless, stooped, but happy, tidy, lively, looking like brother and sister, not like man and wife.

"I still remember your grandfather, your great-grandfather; he was a fine Jew, very fine, really fine, not like today's Jews—no, really not! We got to know him, I think—how *did* we get to know your great-grandfather?"

He sucked in his lips over his toothless gums and told me stories from bygone days and as he remembered *those* years, he became more animated, fresher, younger.

"Listen, my sweetheart!" he said to the old woman, "Don't you remember, my soul, the name of the landowner from whom his great-great-grandfather had a lease? Hah, sweetheart?"

"Pan Przsreshrshanski, that was his name, Avreml," she said.

"Yes, you're right, sweetheart, you're right. Pan Przsheshrshanski was his name."

And a peculiar whistle accompanied the name as they pronounced it.

"That couldn't have been too long ago, isn't that so? What do you think, sweetheart?"

"Not long ago, Avremele, not long ago; about . . . about sixty or seventy years ago, not more, not more than seventy," the old woman answered.

And the youthful old man told me all kinds of stories and anecdotes, far into the night.

"Come along, Avremenyu, come to bed now!"

And the old woman led the old man by the hand off to bed the way one leads a small child, and in a few minutes she returned to me alone, dressed for bed, with a white, starched cap on her head and some hairpins in her mouth.

She sat down alongside me for a chat. And we chatted for quite a bit, and we could not have enough of our talk, by which I mean, I wasn't the one talking, *she* was. The old woman talked and I heard her out.

"You cannot imagine," she said to me, leaning on her wrinkled elbows, "You cannot imagine how weak my Avreml has become lately. If he stays up an extra half hour, he tires and must go to bed. But why should I complain? I thank God for it. There are not too many Avremls like my Avreml. I have never ever had any disrespect from him, never heard a cross word, from our wedding till this day, may he live to be a hundred and twenty. What is there more to say? I have no complaints, none at all, and we live happily together, bless God, as He commanded, and we have no complaints to Him either. He has provided for us all these years and we don't, God forbid, have to depend on others for help, praised be God, blessed be He."

"Well, and your children?"

"My children? Ay, ay, ay! The Blessed One has punished me, all our children are dead. We have grandchildren and great-grandchildren and great-great grandchildren, thank the Lord, *kayn eyn horeh*, but no children. They've all died."

The old woman sank deep in thought.

After a few moments she said to me, "What do you think of him?"

"Of whom?"

"Of my Avremele."

I didn't understand what she meant, so I smiled and changed the subject.

We spent a long time together. We spoke about many things and different people; but most of all Avreml, her Avreml, was on her tongue time and time again.

Avreml served as illustration for every subject, some-one with whom to compare every person. Avreml! Avreml! Avreml!

I imagined that sitting across from me was a wife, a young wife, not an old woman of almost a hundred years.

How I would love to know what has become of that couple.

D

The Treasure

On the other side of the mountain, behind the old syna-gogue, a treasure is buried.

That's what they said in our village.

But finding the treasure was no easy task. If all the Jews in the village were to live in harmony and would undertake to find it together, it would be found.

That's what they said in our village.

And if all the Jews were to live happily together, with-out envy, without malice, without quarreling, without bad-mouthing, without gossip, and they joined together, they would find the treasure. If not, it would sink deeper and deeper into the earth.

That's what they said in our village and they began to debate and contradict, to bicker and argue, to name-call and quarrel more and more venomously and all because of the treasure. One said it must be here and another said it must be there, and they couldn't stop debating and contradicting, bickering and arguing, name-calling and quarreling, more and more venomously, and all because of the treasure—and the treasure sank deeper and deeper into the earth.

E

The Nerve!

He sat on the ground near the door of the shul. He sat and counted the groshens, counted the pennies—the pennies he had accumulated during the day.

Twice a week, Monday and Thursday, he went around to all the houses—a *poor* pauper collecting pennies from *rich* paupers. Those two days were *his*.

How brightly shone the sun, how warm were its rays! With one hand in his bosom and the other holding the groshens and pennies, clinking them together, he counted them and added them up. Suddenly . . .

Who was that driving by in that carriage drawn by a team of six horses? Ah! That was the count of the district.

As the horses pulled the carriage by, two clouds of dust were left behind.

The dust covered his eyes and mouth and blocked out the bright sunlight for several minutes.

"How presumptuous! The nerve of that count!" he grumbled into his beard and went back to his work, counting groshens, figuring his take.

F

Dividing Up

It's become a new trend these days: societies, orphanages, schools, institutions. There was a time when we had never heard of such things.

When a poor man died and left a dozen orphans, they were doomed—you might as well throw them into the lake! That's just a way of speaking; it's never happened that living people were thrown into the lake alive! It's just a way of speaking.

I remember it as if it were today. Kasriel, the water-carrier, died and soon after him, his wife, and they left a goodly number of children behind, without a father, without a mother, without a place to lay their heads, without a crust of bread. An uproar, an uproar arose in town, an uproar among the poor folk.

"Murderers! Monsters! Devils! Why doesn't anyone speak out? How can you let so many children die of hunger? Why don't they do something? Where are our rich folks? The wealthy ones?"

The rich folks, the wealthy ones, were busy with their own affairs, and the poor folks kept making a racket and protesting until night fell and a meeting was held at the rabbi's. It was decided the children would be divided up.

A great squabble broke out over how to divide them up; volunteers for such a good deed were many, but children—only seven.

G

Two Souls

"Have you gotten everything ready? Take these two and deliver them to earth and come right back."

So said God, blessed be His name, to an angel, indicating two sinful souls to him.

And the angel took the two sinful souls under his wings and flew down with them to earth.

And the night spread its dark wings over the earth and it became dark.

And a cold wind, a strong wind gusted and swirled through the windows, through the door, through the wall of a small, broken down shack. In that small, broken down shack, on a bed of straw, lay a sickly, emaciated woman. The woman was writhing, writhing in pain—she was in labor.

And a cold wind, a strong wind gusted and swirled and could not pass through the brick walls and tall doors and windows of a wealthy house. Inside the elegant, wealthy house, comfortably bedded down in satin and silk, lay a healthy, pretty woman. The healthy, pretty woman was writhing, writhing in pain—she was in labor.

The angel quickly deposited the two souls.

"Go, children," he said to them, "go, brothers, suffer in this world for a while!"

And on that night two baby boys were born: one on the ground, on straw—to hunger, to need, to misery—another mouth to feed. And the other—on satin and silk, in joy, to wealth, to happiness, to luxury, to pleasures, to all the rewards of the world.

"Why?" the angel asked the Almighty One. "Is that just? One to have everything, the other to have nothing? One on straw, the other on satin? One to luxury, the other to need?"

"Look down and be silent!" answered the Ruler of the world.

Twenty years passed.

And the night spread its dark wings on the earth and it became dark.

And a strong wind, a cold wind gusted and swirled and blew through the windows, through the door, through the walls of a small, broken down shack. From the small, broken down shack was heard a voice, a pleading voice:

"God Almighty! Beloved God! Hear my plea, hear my weeping; let me die, take me from this earth, I cannot suffer any longer!"

"No, live on, live on, suffer—live long, live long my child!"

And a strong wind, a cold wind swirled and gusted and could not pass through the brick walls and high doors and windows of the elegant, wealthy house. From the elegant, wealthy house was heard a voice, a pleading voice:

"God Almighty! Beloved God! Hear my plea, hear my weeping. Take away the Angel of Death from me. I want to live. A shame to waste such a good life. I am too young, I don't want to leave this world!"

"No, die! No, die! Say farewell—enough, you've had your good times, my child!"

And a strong wind, a cold wind swirled and gusted that night, and the sinful soul in the happy house, the son of the healthy, rich mother, unwillingly rose up to heaven.

And a strong wind, a cold wind gusted and swirled a long time, and the sinful soul in the broken down shack, the son of the sickly pauper, unwillingly lived on, lived on!

H

I Am Ashamed

I had a friend. We studied at the same school. We lived together, did foolish things together, shared joys and sorrows.

What is called blind fortune, success, smiled upon my friend and made him happy. Things became better and better for him, and he rose higher and higher.

And I remained behind.

We had not seen or met each other in a very long while. We went our separate ways and lived in different cities.

Once I came to the city where my friend lived and passed my friend's fabulous home and I stopped in front of it. "Should I go in or shouldn't I?"

And I went in.

Imagine! He recognized me!

"So how are you, brother? How are things going for you?"

We stood in the entryway of the house for a long time; he did not invite me inside.

He realized I was wondering about this and said to me, looking at my clothes,

"Please excuse me, dear brother, don't be offended, I beg you, forgive me, I cannot, *I am ashamed!*"

"You are ashamed? You are ashamed of me?"

"Ah, no, heaven forbid, that's not what I meant, that's not what I was saying! I said I was ashamed of . . . of my wealthy house . . . for you, for my old friend, for . . . for . . . tell me, where do you live? Where are you staying? I will come, I will go to your place, be your guest!"

He glanced down at my run-down, worn-out boots and turned red with embarrassment.

I understood him and forgave him with all my heart, with all my heart!

I

Where the World Ends

There, on the other side of the cemetery, behind the town, the sky meets the earth.

There, on the other side of the cemetery, behind the town, is where the world ends.

That's what we schoolboys reasoned, and we decided among us that when we gathered together Sabbath afternoon, when everyone, all the Jews, all the townspeople were sleeping their sweet Sabbath sleep, we would head out for where the world ends.

We walked, maybe an hour, or two, or three—I don't know; but with God's help, we arrived safely at the windmill.

There, at the windmill, we sat down to rest. And then we laid ourselves down, we stretched out on the green grass, on the sweet-smelling grass and napped a while.

Each of us was absorbed in his own thoughts, his own fantasies. It was still. No one spoke a word; no one wanted to be distracted, no one wanted to distract anyone else.

"Where *does* the world end?" one of us said.

"Right here, silly!" another boy answered.

And we all agreed that right there, just beyond the windmill, was where the world ended, that beyond the mill would be the ·*harei khoshekh*, the dark mountains, which are covered with black grass and where are found, to this day, little Jews with beards down to their toes, the little Jews that God had driven there because of their tongues, their long tongues with which they had slain one another. And beyond the mountains was the frozen ocean to which the stormy wind drove all the vessels and ships and from which no one ever returned.

"Get to the synagogue! Scoundrels! To the synagogue! Fine lads! Shouldn't you be sitting in the synagogue Sabbath afternoon and studying a chapter rather than wasting your time, along with the peasants, behind the mill? Get to the synagogue, ignorant peasants!"

That was Motti "Redcheek," a fine Jew, a scholarly businessman who had his own house and his own seat at the eastern wall of the synagogue, the third seat from the Holy Ark.

J

Angel of Death

I heard it in school, my rebbe told me. My rebbe, Reb Meier, blessed be his memory.

He told us frightening stories about how people die, about the Angel of Death covered with a thousand eyes from head to foot, about the Angel of Blood with the iron rods who enters into the grave carrying a decree:

"Villain! What is your name? Villain! How are you called? In matters of the Torah, what have you learned?"

And many more horrible, really frightening stories. A chill would pass over our bodies, our hair would stand on end.

But more frightening than anything for me was the Angel of Death, covered with the thousand eyes from head to toe. And I was certain that if I were to meet this personage, I would surely die out of sheer fright alone.

Ah, how times change.

Now, when I see "him" almost every day, I am no longer astonished.

I sense "him" near me; I hear "his" breathing close by; I know, I hear, that "he" is following me in my every footstep—and it doesn't bother me!

"Come now, faster, faster!" "he" says to me. "Make your will and come . . . "

"Tomorrow, God willing, tomorrow!" I answer "him" and put "him" off for another day.

Thus, as you see, we deceive each other. "He" says to me: "Your will!" And I say to "him," "Tomorrow . . . tomorrow . . . tomorrow . . ."

The Youngest
Seder King
(*A Story in Honor of Passover*)

A

hat a lucky child, that Yuzek! Everyone loved him, everyone fussed over him, made allowances for him, kissed him, cuddled him.

And who was this all about?

Yuzek!

"Parents don't spoil an only child as much as those two sisters, Sara and Rivka, spoil their little brother. Yuzek, Yuzek, and still Yuzek! 'Yuzek, please eat! Yuzek, please drink! Yuzek, please sleep! Yuzek, here's a sweet! Yuzek, we're sewing you a new pair of trousers for the holidays! Yuzek, you're going to go to the bathhouse before Passover! Yuzek, you're going to conduct the seder for Passover!' Yuzek, Yuzek and still Yuzek—it's become tiresome to hear! They're taking a gem of a child and ruining him!"

So said the ladies who lived together with the sisters, all the while sneaking into Yuzek's hand a piece of honey cake, a strudel, a roasted chicken liver, a little jam.

They all did it out of pity. He was, after all, a poor little orphan!

B

There was a Jew named Raphael who was poor all his life, and an asthmatic to boot, with peculiar musical lungs. When he breathed in and out, it sounded like a bow scraping across the strings of a violin. This Raphael was an honest man but, may he forgive me, he was also a luckless *shlimazel*, an impractical man. Perhaps it was because he was so honest that he was a luckless *shlimazel*. On the other hand, perhaps it was because he was a luckless *shlimazel* that he had to be so honest. They said about him in Kasrilevka that if Raphael were not a *shlimazel*, he would have made a lot of money.

And he might have had all that money in hand because he had been the foreman at Reb Simkha'le Viner's distillery, and aside from his salary, he solemnly swore that he never profited from any other outside income.

Reb Simkha'le Viner was lucky to have an honest foreman. He respected him for it, paid him exactly six rubles a week, sometimes added a ten ruble coin for the holidays, didn't charge him for Passover wine, and a bottle of Passover whisky—no questions asked. How else could it be? Wasn't Reb Simkha'le a person who understood how to show appreciation? But Raphael, the foreman, contracted rheumatism and finally a cold in the lungs in the distillery, and that's when those whistling, singing musical sounds began in his chest. Who was to blame? To be healthy—that was a gift of God. The healthiest person can drop dead suddenly, God forbid. Our sages have long said that . . . but you probably already know what our sages said.

At any rate, Raphael's chest whistled and wheezed and sang until one time, it was between Passover and Sukkos, he lay down with a high fever and never got up.

C

Raphael died and—ay-ay-ay!—what a funeral he had! Reb Simkha'le went all out! He himself carried Raphael's body out on the funeral stretcher, he himself helped carry him on his shoulders, he himself followed him to the holy place, making sure he had a fine grave, he himself supervised the digging of the plot, threw in the first spadeful of soil and when the child, Yuzek, chanted the first Kaddish with Ozer, the sexton, over his father's grave, Reb Simkha'le wept. My, how he wept!

"No one can know! No one can know!" he told each person separately afterwards, "It is such a loss, such a loss, it is enormous!"

And to the widow he said: "Don't cry, I will not forsake you and your orphans. Trust first in God, then in me . . ."

And Reb Simkha'le kept his word, as much as possible. The first few weeks he paid the widow the same wages that Raphael used to receive. True, she had to go ask for it, not once but several times, and that was for her not too pleasant; but I ask you, what did you expect? He should deliver the wages to her home? Seems to me it's enough to pay a person's wages after his death!

"You're coming to ask me for money," he once said to her, "as if you are entitled to it, as if you had invested in my distillery."

That day the widow cried more than when Raphael was buried. When her two daughters, Sarah and Rivka, found out why their mother was crying, they made her vow she would not go back to Reb Simkha'le.

"But what will we do?"

"What everyone else does: we will be servants, we'll wash clothes, we'll sew on a machine."

Sewing on a machine was then in Kasrilevka a popular occupation. One could earn two zlotys a day if one were willing to sit at the machine sixteen or seventeen hours a day. Getting work was no problem either; if not clothing, it was underwear, or it was hemming handkerchiefs. The hardest part was obtaining a sewing machine, harder still, two sewing machines!

True, sewing machines were available on installment. But where would they get the few rubles for the first payment?

"Go ask your rich friend," the neighbors suggested to the widow, "Tell him that the girls will work it off."

D

That's easy to say: go ask your rich friend! But what doesn't a Jew do to make a living? The widow went to Reb Simkha'le Viner and found him at the best possible time, right after eating. Everyone knows that when you need to come to someone for a favor, you should only track him down after a meal; after a meal a person is a softer touch than before a meal—before a meal a person is a beast.

"What's on your mind?"

The widow laid out her proposal about the sewing machines.

Reb Simkha'le listened carefully, picked his teeth, got red in the face, perspired a bit, and dozed off. He didn't fall asleep, God forbid, just snoozed, looking at her with half-closed eyes, thinking in the meantime about business matters and about his digestion. Reb Simkha'le was fleshy and over-weight. His doctors had ordered him to eat more meat and less starchy foods; and wouldn't you know, Reb Simkha'le really loved starchy foods: bread, noodles, kugel, anything made of flour. He knew it wasn't good for him, but when he saw it, he ate it, and after he ate it, he was sorry.

"So how are things going for you?" he said to the widow when she had finished and he had stopped dozing, gazing at her with half-shut eyes.

"How should things be going for me?" the widow answered, "You hear how things are going, may all my enemies have things go as well for them! That's why if I had money for a sewing machine, for two sewing machines, at the very least one sewing machine . . ."

"What sewing machine?" he said in surprise, now looking at her with open eyes.

"I already told you that my daughters want to do sewing, to become seamstresses, to sew on a machine, we don't have a machine and we really need two sewing machines to be paid out on installments."

"That's a good thing, a very good thing, seamstresses, sewing, earning money, excellent, very good!"

But at the same time a thought flew through his mind: "How come my stomach feels so bloated? It seems to me I haven't eaten that much today!" And one eye seemed to get smaller. But as the widow remained silent, he sat up and spoke further to her:

"Well, very fine, sewing, excellent, why not?"

"I wanted to ask you, Reb Simkha'le, you've done so much for our sakes, perhaps it would be possible that . . ."

Upon hearing the possibility of a request for a loan, an advance of money, Reb Simkha'le sat bolt upright.

"That what?"

"That you could lend us the first payment for the sewing machines."

"Which sewing machines?"

"The ones I'm telling you about, two sewing machines for my daughters, at the very least one sewing machine."

"What do I have to do with sewing machines? Where do I come to sewing machines?"

"Money!" said the widow, "My daughters will buy the sewing machines themselves. They sell sewing machines on time. If I put down fifty and in three months I pay another twenty-five, and then in . . ."

"I know, I know, you don't have to tell me. As far as I'm concerned, they can do without sewing machines. Who ever heard of sewing machines!"

"Then how will they be able to sew? By hand you can't get enough work done in time; all seamstresses have sewing machines nowadays."

"You want them to be seamstresses? Oh, how terrible, how terrible! If your husband were to rise from his grave and hear that you want to make your daughters seamstresses, he would die all over again. Don't you know your Raphael was an honest, an observant Jew. Men like Raphael are not to be found! If Raphael were to hear seamstresses, he wouldn't be able to bear it! He would—I don't know what!"

Reb Simkha'le spoke from the heart. He really meant what he was saying. And the more he spoke, the louder he raised his voice:

"Seamstresses? Heh! Fine work for a Jewish girl! Heh! We know what a seamstress is! And Jewish girls at that! Heh! Raphael's daughters seamstresses! And how about me? You know your Raphael grew up in my house? I made a man of him, first God, then I. And who made his wedding if not I? Heh! And you want me to allow such a thing? Heaven forbid! What do you think I am? A stone? A bone? A piece of wood? Heh!"

As for the widow—she came empty-handed and she left empty-handed.

She made a holy vow, swore most earnestly, may she not see her children grow up, that her foot would never cross Reb Simkha'le's threshhold again—better to become a servant!

E

But it's easy to say, "become a servant!" Raphael, the foreman's wife, a respectable housewife like all Kasrilevka housewives, become a servant? Stand at a stranger's oven? Sit at a stranger's table? Better to die than live like that! And the widow wished she were dead. And this once, God, the great almighty God, He who is a father to orphans and a comfort to widows, was merciful to the poor widow and didn't permit her to suffer for long on this earth, granted her an easy death, following some sort of internal swelling. She suffered some but only languished altogether a little over a month and died.

It so happened that in Kasrilevka at that time, except for babies, no one died, and the widow was buried near her husband, one grave next to the other—this was their good fortune! And now Yuzek had to say Kaddish for both his father and mother, and from that time on Yuzek became beloved and precious to everyone who heard him chanting the Kaddish in the synagogue, standing on a bench, screetching in his childish voice, "*Yiskadal v'yiskadash . . .*" Everyone who saw this young boy with his round little hat, his dark eyes and rosy cheeks standing on a bench in the synagogue and heard him chanting the Kaddish, was riveted to the spot, sighed and turned inward to thoughts that were neither hopeful nor happy, because everybody can, God forbid, die, everybody has children who can be orphaned, may it never happen! And everyone pushed a little something into his hand—a kopek, an apple, out of pity and charity for orphans.

The truth was Yuzek was a gifted child with the kind of face that said, "Love me," and he was also smart, the smartest boy in his school; Reb Noah, the teacher, couldn't praise him enough and the whole town lauded him.

"They really praise Raphael the foreman's son, don't they?"

"Yuzek? They say he'll grow up to really be somebody!"

"And where do you find such a rarity? Among poor people, on the trash heap!"

"It's always like that. Who goes on living? Old Moshe-Aharon—can't walk, can't talk. Who dies? Reb Simkha'le's son-in-law—strong, healthy, a father of children, a young man with money—he goes and dies!"

"You talk about Reb Simkha'le's son-in-law? How about Paysi, the rich man's daughter-in-law?"

"How is she managing?"

"I wouldn't call it managing! They've already brought the specialist from Yehupetz down three times."

"Really? I should earn half as much as that will cost them, God in heaven!"

"That's the world for you!"

"That's the way the world goes!"

That was how people in Kasrilevka talked, criticizing the work of the Almighty: why He grants years to some and not to others. Why He grants riches to this one and to that one nothing! Why He grants bright children to this one and not—oh, the devil take it all! It never occured to them to ask how these bright children survived. What did they eat? Who clothed them? Why didn't they freeze during the long winters in cold cellars? Why didn't they grow up crippled, hunchbacked, destined to be paupers, unwanted, miserable souls on earth?

Luckily the sisters, Sarah and Rivka, were able to scrape together enough money for a sewing machine and for that they had to thank their three friends, Basya the healer, Pessi the sexton's wife, and Sosi the used goods dealer, who shared a house with them. The three of them were able to put together enough money for the down payment, the rest would be paid out and lo and behold—they had a sewing machine. What's so remarkable about that? They were human beings, after all. What else could two grown girls do with a young orphan boy to support? Even a snake, they say, looks out for its young. Can a human being do no less?

One problem, however, was that the sewing machine clattered away day and night, because there was, thank

God, much work to be had and both sisters worked at the sewing machine, taking turns—while one sister sewed the other was cooking at the stove and then when the other sister was sewing on the machine, the other one was preparing the supper. The sewing machine never stopped clattering and the neighbors were holding their heads and quietly grumbling:

"What a noisemaker!"

F

But God is merciful; He sends a remedy for every ailment. The remedy was Yuzek. Every family experiences a time that is bleak and dark, times are bad, business is not going well, the heart is heavy. Then along comes a little squirrel and the entire household is transformed. At first the little squirrel squalls, screams at night with bellyaches, doesn't let anyone sleep. But soon it grows some, stops crying, opens its eyes and looks around, like a real person: "See how it's looking around! So, little one! So, tiny one!" The little squirrel opens its mouth, sticks out its tongue and begins to laugh and everyone feels bright and happy, "Just look, look, it's laughing, I swear, it's laughing!" Such joy, such an event, such a celebration! The whole house is filled with the baby, people carrying it around, forgetting their problems, life's bitterness seems sweeter, there is nothing but pure delight!

That was how it was with our Yuzek. Yuzek was the beloved little squirrel whom everyone adored and made a fuss over. Before Passover, they outfitted him like a prince in a little coat and trousers with suspenders, had a pair of little boots made for him and bought him a new cap. The women promised to give him nuts and stuffed him with fried matzo-meal pancakes, ruining his stomach and almost killing him with kindness.

"Who asked you to stuff him like that?" the sisters rebuked the women.

"Sha, sha, look at them, will you! We give the child a pancake with shmaltz and look how they're carrying on!"

That was the way the women justified themselves, and Basya the healer did everything she could to save the child. The night before Passover they gave Yuzek a clean shirt and three groshens and sent him off to the baths. When he returned, they dressed him in his new outfit and he shone like the sun.

"A royal child!" they exclaimed to one another.

"May no evil eye befall him, may no angry eye harm him!"

And Yuzek took the little prayer book and went off to pray at the synagogue, said Kaddish, and returned home with a cheerful holiday greeting for all. He found the table laid out with matzos, a decanter of raisin wine, bitter herbs, grated horseradish, chopped apples and honey, potatoes, and salt water. They had everything, everything that was needed, except for one thing: there was no one to conduct the seder.

There was no seder King!

G

All three friends were without husbands. Two were widows and one was divorced. None of them had any children. In fact, they did have children but not living with them; the children had long ago left home, dispersed throughout the world: one was a craftsman, one worked in a shop, another was far, far away in America. It was luck, or the lack of it, that had brought these three women together in the same house, the house of Basya the healer, who owned it and was of the three the most well-to-do.

Although they lived under one roof, cooked at one stove, made bread at the same kneading trough, each had her own table because it was difficult for three women to keep house and get along together. If you see women nowadays being friendly, kissing one another when they get together for a visit, sitting together and cracking nuts, don't be surprised. It's only because they don't live under the same roof, don't cook at the same stove, and don't make bread at the same kneading trough.

Of the three hundred sixty five days of the year, our women quarreled for about three hundred of them, but I don't know what you consider to be quarreling. They never took anything from one another, didn't insult one another, didn't offend each other's dignity, God forbid. It was simply a matter of three different personalities not always agreeing. For instance, Pessi the sexton's wife liked to bank the fire in the stove and cover it with an oven lid. What was wrong with that? But Sosi the used goods dealer had the habit of putting a pot of chicory on the hearth in the morning. That too, didn't seem too terribly wrong. She certainly wouldn't push her little pot of chicory in among the pots reserved for meat. But Pessi the sexton's wife said that wasn't a good idea because on account of a pot of chickory you could ruin the challah in the oven. Said Sosi the used goods dealer, "Let all her enemies be ruined!" Pessi the

sexton's wife said that apparently she had quite a few enemies. Sosi the used goods dealer then said, "I can't complain, I have enough of them, may they wither." Said Pessi
the sexton's wife: "Since when have you become so full of
talk?" Then Sosi the used goods dealer said: "Ever since
I moved into this God-forsaken place." So Basya the healer,
the landlady of the house, who was standing off to the side,
her headscarf tucked behind her ears, a rolling pin in her
hands, rolling out a sheet of noodles for the Sabbath,
chimed in: "I don't know why you feel it's so God-forsaken.
Is it the little rent you pay?" Sosi the used goods dealer
answered: "It's easy for you to say, you're a property owner
and have, *kayn eyn horeh*, lots of money!" Then Basya the
healer commented: "What difference does it make to you
whether I have a lot or a little money? Have I ever taken
anything from you?" Sosi the used goods dealer responded:
"What is there to take? My poverty? Take it!" So Basya the
healer retorted: "Keep it for yourself in good health!"

Pessi the sexton's wife spoke up: "No one is safe from
poverty! We know plenty of capable housewives who own
their own homes and still end up paupers!" "Worse than
paupers," put in Sosi the used goods dealer. That made
Basya the healer angry and she lashed out at Sosi the used
goods dealer. Then Pessi stood up for Sosi and soon a
shouting match broke out among the three women, a mish-
mash, a flood of loud words, a hurling of insults and accu-
sations: "She calls herself a peacemaker!" "What do you
think of the nerve of that woman!" "If you don't like it you
don't have to marry me!" "Be quiet, big mouth, because
you might catch a fireplace poker in the head." "I don't
know which of you is worse." "Look who's talking!" "Take
that!" "Both of you take that!"

Do you think it was as bad as it sounds? Blows? God forbid! Tongues stuck out, a nose thumbed, and that was all.

H

Don't be offended by what I am about to tell you: I'm afraid that whenever you yoke three modern women together and squeeze them under the same roof, as our three women were squeezed together, I cannot guarantee what would happen; it's possible nothing would happen, and it's possible it would turn nasty, even nastier than with my three neighbors. I don't mean to insult anyone—talking, just talking . . .

But I return to my women. In spite of all the quarrels and the nasty exchanges that would erupt among them, they did not remain enemies for long, God forbid, because in truth, what did they have against one another? Did they threaten each other's livelihoods? One moment they fought and the next they made up. And invariably when Passover came they genuinely got along, worked together as one soul. All three baked matzos on the same day, all three put up their crocks of borscht, all three bought a sack of potatoes together to save money, and all three sat down to the seder table at the landlady's, Basya the healer, and together they held high the seder plate quietly repeating word for word as Basya read aloud from the Yiddish translation of the Haggadah.

In the past when Basya's husband, Yisroel the healer, was still alive, he would preside at the seder. After Yisroel the healer died, one of the women's sons led the seder. But now that all the children had dispersed, one this way and one that, and all that remained in the house was one male, Yuzek, the women wondered if perhaps Yuzek could conduct the seder this year. Yuzek had been studying Torah for a long time, he was fluent in Hebrew—why shouldn't he be the man of the house, the seder King?

"Yuzek, do you want to be the seder King?"

"The seder King? Why not? Who would turn down a kingdom?"

"God help the kingdom if Yuzek is the king!"

And the three women and the two sisters prepared a tall pile of pillows as his throne, and when Yuzek returned from the synagogue with his cheerful "*Goot Yontev*," he seated himself upon the seder King's throne in his brand-new holiday clothes, like a true seder King.

I

There are three actions: yawning, laughing, and crying—those are behaviors that are contagious. We have no control over yawning, laughing, and crying.

Almost at the high point of the seder, after the youngest seder King Yuzek the orphan had finished the lovely, "We are bound to thank and praise Thee" and the melodious "Halleluiah," and was raising the second cup of wine, beginning to recite the prayer with which to drink the wine and as he started to bring the wine to his lips, there arose from the women a lamentation as if they were keening for the dead.

How this happened, which of them first began to weep, is difficult to say. After Yuzek recited the *kiddush* and began to sing, "Slaves we were," one of the two sisters remembered that just a year ago at that time they were also sitting at the seder but it was a quite different seder. Their father and mother were alive and the two sisters had new dresses sewn for them for Passover. They could never have dreamed that this year they would need to be sitting at a stranger's table with strange women and that Yuzek would be presiding over the seder. One of the sister's eyes began to blink and her lower lip trembled. Looking at her, the other sister let fall one teardrop after another. And looking at them both, one of the three neighbors remembered her own sorrow. When Nati the sexton, her husband was still alive she was happy, that is, she was never really happy but certainly happier than she was now that she was called the assistant sexton's wife because Ozer the sexton, who used to be the assistant sexton to Nati, had been promoted after her husband's death from assistant sexton to sexton, and his wife Gnessi had become so puffed up, my God! you couldn't get near her!

As Pessi the sexton's wife was thinking these thoughts, she made such a sad face that Sosi the used goods dealer had to be stronger than iron to hold back her tears. Sosi was reminded of her own sorrowful life: how her competitors wouldn't allow her to make a groshen, dragged her customers away, tried to ruin her! Now she was remembering her oldest daughter who had died long ago when she was a child, Rossi was her name. If Rossi hadn't died, she would now be a grown-up woman, perhaps even a mother herself. And she also thought of her husband, how much he had suffered all his days, was a miserable cripple, a failure at everything he did, a sickly man. And Sosi the used goods dealer, as she repeated Basya the healer's wife's words from the Haggadah, swaying back and forth with her, suddenly found her face wet with tears.

And even the reader herself, Basya the healer, did not hear the words of the Haggadah that issued from her lips as if of their own accord. She also remembered her own sorrows, her children who left for that far-off America. True, they did write her fine letters assuring her they were making a good living: they were working very hard and were doing as well as anyone else. To prove how well-off they were, they had sent her their portraits, which in America are called "pictures," and promised her that if their businesses would do better, they would send her a few dollars and a ship's ticket and would bring her over to that vast, glorious land, where everybody made a living, where everybody was equal, where a person could fall down on the street from hunger and no one would bother him. May her enemies choke before Basya would go there. She had children here too. Ay, they weren't doing too well here. What could one do? It was up to God. Everything was up to God!

So thought Basya the healer as she read the Haggadah not realizing how she herself was weeping, how her tears were flowing. When the time came to drink the second of the four cups of wine and the youngest seder King paused to sip a little wine, all the women became aware of their crying and Basya the healer scolded them loudly, dried her eyes with her apron and blew her nose:

"Why have you all begun crying in the middle of everything? What is today, Yom Kippur? Or Tisha B'Av? What nonsense!"

The women calmed down as one of them brought the seder King a pitcher of water and a basin with which to wash his hands while another served the hot fish from the oven and a third brought the horseradish. The youngest seder King made a blessing, "*Al akhilat matzo*," the woman responded, "Amen," and the holiday dinner commenced in silence.

My Brother
Elyahu's Drink

A

For one ruble—a hundred rubles! Any one of you can earn a hundred rubles a month and more. All you have to do is read our book costing a mere ruble plus postage. Hurry, buy! Stop what you are doing and take advantage of this great opportunity or you will miss out!"

That is what my brother Elyahu read somewhere in a newspaper soon after he stopped being a boarder in his father-in-law's home. My brother Elyahu stopped being a boarder, not because it was time. They had, in fact, promised him three years' room and board but he was hardly there three quarters of a year. Misfortune had befallen his wealthy father-in-law, Yoneh the baker. He went broke and from a rich man overnight became a pauper. How this happened is another story and I don't have time to tell it now. I'm very busy. I'm making money. I'm hawking a drink my brother Elyahu makes with his own hands. He learned how to make it from a book costing only one ruble and from which you can earn a hundred rubles a month and more. As soon as my brother Elyahu read about that book, he immediately sent off a ruble (his last ruble) by mail and told our mother she need not worry any longer.

"Mama! Thank God, we are in luck! We don't have to worry about money any more. We'll have money up to here" (he indicated his neck).

"From what?" asked my mother, "Did you get a job?"

"Better than a job!" my brother Elyahu answered, his eyes aglow, apparently out of great excitement. He told her that she only had to wait a few days until the book arrived.

"What book?" my mother asked him.

"What a book!" my brother Elyahu exclaimed and asked her if she would be satisfied with a hundred rubles a month. My mother laughed at him and told him she would be satisfied with a hundred rubles a year so long as it was a sure thing. My brother Eliyahu told her that her outlook was too narrow and off he went to the post office where he went daily asking if his book had arrived. It had been over a week since he had sent the ruble and still no book! In the meantime one had to live. "You can't live on air," said my mother. I don't understand what living on air had to do with it.

B

Hooray, the book has arrived! No sooner did we unpack it than my brother Elyahu sat down to read it. Oh my, what didn't he find in that book! So many ways to earn money! A recipe for making the best inks that could earn you a hundred rubles a month. A recipe for making good black shoe wax that could earn you a hundred rubles a month. A recipe for driving out mice, cockroaches, and other vermin that could earn you a hundred rubles a month. A recipe for making liqueurs, sweet brandy, lemonade, soda water, kvass, and other cheaper drinks that could earn you a hundred rubles a month and more.

My brother Eliyahu stopped at the last recipe. First, because you could expect to earn even *more* than a hundred rubles a month. That's what it explicitly said in the book. Second, you didn't have to mess with ink and shoe wax or bother with mice, cockroaches, and other vermin. The question was only which drink to make? For liqueurs and sweet brandy you needed Rothschild's fortune. For lemonade and soda water you needed some kind of gadget that cost who knows how much! So one thing remained: kvass! Kvass is a cheap drink to make and is in demand, especially in a hot summer like this one. From kvass, you must know, our Boruch the kvassmaker became a rich man. He makes bottled kvass. His kvass is known all over the world. It shoots out of the bottles like out of a cannon. What makes it shoot out? No one knows. That's Boruch's secret. They say he adds something that makes it shoot out. Some say raisins. Others say hops. Come summer and he has more than he can handle. That's how much money he earns!

The kvass my brother Elyahu concocts according to the recipe is not bottled kvass and doesn't shoot out. Our kvass is a different kind of drink. How it's made, I cannot tell you. My brother Elyahu doesn't let anyone near while he is making it. Only when he pours the water in are we allowed to look. But when he gets to the serious part, he locks himself in my mother's room. Not I, not my mother, not my sister-in-law Brukha—no one has the privilege of witnessing it. But if you promise me you will keep it a secret, I can tell you what's in that drink because I have seen what he prepares beforehand. Lemon peel, honey, something they call cream of tartar that is as sour as vinegar, and the rest—water. Water is the main ingredient. The more water—the more kvass. The ingredients are all mixed together thoroughly with an ordinary stick, that's what it says in the book, and the drink is ready. Then it's poured into a large jug and you throw in a hunk of ice. Ice is the most important thing! Without ice it isn't worth drinking. I once tasted a little kvass without ice and I thought it was the end of my life!

C

Once the first batch of kvass was ready it was decided I would be the one to peddle it on the street. Who else *but* me? For my brother Elyahu it wouldn't be proper. After all, he was a married man. My mother—certainly not. We would never allow our mother to go around with a jug through the marketplace crying, "Kvass! Kvass! People, kvass!" All agreed it had to be my job. I thought so too. I was thrilled to hear the news. My brother Elyahu began teaching me what to do. I had to hold the jug by a cord in one hand, the glass in the other hand and to get people to stop, I had to sing in a loud voice:

> People, a drink!
> A kopek a glass!
> Cold and sweet—
> Come quench your thirst!

I've already told you that I have a nice soprano voice, inherited from my father, of blessed memory. I sang out loud and clear, turning the words inside out:

> A kvass of sweet glass!
> A person a kopek!
> Quenching and cold—
> Come sweeten your drink!

I don't know whether it was my singing that they liked or that the drink was so good or whether the day was so hot. I sold out the first jug in half an hour and came home with almost three quarters of a ruble. My brother Elyahu gave the money to our mother and soon refilled my jug. He said that if I could run that circuit five or six times a day, we would have earned exactly one hundred rubles a month. Deduct, if you please, the four Sabbaths in the month and you will see how much the drink cost us and what kind of a percentage we could earn from it. The drink cost us very little, one can say, almost nothing. All the money went for ice, making it essential to sell the jugful of drink all the faster so the block of ice could be used for a second jug and for a third jug and so on. I had to move fast with the drink, really run with it, while tagging after me were crowds of Jewish and gentile boys. They mimicked my singing but I paid them no heed. My aim was to empty the jug as fast as possible so I could run home for another one. I don't know how much I made that first day. I only know that my brother, Elyahu, and my sister-in-law, Brukha, and my mother really praised me. For supper I was served a piece of pumpkin and watermelon and two prunes and of course, kvass. We all drank kvass like water. Before going to sleep on my place on the floor, my mother asked me whether my legs ached. My brother Elyahu laughed at her and said I was the kind of boy whom nothing ever bothers.

"Absolutely!" I said, "If you need proof, I'll go out right now with the jug in the middle of the night."

All three laugh at my cleverness. But in my mother's eyes I saw tears welling. Well, that's an old story—a mother has to cry! I wonder if all mothers cry as much as my mother.

D

We were, *kayn eyn horeh*, on a lucky streak. One day was hotter than the next. They were scorchers! People were passing out from the heat, children were dropping like flies. If not for that glass of kvass they would have burned up. I was returning with the jug, without exaggeration, ten times a day! My brother Elyahu would squint into the jug with one eye and say it was almost empty. Then he hit on an idea and poured in a few more pails of water. I had had this idea even before he did. I must confess to you that I did some mischief a few times.

Almost every day I would drop into our neighbor Pessi's, and let her taste a glass of our very own drink. I would also give her husband Moishe, the bookbinder, two glasses. He's a fine fellow. Each child also got a glass of kvass. Let them also know what a good drink we can make. The blind uncle also got a glassful. A pity on him, he was blind. All my friends got some kvass, free of charge, without paying a kopek! But in order to make up for the loss, I added water. For each glass of kvass I gave away free, I added two glasses of water. The same was done at home.

When my brother Elyahu would drink a glass of kvass he would immediately pour in water. He was right. It was a shame to waste a kopek. My sister-in-law Brukha would drink a few glasses of kvass (she was crazy about my brother Elyahu's kvass!) and she would replace them with water. If my mother felt like a glass of kvass (she had to be asked—she wouldn't take any herself!)—fill it up with water!

Anyhow, not a drop was wasted and we were taking in good money, *kayn eyn horeh*. My mother paid off bills and redeemed some necessary items from the pawn shop, like bedding. In the house there appeared a table and a bench. For Sabbath we had fish, meat, and white challah. They promised me that, God willing, for the holidays I would have a new pair of boots. I was sure no one in the world could be as happy as I was!

E

Be a prophet and know that a tragedy would befall us and that our drink would become unfit to drink, good only to be poured onto the slop pile. I was lucky not to have been dragged off to the police station. Listen to this story!

One day I wandered over to our neighbor Pessi's with my jug of kvass. Everyone started drinking kvass, I among them. I figured I was down twelve or thirteen glasses and went to the place for water. But instead of finding the water barrel, I apparently went to the tub where the laundry is washed and poured in fifteen or twenty glasses of soapy water into my jug and went merrily on my way down the street singing a new song that I myself had made up:

People, a drink!
Like nothing you've ever tasted!
Only a kopek,
Your money won't be wasted!!

I was stopped by a man who paid me a kopek and asked for a glass of kvass. He downed the glass and screwed up his face:

"Little boy! What kind of drink is this?"

I paid him no heed. Two more people were waiting to be served. One sipped half a glass, the other a third of a glass. They paid, spat out the drink and walked away. Another brought the glass to his lips. He tasted the drink and said it smelled like soap and tasted salty. Another looked at the glass and returned it to me, saying:

"What is this?"

"It's a drink, that's what it is," I said.

"A drink?" he exclaimed, "That's a stink, not a drink!"

Another person came over, tasted the drink and splashed it right in my face. In a minute I was surrounded by a whole circle of men, women, and children. All were yammering, gesticulating, fuming. A Russian policeman came by and seeing an angry crowd asked what was going on. They told him. He peered into my jug and asked for a sample. I poured him a glass of kvass. The Russian policeman drank it down and spat it out, becoming enraged.

"Where did you get this slop?" he demanded.

"It's from a book," I said to him, "my brother's business. My brother made it himself."

"Who is your brother?" he asked me.

"My brother Elyahu," I answered him.

"Who is this Elyahu?" he asked me.

"Speak not, foolish youth, concerning thy brother!" several Jews spoke in a mixture of Hebrew and Yiddish designed to baffle the policeman's understanding. The crowd became unruly, noisy, ready to riot. New people kept arriving on the scene. The Russian policeman held me by the hand and was about to haul me and my drink right over to the police station. The shouting became louder. "An orphan, a poor orphan!" I heard from all sides. My heart told me I was in a tight spot. I looked at the crowd surrounding me.

"Jews, have pity!" I exclaimed.

They tried to bribe the Russian policeman but he refused. One of the men, an old Jew with shifty eyes, cried out to me in a mixture of Hebrew and Yiddish:

"Mottl! Pull thy hand away from the Russian policeman and take to thy heels as fast as thou canst!"

I tore away and ran full speed home.

Half dead, I burst into my house.

"Where's the jug?" my brother Elyahu asked.

"At the police station!" I answered and ran into my mother's arms, in tears.

We Flood the
World with Ink

A

Oh, was I a fool! Because I had sold soapy, spoiled kvass, I thought surely they would behead me! But in the end nothing happened. My fears were groundless. "Didn't Yente sell tallow for goose-fat? And didn't Gedalye the butcher feed the whole town an entire year with *treyf* meat?" That's how our neighbor, Pessi, consoled my mother. My mother! She takes everything to heart. That's why I love my brother Elyahu. My brother Elyahu doesn't think worse of himself because we were burned by the kvass. So long as he has the book, he's happy. He bought a book for a ruble. The book is called, "For One Ruble—a Hundred!" He sits and learns it by heart. In the book are endless recipes for making money. He knows almost all the recipes. He knows how to make ink, how to make shoe wax, and how to get rid of mice, cockroaches, and other vermin. He decided to make ink.

Ink, he said, is a good product. Everyone has to write. He asked Yudel the writing teacher how much he spent on ink. He said: "A fortune!"

Yudel the writing teacher teaches writing to about sixty girls. Boys don't study with him. They're afraid of him. He spanks them or strikes them over their hands with a ruler. You can't hit girls. You certainly can't spank them. I'm sorry I wasn't born a girl. First, I wouldn't have to pray every day. I'm sick of it. Every day the same thing. And then, I wouldn't have to go to Hebrew school. I go to Hebrew school half a day. What I learn you can put on the head of a pin, but of slaps there are more than enough. You think from the rebbe? No, from his wife, the rebbitzin. What business is it of hers that I feed the cat? You should see her cat—God's pity on it! She's always hungry. She constantly mews quietly to herself, with a whine like that of a human being, forgive the comparison. It can tear your heart out! But they have not one drop of pity. What do they have against her? If she so much as goes over to sniff someone, they scream at her: "Scat!" And she scurries off in a shot. They don't let her get away with anything. Once she was lost for a few days. I thought she was dead for sure. But it turned out she had had kittens. . . . But I must return to my brother Elyahu's ink.

B

My brother Elyahu says that the world isn't what it used to be. Once, when you wanted to make ink, he says, you had to buy black walnuts, chop them up, cook them on the fire for who knows how long, and then pour in some copperwater; and in order to make the ink shiny you had to add sugar—a big fuss! Today, he says, it's easy as pie! You buy, he says, powder and a bottle of glycerine at the apothecary, mix them with water, boil it on the fire— presto! Ink. So says my brother Elyahu.

He went off to the apothecary and brought back a bag full of the special powders and a large bottle of glycerine. Then he locked himself up in my mother's room and did something. What—I don't know. It's a secret. With him everything is a secret. When he has to tell my mother, for example, to give him the pestle from the mortar, he calls her over to the side and whispers: "Mama! The pestle from the mortar." He mixed the powders and the glycerine in a very large pot (he bought a new pot). The pot full of the mixture was shoved into the oven and he whispered to my mother to lock the door. We couldn't imagine what was going on. My mother kept glancing at the oven every minute fearful it would explode. Then we rolled in the kvass jug. Carefully we removed the pot from the oven and carefully poured the mixture into the jug. Then we began to pour water in until the jug was filled a little more than half way. My brother Elyahu said: "Enough!" and consulted the book, "For a Ruble—a Hundred Rubles." He read and in a whisper asked for a pen and a white sheet of paper. "The ones we write petitions with," he whispered in my mother's ear. He dipped the pen into the jug and began to write something on the white sheet of paper with a swirl and a flourish. He showed the writing first to my mother, then to my sister-in-law Brukha. Both looked at it and said to him:

"It writes!"

They got back to work. After pouring in a few more pails of water, my brother Elyahu raised his hand and said:

"Enough!" Again he dipped the pen into the jug, again he wrote something on the white sheet of paper and again showed the writing first to my mother and then to my sister-in-law Brukha. Again they both looked at the paper and said:

"It writes!"

This they did several times until the jug was full to the brim. There was no room for any more water. Then my brother Elyahu raised his hand and said: "Enough!"—and the four of us sat down to eat.

C

After supper we busied ouselves pouring the ink into bottles. My brother Elyahu had collected bottles from all over. All kinds of bottles and flasks. Big and little. Beer bottles, wine bottles, kvass bottles, whisky bottles. And just plain bottles. He also bought up old corks to save money. He bought a new funnel and a tin quart measure with which to pour the ink from the jug into the bottles. Here he again whispered into my mother's ear to lock the door. Then the four of us got down to work.

The work was divided evenly. My sister-in-law Brukha rinsed out the bottles and handed them to my mother. My mother examined each bottle and gave them over to me. I had to place the funnel into each bottle, holding the funnel in one hand and the bottle with the other. And my brother Elyahu had only one job: pouring the ink from the jug into the quart measure and then through the funnel into the bottles. The work was very enjoyable and pleasant. The only problem was the ink. It stained your fingers, your hands, your nose, your whole face. Both of us, I and my brother Elyahu, looked black as devils. It was the first time I ever saw my mother laugh. And you can imagine my sister-in-law, Brukha—she almost split her sides laughing. My brother Elyahu hates when someone laughs at him and he became angry at my sister-in-law Brukha and demanded to know why she was laughing. That made her laugh even harder. He became even angrier and she laughed all the more. The laughter kept coming in uncontrollable spasms! My mother finally begged her to stop and she told us to go wash up. But my brother Elyahu didn't have the time. The last thing he had on his mind was washing. All he thought of was filling the bottles.

Finally all the bottles were filled. No more bottles! Where to get more bottles? He called my sister-in-law Brukha off to the side, gave her money, and whispered in her ear to buy some more bottles. She heard him out, looked him in the face and burst out laughing. He became angry and called my mother over to tell her the same secret. My mother went off to buy bottles and we continued pouring water into the jug. Not all at once, you understand, a little at a time. After each pailful of water, he raised his hand and said to himself: "Enough!" Then he dipped the pen into the jug and wrote on the white sheet of paper and said to himself:

"It writes!"

He did this several times till my mother came back with a new supply of bottles. We got back to our original task of pouring ink from the jug to the bottle, till we again ran out of bottles.

"How long can this go on?" said my sister-in-law Brukha.

"*Kayn eyn horeh*, why stop a good thing?" said my mother, and my brother Elyahu shot an angry look at Brukha, as if to say:

"You are my wife, but you're also a dunce, may God have pity on you!"

D

How much ink we made—that I cannot tell you. I'm afraid it was as much as a thousand bottles! But what good was it, there was no place to get rid of the ink. My brother Elyahu had looked everywhere. Selling the ink retail, bottle by bottle, one at a time, didn't make sense. That's what my brother Elyahu said to my neighbor's husband, Moishe the bookbinder. When Moishe came into our house, and when he saw all those bottles, he sprang back in fright. My brother Elyahu saw this and there followed a strange conversation between the two. I will relate it to you word for word:

ELYAHU: What scared you so?

BOOKBINDER: What's in those bottles?

ELYAHU: What could it be? Wine!

BOOKBINDER: Wine? That's ink!

ELYAHU: Why ask then?

BOOKBINDER: What are you going to do with so much ink?

ELYAHU: Drink it!

BOOKBINDER: No, stop joking. You're going to sell them retail?

ELYAHU: What am I, crazy? If I sell them, I'll sell them ten, twenty, fifty bottles at a time. That's called "wholesale." Do you know what "wholesale" means?

BOOKBINDER: I know what "wholesale" means. To whom are you going to sell it?

ELYAHU: To whom? To the rabbi!

And my brother Elyahu went off to the stores. When he came to this big wholesaler, the wholesaler wanted to examine a bottle. Another wholesaler wouldn't even take the bottle in his hand because it didn't have a label. "On the bottle," he said, "there has to be a nice label with a design." My brother Elyahu said to him: "I don't make designs, I make ink." The other one answered: "Suit yourself."

Then he hurried off to Yudel the writing teacher who said something very nasty to him. He had already bought a summer's supply of ink. My brother Elyahu asked him: "How many bottles of ink did you buy?" Yudel the writing teacher said: "Bottles? I bought one bottle of ink that will last and last and when I run out I'll buy another bottle." How do you like that business! Only a scribbler can think like that! First he said he spent a fortune on ink and now he buys a bottle of ink that will last forever. My poor brother Elyahu was beside himself. He didn't know what he would do with so much ink. Originally he had said he wouldn't sell any ink retail, only wholesale. Now he thought better of it. He would begin, he said, to sell it retail. I would like to know what "retail" means.

This is what "retail" means. Just listen.

E

My brother Elyahu brought back to the house a large sheet of paper. He sat down and printed on it in large block letters:

INK SOLD *WHOLESALE* HERE
RETAIL—GOOD AND CHEAP

The two words, "wholesale" and "cheap" were written so large they took up almost the whole sheet. When the lettering had dried, he attached the paper on the outside of our door. I saw through the window how many passersby stopped to look. My brother Elyahu also looked out the window and cracked his knuckles. That was a sign that he was upset. He said to me:

"Do you know what? Just go and stand by the door and listen to what they're saying."

I didn't need to be asked too long. I stood by the door and listened to what they were saying. I stood there half an hour and came back into the house. My brother Elyahu came over and asked me quietly:

"Well?"

"Well what?"

"What did they say?"

"Who?"

"The people who passed by."

"They said it was nicely printed."

"And nothing more?"

"Nothing more."

My brother Elyahu sighed. Why was he sighing? My mother had the same question.

"Why are you sighing, silly? Wait a little. Do you expect in one day to sell out all the merchandise?"

"At least one sale!" said my brother Elyahu, his voice choking.

"You're a great fool, I tell you. Just wait, my child, you will, God willing, make a sale."

That is what my mother said and set the table. We washed and sat down to eat. The four of us squeezed in all together in one tight space. Because of all the bottles it was terribly crowded in the house. We had just made the blessing over the bread when a strange young man arrived. He was already betrothed to be married. I knew him. His name was Koppel. His father is a ladies' tailor.

"Do you sell single bottles of ink here?"

"Yes, what do you want?"

"I want some ink."

"How much ink do you need?"

"Give me a kopek's worth of ink."

My brother Elyahu was really beside himself. If he hadn't been ashamed in front of my mother, he would first have slapped this betrothed Koppel a few times and then thrown him out of the house. He controlled himself and poured out a kopek's worth of ink. Less than a quarter of an hour later, a young girl came in. I didn't know the young girl. She picked her nose and spoke to my mother:

"Do you make ink here?"

"Yes, what do you want?"

"My sister wants to know if you can lend her a little ink. She has to write a letter to America to her future husband."

"Who is your sister?"

"Basya the seamstress."

"Ah? Look how she's grown up! *Kayn eyn horeh*! I didn't recognize you. Do you have an inkwell?"

"Where would we get an inkwell? My sister wants to know if you have a pen and as soon as she finishes writing the letter to America, she'll give you back the ink and the pen."

My brother Elyahu had vanished from the table. He was in my mother's room. He was pacing quietly, head down, biting his nails.

F

"Why did you make so much ink? It looks like you wanted to supply the whole world with ink in case there was a shortage of ink."

That's what our neighbor's husband, Moishe the bookbinder, said. What a strange man that bookbinder! He has the habit of rubbing salt in your wounds. Usually he's a tolerable fellow, just a bit of a pest. He likes to get under your skin.

But my brother Elyahu really got back at him! He told him he would do better to pay attention to his own affairs and be careful not to mix up the books he was binding, not to bind together a Haggadah with the High Holiday penitential prayers. Moishe the bookbinder knew very well what that dig was about! He had once been engaged by a coachman to do a job. The coachman had given him a Haggadah to bind but a misfortune occurred: by mistake, the bookbinder bound in together with the Haggadah a section of the penitential prayers. The coachman would most likely never have found the mistake but his neighbors overheard the wagon driver sing out in a sorrowful tone from the penitential *Slikhot* prayers of the High Holidays instead of the welcoming prayer for Elijah at the Passover seder and everyone started to laugh. The following morning the coachman went to our neighbor the bookbinder and wanted to tear him limb from limb.

"Villain, what did you do to me? Why did you stick in an unkosher prayer in my Passover Haggadah? Right now I'm going to rip the guts out of your belly!"

Yes, we had quite a jolly Passover at the time.

But don't be upset that I brought in another story. I'll soon come back to our lucrative business ventures.

After the Flood
(of Ink)

A

M y brother Elyahu was beside himself with worry. What to do with all that unsold ink?

"Still with the ink?" my mother said to him.

"I'm not talking about ink!" my brother Elyahu answered. "To the devil with the ink! I'm talking about the bottles! There's a fortune in those bottles! We have to make sure to empty the bottles and get our money out of them!"

Everything has to be turned into money! My brother Elyahu decided we had to get rid of all that ink no matter how. But that was the problem—where to pour it all? It could be embarrassing. "There's nothing for it," said my brother Elyahu, "We'll have to wait till night. At night it's dark, no one will see."

Night fell at last. Out of spite, the moon was shining like a lantern. "When you need it, it hides. But look at it now. As if we'd sent for it!" said my brother Elyahu as we carried out bottle after bottle and—splash! poured the ink on the street. A huge puddle grew in one place where we were pouring the ink. "We shouldn't pour it all in one place," said my brother Elyahu and I obeyed him. I found a fresh place to pour each bottle. Splash! against a neighbor's wall! Splash! against another neighbor's fence! Splash! all over two goats chewing their cud in the moonlight!

"That's enough for tonight!" my brother Elyahu said and we went to bed. It was quiet and dark. We could hear the crickets. The cat was purring under the stove. That sleepyhead. Day and night all she desires is to warm herself and doze. I heard footsteps on the other side of the door. Could it be some bad person? It was my mother who wasn't sleeping. It seemed she never slept. I could always hear her cracking her knuckles, sighing and groaning and talking to herself. That was her habit. Every night she talked her troubles out. To whom was she talking? To God. Every other minute she would let out an, "Oy, God! God!"

B

I was lying on my bedding on the floor and heard a hubbub of familiar voices in my sleep. Slowly I opened my eyes—it was already broad daylight. The bright light of the sun had burst through the window. It was calling me outdoors. I tried to remember what had happened the night before—aha! Ink! I jumped up and quickly dressed. My mother was teary-eyed (when wasn't she teary-eyed?). My sister-in-law Brukha was furious (when wasn't she furious?). And my brother Elyahu was standing in the middle of the room, hanging his head, trying to look innocent as a lamb. What was happening? A great deal! Once our neighbors had awakened in the morning all hell had broken loose. You would think they were being slaughtered! One neighbor's wall had been splashed with ink. Another neighbor's fence, a new fence, had ink poured all over it. A third neighbor had two white goats and now they were black, unrecognizable. This all might have been tolerated had it not been for the *shokhet's*, the ritual slaughterer's, stockings. A new pair of white stockings that his wife had hung to dry on our neighbor's fence were ruined. Someone had suggested she hang her stockings on a neighbor's fence. To keep the peace my mother promised to buy her a new pair of stockings. But what about the wall? And the fence? It was decided that my mother and my sister-in-law Brukha would very kindly take two brushes and whitewash the stains.

"You're lucky you happen to live next door to decent neighbors. If you had splashed ink on Menasha the healer's garden, you would know what kind of God we have!" said our neighbor, Pessi, to my mother.

"What are you talking about? Do you mean you need luck to have bad luck?" my mother answered her and looked at me meaningfully.

What do you think she meant?

C

"Now I'll be smarter," my brother Elyahu said to me, "Just wait till nightfall and we'll take the bottles down to the river."

Right, as I am a Jew! What could be smarter than that? All the filth is poured into the river anyway! That's where they wash laundry, water horses, and that's where the pigs wallow. I know that river well. I used to catch fish in it. You can easily see why I was looking forward to going to the river. As soon as night fell, we loaded baskets full of bottles and carried them to the river. We poured out the ink, carried the empty bottles back home and took another load of full bottles. We worked all night. I hadn't had such a happy, enjoyable night in a long time. Just picture it: the town was asleep, the sky was full of stars, the moon was reflected in the river. It was peaceful and quiet. A river is like a living thing. After Passover, when the ice melts, it performs wonders! It swells, spreads itself out and pours over its banks. And then it grows smaller, narrower, and shallower. By the end of summer, the river quiets down and takes a nap. Occasionally some creature in the bottom mud goes: "Bul-bul-bul." A pair of frogs reply from the other side: "Krua-krua!" It's an embarrassment, not a river! It's easy for me to cross it by foot from one side to the other without even taking off my trousers!

Because of our ink the river became a little wider. Imagine, we poured in about a thousand bottles of ink, toiling like oxen! We slept afterwards like the dead. My mother woke us with a lament:

"Woe unto me and my miserable life! What have you done to the river?"

It appeared we had brought a catastrophe down on the whole town. The washerwomen didn't have anywhere to wash their laundry. The coachmen didn't have anywhere to water their horses. The water-carriers were uniting to come after us. That was the good news our mother brought. But we weren't going to wait. We were not anxious to learn what the water-carriers had in store for us. I and my brother Elyahu decided we had better take off as fast as our legs would carry us and pay a visit to his friend, Pinni.

"Let them look for us there if they want us!" my brother Elyahu said to me as he took my hand and we sped down the hill to his friend, Pinni. When we meet again, I'll tell you all about my brother Elyahu's friend, Pinni. It's worth your while to get to know him: he also has lots of good ideas.

The Neighborhood Sneezes

A

Guess what we're breaking our heads over these days? Mice! All week my brother Elyahu has been studying his little book on how to make money with little investment, "From One Ruble —A Hundred Rubles." He's already learned, he says, how to drive out mice, cockroaches, and other vermin. Rats too. Just let him put a powder in the right place, and not one mouse will be left! They'll run away. Or die. No more mice! How he makes it, I don't know. It's a secret. Only he and the book know the secret, no one else. He keeps the book in his bosom pocket, the powder in a paper. The powder is reddish and ground fine like snuff. It's called "shemeritzi."

"What is shemeritzi?"
"Turkish pepper."
"What is Turkish pepper?"

"If you don't stop these 'what-is's,' you'll find your head going through the door!"

That's what my brother Elyahu says to me. He hates to be asked questions just when he's in the middle of work. I look on and keep my mouth shut. I see that along with the red powder he has another powder. It also works on mice. But you have to be very careful with it!

"Deadly poison!" my brother Elyahu says maybe a hundred times to my mother, Brukha, and me. Especially to me, lest God forbid, I touch it—it's poison!

We make our first test on our neighbor Pessi's mice. An endless horde of mice live there. Her husband is a bookbinder. Moishe. is his name. His house is always full of prayer books. Mice love prayer books. And not so much the prayer books as the glue with which the books are held together. But as long as they're eating the glue they might as well eat the prayer books too. They do enormous damage. Once they gnawed through one of his holiday prayer books, brand new, right where "THE KING" was printed in large letters. They really loved those words, "THE KING!" They only left the crown of the letter *lamed*.

"Let me at them for one night!" my brother Elyahu pleads with the bookbinder. The bookbinder won't have it. He says:

"I'm afraid you'll ruin my prayer books."

"How will I ruin your prayer books?" my brother Elyahu asks him.

"I don't know how but I'm still afraid. These prayer books belong to other people."

Argue with a bookbinder! But we finally did manage to have him agree for us to spend just one night there.

B

That first night didn't work out too well for us. We didn't catch one mouse! But my brother Elyahu says it was a good sign. The mice, he says, sniffed out our powder and ran off. The bookbinder shook his head and smirked. Apparently he didn't believe this. Still and all word got around town that we could drive away mice. It was our neighbor, Pessi, who got the word around. She went off one morning to the market and spread the word all over town that "no one drives mice away like they drive mice away." She made our reputation. Before the mice it was the kvass she trumpeted all over town and after that she trumpeted far and wide that we made the best ink in the world. But what did her trumpeting help when no one needed ink? But mice are not the same as ink. Mice are everywhere, in every house. Every homeowner has a cat. But what good is one cat against so many mice? And especially rats! Rats are as afraid of a cat as Haman is of a Purim noisemaker. In fact, a cat itself is afraid of a rat. That's what Berreh the shoemaker says. He tells terrifying tales about rats. People say he is a big exaggerater, but even if what he says is only half true, it's still bad. He says that rats ate up a pair of new boots. He swears up and down and you must believe him. He says that he himself saw two big rats come out of their nests and before his very eyes eat up a pair of boots. It was at night. He was afraid of coming too close to them—two huge rats, as big as calves. He chased them from a distance, whistled at them, stamped his feet, screamed: "Kish-kish-kish-kish!" Nothing helped. He threw the heel of a boot at them, but they just glanced at him and went about their business.

Then he threw the cat at them. They attacked the cat and ate her up too. Nobody wanted to believe him but if a person swears, you have to believe him.

"Give me just one night," my brother Elyahu said to him, "and I'll drive out all the rats!"

"Ah, with the greatest pleasure!" said Berreh the shoemaker, "I'll thank you for it!"

C

We sat through one whole night at Berreh the shoemaker's, who himself sat with us. Ah, what wondrous tales he told us! He was a veteran of the Turkish War stationed in a place called Plevne. "They were shooting with cannons. Do you know how big a cannon is? You can be sure that one cannonball is bigger than this whole house and they shoot a thousand such cannonballs in one minute. What do you think of that? When that cannonball flies through the air, it screams so loud you can go deaf." Once he was standing guard, as Berreh the shoemaker told it, when suddenly he heard a bang and something was carrying him up in the air, high up, way above the clouds, and there the cannonball exploded into a thousand pieces. It was just lucky, he said, that he fell on a soft place. Otherwise he would have broken his head. My brother Elyahu listened to this tale and his eyebrows smiled. That is to say, he himself wasn't laughing, but his eyebrows were laughing. A strange laughter. Berreh the shoemaker didn't notice this. He didn't stop telling his fantastic tales. One story was more scary than the next. And that's how we spent our time until daybreak. And rats? Not a one.

"You're a magician!" said Berreh the shoemaker to my brother Elyahu. And he went out into the town and told everyone about this miracle, how with a magical incantation we drove away all the rats in one night. He swore that he himself saw how after my brother Elyahu muttered something the rats came out of their nests and ran down the hill to the river, swam across the river and kept running, he did not know where to.

D

"Are you the people who drive away mice?" asked all the people who come to hire us to drive away the mice with our magical incantation.

But my brother Elyahu is an honest person. He hates lies. He says he doesn't drive away mice with a magical incantation but with a powder. He has a kind of powder that once the mice smell it, they run away.

"Let it be a powder, let it be whatever you want, so long as you drive away the mice! How much will it cost?"

My brother Elyahu hates to bargain. He says that for the powder it will cost so much and for the labor so much and so much. As you might expect he keeps on raising the price. Actually, it isn't he who raises the price, but my sister-in-law. "Make up your mind," she says, "If you're going to eat pig, let the fat run down your beard. If you're going to be a mouse catcher, at least make some money out of it."

"Nu, and where is fairness? Where is God?" my mother interjects. And my sister-in-law Brukha snaps at her:

"Fairness? *There* is fairness! (She indicates the stove.) God? *Here* is God! (She slaps her pocket.)"

"Brukha! What did you say? God be with you!!!" my mother cries out, wringing her hands.

"Why are you wasting your time talking to a fool?!" says my brother Elyahu to my mother, pacing around the room, twisting his beard. He has quite a full beard. It grows like crazy. He twists it and it grows in a weird way. Of all places, it grows thickest on his throat. His face is smooth but his throat is hairy. Have you ever seen such a beard?

Any other time, my sister-in-law Brukha would have ruined his day at the very least, for calling her a fool, but this time she ignored it because he was earning money. Whenever my brother Elyahu is earning money, he becomes a bigshot in her eyes. I am also more valued in her eyes because I help my brother earn money. Usually she calls me "*shlepper*," or "*shlimazel*," or "poor excuse of a kid." Now she is more endearing—she calls me "Mottele":

"Mottele! Hand me my shoes."

"Mottele! Draw some water for me."

"Mottele! Take out the garbage."

If you earn money, they talk to you different.

E

The trouble with my brother Elyahu is that he overdoes things. When he made kvass—it was a barrelfull. Ink—a thousand bottles. A powder for mice—a full sack. Our neighbor's husband, the bookbinder, told him, "Why do you need so much powder?" I don't think my brother Elyahu appreciated this. Had they at least locked the sack up in a closet . . . but no, they all went off and left me alone with it. Was it my fault that I rode the sack as if it were a horse?

Be a prophet and know the sack would burst and all this yellow stuff would come pouring out! It was the powder that my brother Elyahu used to drive the mice away. It had such a sharp smell you could faint from it! I bent down and tried to sweep up what had spilled but was seized by a fit of sneezing. Had I inhaled a whole box of snuff, I wouldn't have sneezed as hard. I sneezed and sneezed till I finally ran outside hoping to stop sneezing. Guess what happened? Along came my mother who saw me sneezing. She asked me: "What's the matter?" All I could do was answer her with sneezes and more sneezes! And again sneezes!

"God help me, where did you catch such a cold?" said my mother, wringing her hands. I couldn't stop sneezing and pointed toward the house. She went in and soon ran back out sneezing even worse than I. Along came my brother Elyahu and saw us both sneezing. He asked: "What's the matter?" My mother pointed toward the house. He went in and came bounding out shouting:

"Who did th- katchoo! Katchoo! Katchoo!"

It's been a long time since I had seen my brother Elyahu so angry. He came at me with both hands. It was just lucky he was sneezing or else I would really have gotten it. Along came my sister-in-law Brukha and found all three of us holding our sides sneezing.

"What's going on here? Why this sneezing all of a sudden?"

What could we tell her? Could we so much as utter a word? We pointed toward the house. She went in and ran right out again, red as fire, and assailed my brother Elyahu:

"What did I tell—katchoo! Katchoo! Katchoo!"

Along came our neighbor, Fat Pessi. She spoke to us but none of us could answer her with so much as a word.

We pointed toward the house. She too went in and came running out again:

"What have you—katchoo! Katchoo! Katchoo!"

Our neighbor waved her hands in the air. Along came her husband the bookbinder, looked at us and laughed:

"What is all this sneezing about?"

"Just go in there—katchoo! Katchoo! Katchoo!" we said and pointed toward the house. The bookbinder went into our house and ran out laughing:

"I know what it is! I smelled it! That's shemer—katchoo! Katchoo!"

He grabbed his sides and started sneezing. With each sneeze he lifted himself up on his tiptoes. Within half an hour all our neighbors and their neighbors and their uncles and aunts and third cousins and their friends—the whole neighborhood, from one end to the next, was in a sneezing fit!

Why was my brother Elyahu so frightened? Apparently he was afraid they would let out their anger for the sneezing at him. He took me by the hand and, still sneezing, we ran down the hill to his friend Pinni. It took a good hour and a half before we could even speak like human beings. My brother Elyahu told his friend Pinni the whole story. His friend Pinni listened thoughtfully, like a doctor listening to a patient. When my brother Elyahu finished, his friend Pinni said to him:

"Give me that book."

My brother Elyahu took the book out of his bosom pocket and handed it to his friend Pinni. His friend Pinni read the title, "From One Ruble — a Hundred Rubles! Remedies Made From Ordinary Ingredients. With Your Own Hands, Make a Hundred Rubles a Month and More." He took the book and tossed it into the stove, right on the fire. My brother Elyahu lunged with both hands to the fire. His friend Pinni held him back:

"Slow down, not so fast!"

After a few minutes my brother Elyahu's book, about making a hundred rubles a month and more, was a pile of ashes. One unburned page remained on which you could barely make out the word: sh-e-m-e-r-i-t-z-i."

David, King of Israel

A SHORT INTRODUCTION

Old images from the past, rise from your graves! In the eyes of our youth you have long been dead. A great shame! Time does not stand still. Images change. One generation shoulders the other aside. Our children will know nothing about you. As with myself you will sink deep into your graves, perhaps be lost forever, as if you had never existed. Rise up, rise up, and let me lead you at least one more time before the eyes of the young. Let our children gaze on you. Show this generation that there once was among us those like yourselves, that you are not figments of the imagination, that you once lived on this earth and that you are still intimately related to them, these your own great-grandchildren.

A

Tightly curled beard and sidelocks white as fallen snow, an old-fashioned three-cornered hat called a Napoleon on his head, a tall, stout staff in his hand with a bone handle, a sack on his shoulders, bent low to the ground, every Friday and every holiday eve he goes from house to house collecting Sabbath challahs for needy Jewish prisoners in jail.

That's old Dodi, or "David, king of Israel," who must be a hundred years old. Everyone knows him and knows what he wants by now: he wants Sabbath challahs for his needy prisoners in jail. No one haggles with him. Whoever has and wants to—gives; whoever doesn't have and doesn't want to—doesn't give. Old Dodi won't be offended. For if everyone had enough to give and everyone wanted to give, who would there be to receive? And if there were no one to give and no one to receive, where would we learn about mercy and charity and good deeds? Why would we need the World Beyond and Paradise? And if there were no World Beyond or Paradise, what would we do with all the pious people in the Other World?

That was how old Dodi used to reason. He believed that whatever path the Lord set him on was a good one: there had to be those who gave and those who received, those who had and those who didn't have, those who sat in prison and those who worried about them and collected challah for them every Friday and holiday eve.

B

Who was this old Dodi, or David, king of Israel, and what was he before he was an old Jew of nearly a hundred years and before he undertook to gather Sabbath challahs for needy prisoners in jail? No one knew.

What did old Dodi live on? Where did he live? How old was he really? Where were his children and grandchildren? No one knew. It was a mystery. There was simply no one who could remember and if you asked him yourself he wouldn't answer. Don't even try it, you'd make it worse because if you allowed yourself to get into a conversation with him, he'd ask you to donate something for his needy Jewish prisoners in jail and no matter what you talked to him about, you'd end up talking about his prisoners!

"Reb Dodi! Where did you sleep last night?"

"Praised be God, it wasn't in jail. Perhaps you have an old coat for my prisoners?"

"Reb Dodi! What happened to your children and all your grandchildren?"

"Praised be God, they wandered off, this one here, that one there, dispersed beyond the seven seas. Some are dead, some still live. Who knows how they live, good or bad, so long as they are not in prison, God forbid. Forgive me for asking, but do you think you might have some old underclothes for my prisoners?"

"Reb Dodi! How old are you, may you live to a hundred and twenty?"

"Praised be God, I'm not a young man. May God grant you no fewer years but more good fortune but most of all may you not know about prison as long as you live. Do you think you might have in your house a pair of old worn-out boots for my prisoners?"

That was old Dodi, or David, king of Israel.

C

So why did they call him David, king of Israel?

Because once a year he was a king, a king for the Jewish children and that once a year was the day of Simkhas Torah.

Come Simkhas Torah, you wouldn't recognize old Dodi. His back erect, his beard and sidelocks combed, his Napoleon three-cornered hat freshened up, his broad white collar smoothed out. Without his staff, without his sack—it wasn't the same Dodi. His face shone, his eyes glowed. In honor of the holiday he had drunk a little whisky and so old Dodi was a different man with a different soul—a lively, happy soul.

Gathering together the youngsters, boys from all the schools, and placing them in circles around himself, old Dodi would stand in the middle, his hands raised to the sky and sing in a loud voice:

"Holy flock of sheep!"

The youngsters answered: "Meh-eh-eh!"

"Who leads you?"

"Our King David, meh-eh-eh!"

"What do they call him?"

"David, King of Israel!"

"Sing out, Jewish children, in a nice melody: David! King! Israel! Lives! And prevails!"

"David! King! Israel! Lives! And prevails! Meh-eh-eh!!!"

Once more:

"Holy flock of sheep!"

"Meh-eh-eh!"

"Who leads you?"

"Our King David, meh-eh-eh!"

"What is he called?"

"David, King of Israel, meh-eh-eh!"

"Sing out, Jewish children, in a nice melody: David! King! Israel! Lives! And prevails!"

"David! King! Israel! Lives! And prevails! Meh-eh-eh!!!"

More children joined the others, the cavalcade grew, the crowd that followed grew larger, the voices grew louder as they circled the entire village. At every *sukkah*, David, king of Israel made a stop. The men brought him whisky. Housewives gave him pieces of honeycake from their aprons. He downed the whisky and distributed the honeycake among the youngsters, singing as he did so:

"Holy flock of sheep!"

"Meh-eh-eh!"

"What am I holding here?"

"Honeycake, meh-eh-eh!"

"Which blessing do you make over it?"

"The blessing over food, meh-eh-eh!"

"Tell me now, who leads you?"

"Our King David, meh-eh-eh!"

"What is he called?"

"David, king of Israel, meh-eh-eh!"

"Sing out, Jewish children, in a nice melody: David! King! Israel! Lives! And prevails!"

"David! King! Israel! Lives! And prevails! Meh-eh-eh!!!"

D

At first glance you would think that it couldn't hurt any-one and no one should care that an old man of nearly a hun-dred drinks a little whisky once a year at Simkhas Torah, becomes a bit tipsy, and pretends to be a king with young-sters running after him bleating like little lambs: Meh-eh-eh. But listen to this story:

At *Slikhos* time, during the High Holidays, they sent to our village this new police chief to lord it over us (the old one had died). As you might expect, a new police chief has to demonstrate his own authority. First of all, they said of him that he was a stickler for the rules, too much so. As soon as he spotted a Jew, he immediately demanded: "Iden-tity papers! What's your name? Where are you from?" And second of all, he was unbribable, but absolutely: not a penny, not a kopek! He was absolutely incorruptible. Natu-rally the word got around town: Bad news! A villain! A Haman!

And so it was. Early the next morning he was seen patrolling the streets, marching through the market, in-specting all the shops and stores, sniffing around the syna-gogue courtyard, looking to dig up some infraction. But what could he have found amiss between semesters when the teachers had long ago emptied the classrooms and he could not find anyone who dealt in false banknotes? And so we paid him no heed.

But God sent him some business: Sukkos! He wasn't pleased, you understand, with the way Jews were erecting their *sukkahs*. It was, he said, a fire hazard. What do you think of that complaint? For thousands of years Jews have been sitting in their sukkahs and have never been afraid of anything and now suddenly they have to worry about fires!

"Tell us what you want, sir."

"I want you to stop building your sukkahs this way, but to build thus and so."

Well, they paid as much attention to him as Haman pays attention to the Purim noisemakers, and they set to work erecting their sukkahs the way they always had, not "thus and so." The police chief sniffed this out and had all the sukkahs demolished.

They sent a deputation to him: "Sir Police Chief! We can't celebrate Sukkos without a *sukkah*!" And he said: "No *sukkahs*!" You could call him names if you liked, but if you pressed him, he would demand your identity papers!

In short, you can imagine that things were pretty bad for us, people were desperate, several families huddled together in one sukkah and quaked with fear lest they be discovered. But the One Above had mercy, the seven days of Sukkos passed without incident, our fears were in vain. Then came the eighth day of the holiday, Simkhas Torah.

E

And on the eighth day of the holiday Simkhas Torah, old Dodi went out with his gang of youngsters into the synagogue courtyard and sang out in a loud voice, as was his habit:

"Holy flock of sheep!"
And the flock of sheep answered:
"Meh-eh-eh!"

Suddenly appearing out of nowhere the police chief stared at this fine scene in great amazement. Very likely he was seeing this comedy for the first time. Old Dodi was scarcely frightened of this new police chief and went on with his usual antics:

"Tell me, Jewish children, who leads you?"

"Our King David, meh-eh-eh!"

"What do they call him?"

"David, king of Israel, meh-eh-eh!"

"Sing out now, Jewish children, in a fine melody: David! King! Israel! Lives! And prevails!"

"David! King! Israel! Lives! And prevails!"

The police chief asked for an explanation. Who was this old man and what were the children singing?

Reb Shepsl the teacher, who had a fine hand for writing Russian, came forward. He tucked his earlocks behind his ears and offered himself as an interpreter:

"He is David the Jewish czar and the children are his serfs."

The police chief clutched his sides and began to laugh. How hard do you think he laughed? He almost burst his sides laughing. And David, king of Israel did not stop singing, "Holy flock of sheep!" And the holy flock of sheep did not stop bleating, "Meh-eh-eh!" until the police chief finally became tired of the goings on, chased the youngsters away and took old David, king of Israel to task: "Your identity papers! Where are you from?" It turned out that the old king of Israel himself didn't know where he was from. And so the police chief sent him packing straight to prison, to join his needy prisoners.

There he would sober up the old drunk, he said.

The following year at Sukkos Jews sat in their *sukkahs* as they did every year. At Simkhas Torah Jews reveled as they did every year. But one thing was missing: nowhere could they find the old David, king of Israel. They didn't hear him singing: "Holy flock of sheep," or the "Holy flock of sheep," responding:

"Meh-eh-eh!!!"

Two Purim
Pastry Gifts

A

t had been a long time since Kasrilevka had had
such a lovely warm spring. Earlier in the day the
ice had begun to melt and the snow had turned
into waist-high mud. The sun was shining. A
lazy breeze was blowing. A foolish calf, believing it smelled
spring in the air, began bleating, raised its tail, lowered its
chin and let out half a "Meh-!" Rivulets of water snaked
downhill, taking with them, wherever they could, a wood
chip, a straw, or a piece of paper. Luckily no one in town
had yet made matzos, otherwise one could surely think it
was Passover time instead of Purim.

In the very center of town, right where the mud was
deepest, two girls met, both named Nekhama. One was
dark-skinned, strong, with thick brows and a short nose,
the other one fair-skinned, sickly, with red hair and a pointy
nose. One was barefoot, with heavy thighs; the other was

wearing shoes that barely held together, wide open at the toes like a mouth begging to be fed. What shoes! As she walked, the shoes squished, the soles flapped on the ground and when the shoes were removed, they weighed a ton. Of such shoes it can be said that going barefoot is better. Both Nekhamas were carrying trays of Purim pastry gifts covered with white napkins, holding them high in the air with both hands. Spotting one another, both girls stopped.

"Ah! Nekhama?"

"Ah! Nekhama?"

"Where are you going, Nekhama?"

"Where am I going? I'm delivering Purim pastry gifts."

"To whom are you delivering Purim pastry gifts?"

"Actually to you. And where are you going, Nekhama?"

"Where am I going? You can see I'm delivering Purim pastry gifts."

"To whom are you delivering Purim pastry gifts?"

"Actually to you."

"What a funny coincidence!"

"Really funny!"

"Well then, let's take a look at your pastry gifts, Nekhama."

"Let's take a look at yours, Nekhama."

And both Nekhamas looked for a place to sit down. Spotting a pile of logs near an inn, they slogged through the clay mud and seated themselves on it, laid the baked goods on their knees, lifted off the napkins and took turns examining the contents of the pastry trays.

First the redheaded Nekhama displayed her goods. She worked for Zelda, Reb Yossi's wife, earning five and a half rubles for a winter's work, including clothing and shoes. You can imagine what clothing and shoes! Well, the dress was a dress, though full of patches, yet still you could call it a dress; but the shoes were men's shoes, having belonged to Zelda's son, Menasha, who had enormous feet and had worn down the outside of the heels. Fine shoes!

Redheaded Nekhama's pastry tray consisted of a fine, large hamantosh filled with poppyseeds, two cushion cakes, one open-faced and filled with honey farfel, the other round and decorated on both sides, a sugar bar centered with a raisin, a large square torte, a nice piece of nut bread, two small angel cakes, and a large piece of carob cake that had turned out better than anything Zelda had ever made. Whether the flour was finer, whether the honey was purer, whether the cake simply came out better, or whether it had been beaten better—who knows. It was as fluffy as a thick feather cushion!

After surveying the redheaded Nekhama's pastry tray, the dark-haired Nekhama uncovered and displayed her tray of baked goods. She worked for Zlate, Reb Isaac's wife, earned six rubles for the winter but provided her own clothing and thus went barefoot, for which Zlate scolded her mercilessly:

"How can a girl go around barefoot all winter? Do you want to catch pneumonia, for God's sake?"

But Nekhama paid as much attention to her as Haman does to Purim noisemakers. She preferred to save her money for Passover. Passover, God willing, she would have a pair of high-heeled boots made with buttons and a new dress with trimming. Koppel the shoemaker, who was courting her, would go wild!

On the pastry tray held by the dark-haired Nekhama were displayed a fine piece of strudel, three large honey bars, a nice sized honey teigl, two cushion cakes decorated with a fish and filled with small, sweet farfel, two large poppyseed cookies, black and shiny and stuffed with nutmeats and glazed with honey. In addition, there lay on the tray, smiling at them, a golden, delicious-smelling orange whose delightful aroma permeated the air.

B

"Do you know what I think, Nekhama? Your Purim pastry tray is much nicer than mine," the redheaded Nekhama complimented the dark-haired Nekhama.

"Eh! Your platter isn't so bad!" the dark-haired Nakhama returned the compliment and poked the hamantash with her finger.

"Now *that's* a hamantash!" the dark-haired Nakhama said, her mouth watering, "That's what you call a *real* hamantash! To tell the truth, I resent it that my mistress will be getting such a delicious hamantash, may a boil that size grow on her face, God in heaven! You know, Nekhama, I haven't had a bite to eat today. I would love to have just a tiny taste of that hamantash."

"And do you think *I've* eaten anything today? May *they* eat as much the rest of their lives!" said the redheaded Nekhama, looking about her. "Go ahead, listen to me, Nekhama, break the hamantash in half and we'll both feel better. Who says there has to be a hamantash on a Purim pastry tray? Your Purim pastry tray doesn't have one."

"You are absolutely right!" said the dark-haired Nekhama, breaking the hamantash in two and sharing it with the redheaded Nekhama.

"Let me tell you, it's scrumptuous, truly! Too bad there aren't any more. In return for your hamantash, Nekhama'nyu, you have coming to you a piece of honeycake from my Purim tray. For the amount of money we're making today, they can have one less piece of honeycake and one more boil. Can you imagine how much I've made from early in the morning till now? Guess! Barely one gulden and two groshens. And wouldn't you know there were holes in the groshens. How much did you make, Nekhama, dearie?"

"I didn't even make that much, may a plague descend on them!" said the redheaded Nekhama, biting off and swallowing down big chunks of honeycake like a goose. "I hope I make a gulden for the whole day!"

"Those highfalutin' ladies can go to the devil!" said the dark-haired Nekhama, licking the honeycake crumbs from her fingers. "I came to Khiena the notions seller's door with a Purim pastry gift, she took it from me, scratched around in her pocket and told me to 'come back later,' may a violent death come back later to her!"

"Exactly what happened to me with Kayli, Reb Aaron's wife," said redheaded Nakhama. "I came to her door with the pastry gift and she handed me a sugar cookie to eat on my way, may God hand her a new soul and— "

"And toss the old soul to the dogs!" the dark-haired Nekhama completed her sentence and took one of Zlate's two sugar bars and broke it in half. "Here, eat, my soul. May worms eat them! I could care less if your mistress has one less sugar bar!"

"Oh, my God!" the redheaded Nekhama sprang up with a start and began to wring her hands, "Just look, my sweet, what's become of my Purim pastry tray!"

"Who'll tell them, silly girl?" the dark-skinned Nekhama soothed her, "Don't worry, they're up to their ears in pastry trays all day long and will never notice."

And both Nekhamas covered their pastry trays with their white napkins and made their way over the mud, one this way, the other that way, as if nothing had happened.

C

Zelda Reb Yossi's wife was a round-faced woman and rather attractive. She stood wearing a red silk apron with white polka dots as she set out the baked goods on the Purim pastry trays she would be sending out and arranged in order those she had received.

Reb Yossi Henpecked (that was his nickname in Kasrilevka) was lying on the sofa snoring away while Menasha, their eighteen-year-old son, who had red cheeks and wore a long, shiny coat, kept sneaking around his mother, constantly snatching a piece of honey cake, a few pieces of mandelbrot or a poppyseed cooky. He had so stuffed himself with all those goodies that his mouth was constantly filled and his belly had begun to rumble.

"Menasha, don't you think you've had enough, Menasha?" his mother kept asking.

"Enough, enough!" said Menasha, stuffing his mouth with yet another piece. "The last one," he said, licking his lips.

* * *

"Happy Purim! My mistress has sent you a Purim pastry gift!" announced the dark-haired Nekhama, delivering the covered tray to Zelda.

"Whom do you work for?" Zelda asked her with a friendly smile, taking the platter from her hands.

"For Zlate, Reb Isaac Brismaker's wife," the dark-haired Nekhama answered, waiting for the tray to be emptied and returned.

Zelda put one hand in her pocket to tip the girl for her trouble and with the other hand she uncovered the tray and stood aghast.

"What is this? Menasha, take a look!"

Menasha looked at the tray, grabbed his sides and bent over double with such laughter that Reb Yossi Henpecked almost fell off the sofa from fright.

"Ha? What is it? Who's there?"

"Take a look at this Purim pastry tray!" said Zelda and folded her arms across her stomach. Menasha couldn't stop laughing and Reb Yossi Henpecked spat, turned his face to the wall and went back to sleep.

Zelda flung the tray and napkin at Nekhama and said to her:

"Tell your mistress that we hope that next Purim she still won't be able to afford a better Purim pastry tray than this one."

"And the same to you!" said the dark-haired Nekhama and took the platter.

"Go to the devil!" Zelda said in a rage. "What a sassy girl! What do you say to that, Menasha?"

D

Zlate Reb Isaac's wife was a woman who gave birth to a child every year and never stopped doctoring herself. She was so exhausted from handing out and receiving Purim pastry gifts that she had to sit down on a chair, while continuing to boss her husband, Isaac Brismaker (that's what he was called behind his back because he had a son every year for whom they had to have a circumcision, or *bris*).

"Isaac, take this piece of torte and put it here, and take this piece of nutbread and the three poppyseed cookies from there and put it here, Isaac, and hand me that cushion cake with the farfel, no, not that one, that one! Come on, move, Isaac! Look at how I have to teach him like a little child learning ABC's! And take that little honey cake, the bigger one, and put it there, that's the way, and slice the torte in two, too big a piece of torte, what a waste. Get out of my way, little brats, shoo!"

Those last words were shouted at a pack of youngsters who flocked around her with bare bellies, gazing at the sweets hungrily and licking their lips.

The children kept sneaking up from behind hoping to snatch a piece of honey cake from the table, but their mother would catch them and bestow a slap or a shove or a pinch.

* * *

"Happy Purim! My mistress has sent you a Purim pastry gift!" announced the redheaded Nekhama and handed Zlate the covered tray.

"For whom do you work?" Zlate asked her with a friendly smile, removing the tray from her hands.

"For Zelda, Reb Yossi Henpecked's wife," said the redheaded Nekhama and waited for the tray to be emptied and returned.

Zlate put one hand in her pocket to tip the girl for her trouble and with the other hand uncovered the tray and stood aghast.

"May all the ugly, awful, evil, deadly nightmares descend upon my enemies' heads and afflict their hands and feet and their very lives! Take a look at these Purim pastries! She's making fun of me, as only a frivolous woman like that can!"

"Here, take this back to your mistress!" said Zlate and flung the tray and the napkin right into the redheaded Nekhama's face.

E

Reb Yossi Henpecked and Reb Isaac Brismaker were both shopkeepers in Kasrilevka, whose shops stood right next to one. another. And though they were competitors and tried to take customers away from each other, nevertheless they got along well. They would borrow money occasionally from one another, attended each others' family celebrations, shared holidays and a *kiddush* as befits close neighbors. Summers they sat all day in their shops and played dominoes together and winters they would visit each other to try to keep warm. The wives were congenial as well, gossiped about everyone, borrowed ingredients if they ran short, entrusted one another with their deepest secrets, almost never squabbled and even if they did once in a while over a trifle, they quickly made up. In short, they had a cozy relationship.

The morning after Purim, when Reb Isaac Brismaker went to open his shop, Reb Yossi Henpecked was already standing at the door of his own shop all puffed up like a turkey waiting for Reb Isaac to come over and wish him a good morning so he could give him the cold shoulder. Reb Isaac, who had been riled up by his wife, opened his shop, stood himself at the door and waited for Reb Yossi to approach *him* with the usual morning greeting so that he could snub *him*. And so the two stood facing one another like gamecocks, waiting to see who would be the first to begin. They would both have stood there that way all day had not both their wives arrived from the market, both with flushed faces and eyes burning with rage.

"Isaac, why aren't you thanking him for that fine Purim pastry tray, Isaac, that his darling sent?" Zlate said to her husband.

"Yossi, why don't you remind him of yesterday's Purim pastry tray?" Zelda said to her husband.

"Isaac, do you hear that, Isaac, she's teasing us! Why don't you say something to him, Isaac?"

"Why should I say anything to old Henpecked over there?" Reb Isaac said loud enough for Reb Yossi to hear him being called Henpecked.

"I'm afraid to start up with a Brismaker," Reb Yossi said loud enough for Reb Isaac to hear him being called Brismaker.

When you think about it, what is so insulting about the name "Brismaker"? Every Jew whose wife gives birth to a son, after all, makes a *bris* on the eighth day.

But Reb Isaac could put up with anything in the world except the nickname "Brismaker." That was for him a thousand times worse than the worst curse! He was capable of tearing the perpetrator to pieces!

The same was true of Reb Yossi. If you were to slap him hard three times it would bother him less than the word "Henpecked."

People came running from all over the marketplace and were barely able to pull them apart. They wanted to find out what could possibly have happened to cause two close neighbors and good friends to suddenly be pulling each other's beards. But Reb Yossi and Reb Isaac and Zlate and Zelda were all shouting at the same time, making such a din and yelling at one another so loudly that all they could make out were the words, "Purim pastry gifts! Purim pastry gifts!" and nothing else. What did they mean by "Purim pastry gifts"? It was impossible to figure it out.

"If you don't report this Henpeck to the magistrate, say goodbye to your life!" Zlate screamed at her husband. And Reb Yossi appealed to the crowd in the marketplace:

"Jews, you are witnesses that this vulgar woman called me Henpecked! I'm going right to the magistrate to report her and her husband, Brismaker."

"Jews!" Reb Isaac cried, "Know that I will call you as witnesses before the magistrate that this . . . this . . . this . . . I won't call him by his fine name, has just called me Brismaker!"

Within an hour both of them were standing before Yudel the scribe, both had presented witnesses and each reported the other to the magistrate in the complaint prepared by the scribe.

F

The Kasrilevka magistrate, Pan Milinyevski, a stout landowner with a long beard and high forehead, had been magistrate for so long that he was well acquainted with all the townspeople, knew each of its citizens intimately, especially its Jews. He knew each Jew's character through and through, spoke Yiddish as well as any Jew, and was smart as a whip into the bargain. It was said of him in Kasrilevka that he had a "Jewish head on his shoulders."

In the Fall, soon after Sukkos time, he would be besieged with complaints, all from Jews, may they live and be well—not, God forbid, about thefts, robberies or assaults—no! But for affronts, quarrels over who was called to the Torah on Sabbath and other matters of precedence in the synagogue. Pan Milinyevski hated to stand on ceremony with the Kasrilevka Jews or to get into tangled debates with them. Nor did he allow them to speak too long because he knew it would be endless. If they were willing to compromise, well and good (Pan Milinyevski was a man of peace), if not, he put on his chain of office and laid down the law—no exceptions, no nonsense, no favorites.

Exactly two weeks before Passover the case of the Purim pastry gifts was tried. The magistrate's chamber was packed with men and women, almost all of whom had been witnesses. There was no room to budge.

"Isaac, Yosske, Zlate, Zelda!" Pan Milinyevski called out and from the front row Reb Yossi Henpecked and Isaac Brismaker with their wives stepped forward. And before the magistrate could utter a word, all four of them suddenly began shouting at once, and louder than the rest, as usual, the wives.

"Sir Magistrate!" said Zelda, shoving her husband aside and pointing at Zlate, "This vulgar woman sent me a Purim pastry gift that was an insult in the eyes of the neighbors! A sliver of strudel and a few measly sugar cookies, just to ridicule me, to embarrass me, tphoo!"

"Oy! Oy! Oy! I can't bear this!" screamed Zlate, beating her breast, "I won't live through this!"

"Amen!" said Zelda.

"Be still, blabbermouth! Sir Magistrate, as I live, I sent her two cushion cakes, a nice nut cake, a honey cake, may she suffer for it, and a torte. May she have a hundred boils on her face, woe is me!"

"What torte? I never saw a torte!"

The magistrate tried to calm the wives, at first with gentle tact, then with threats and ringing his bell for quiet, but when he saw it was in vain, that it was impossible to make them shut their mouths, he drove the wives out onto the street so there could be quiet in his chambers and he could hear what they were saying. He advised the men to consult the rabbi.

"Go ask your rabbi," he said, "Go to your rabbi and ask him about the torte." And the whole crowd went off to see the rabbi.

G

Reb Yozifel the rabbi, as we all know, was, blessed be God, the kind of man who could bear up under anything. He didn't mind hearing out each person until he had finished. Reb Yozifel was of the opinion that every person, no matter how much he spoke, had at some point to stop because a person, he said, was not a machine. But the problem was that this time all four spoke at once, outshouting one another besides having bystanders adding their opinions. But what did that matter? Everything on earth had to come to an end. When all had had their fill of talking, accusing, and fighting, and things quieted down, Reb Yozifel addressed himself to both parties, slowly, calmly, as was his manner, and with a sigh:

"Ah-ah-ah! Soon, soon we will be celebrating such a holiday, such a blessed holiday, Passover! Imagine—Passover! Our ancestors fled from Egypt and crossed the sea, such a sea, on dry land! They wandered in the desert for forty years, forty years! Received the Torah on Mount Sinai, and such a Torah, in which it is specifically written: 'Love thy neighbor as thyself.' And alas, we see Jews quarreling because of our many sins, tearing each other's beards, and over what? Over nonsense, foolishness. It is blasphemous, I say, disgraceful in the eyes of the Gentiles. Better to think of providing the poor with matzos for Passover. And how about eggs and chicken fat and vegetables—that they surely do not have. At the very least, matzos, God in heaven, matzos for Passover! Imagine—Passover! Such a holiday! Our ancestors fled from Egypt and crossed the sea, such a great sea, on dry land, wandered in the desert for forty years, forty years! Received the Torah on Mount Sinai, such a Torah, such a Torah! Hear my words, Jewish children, forgive one another, make peace and go home, enjoy good health and keep in mind that we will soon be celebrating such a holiday, such a great, such a blessed holiday!"

One by one the crowd began to disperse from the rabbi's house, shaking their heads at Reb Yozifel's decision with a saying the Kasrilevka wags use: "It's not a sentence but a sermon." But in their hearts they each felt that Reb

Yozifel was right and they were ashamed to repeat the story about the Purim pastry gifts.

* * *

On the first morning of Passover, after synagogue services, Reb Yossi Henpecked (he was the younger of the two) went to Isaac Brismaker's house for the *kiddush* and praised his Passover wine as the best in years as he licked his fingers after eating Zlate's dumplings. On the second morning of Passover, Reb Isaac Brismaker (he was the older of the two) went to Yossi Henpecked's house for the *kiddush* and couldn't find enough nice things to say about his raisin wine or about Zelda's dumplings. And in the afternoon after dinner, when Zelda and Zlate got together and talked about the Purim pastry gifts, the truth rose to the surface like oil on water and both servant girls, the two Nekhamas, received their just desserts: immediately after Passover they were sent packing.

Song of Songs
(*A Children's Tale*)

A

uzi is her name, derived from Esther Libeh, affectionately called Libuzi, shortened to Buzi. She is a year or two older than I am and together our ages don't add up to twenty. Sit down, if you like, and figure out how old I am and how old she is. But that's not what's important. I'd rather tell you her life story.

My older brother, Benny, lived in a small town, owned a mill, could shoot a gun, ride a horse, and swim like a demon. One summer he went swimming in the river and drowned. To him the old saying applied: "Only good swimmers drown." He left behind a mill, two horses, a young widow, and a child. The mill was abandoned, the horses were sold, the young widow remarried and moved far away and the child was brought to us.

That was Buzi.

B

It was easy to understand why my father loved Buzi as if she were his own child, and why my mother doted on her as if she were an only daughter. She was their solace for their great loss. But I? Why was it that when I came home from *cheder* and didn't see Buzi, I would lose my desire to eat? And why was it that when Buzi was there, the house would brighten and the dark corners disappear? And when Buzi spoke to me, why did I lower my eyes? And when Buzi laughed at me, why did I cry?

And when Buzi . . .

C

I always look forward to the sweet beloved holiday, Passover. Then I will be free from school. I will play at nuts with Buzi, romp outdoors, run down to the river. There I will show her how the ducklings swim in the water. Whenever I tell her anything, she doesn't believe me. She laughs. She just doesn't believe anything I tell her. I know, because she only laughs at me and doesn't say anything. And I hate it when anyone laughs at me. Buzi doesn't believe that I can climb the tallest tree (if only I wanted to!). Buzi doesn't believe that I can shoot (if only I had something to shoot with!). Just wait till Passover, that sweet beloved Passover, when we can go outdoors in the fresh air, out of sight of my parents—then I'll show her some tricks. She will be amazed!

D

At last the sweet beloved Passover has come.

They've outfitted us both like royalty for the holiday. Everything we are wearing is spanking new and in the latest style. I look at Buzi and am reminded of the "Song of Songs" I studied before Passover with the rebbe in *cheder*. One verse after another comes to mind:

> *Behold, thou art fair, my love; behold, thou art fair. Thine eyes are as doves. Thy hair is as a flock of goats, that lie along the side of Mount Gilead. Thy teeth are like a flock of ewes that are newly shorn, which are coming up from the washing; whereof every one hath twins, and none is bereaved among them. Thy lips are like a thread of scarlet, and thy mouth is comely. Honey and milk are under thy tongue.*

Tell me, why is it, I ask you, that when I look at Buzi I am reminded of the "Song of Songs"? Why is it that when I am studying the "Song of Songs," I think of Buzi?

E

A rare day before Passover. A bright day. Warm outdoors.

"Are we going?"

That's what Buzi says to me, and I feel I am burning with eagerness. My mother does not spare the nuts. Our pockets are crammed with nuts. She makes us promise not to crack the nuts before the seder but we can play with the nuts as much as our hearts desire. We take off. The nuts rattle in our pockets. The day is lovely. The air is clear. The sun is high in the sky, looking down on us now from the other side of town. All around it is wide open, spacious, mild, and free. Newly sprouted blades of grass, fresh and quivering, push up through the earth on the hillside on the other side of the synagogue. With high-pitched cries, a flock of swallows fly over our heads in a straight line. And again I am reminded of the "Song of Songs":

The flowers appear on the earth; the time of the singing of birds is come, and the voice of the turtle is heard in our land. I feel strangely weightless. I imagine I have wings and at any moment I will rise up and soar.

F

A strange din arises from the town. A roaring, seething, boiling. It is a rare day just before Passover! A bright day. Warm outdoors. At that moment the whole world takes on a new appearance to me. Our courtyard is a castle ground. Our house is a palace. I am a prince. Buzi is a princess. The logs of wood piled next to the house are cedars and fir trees that are mentioned in the "Song of Songs." The cat sunning itself by the door is one of the young deer mentioned in the "Song of Songs." Beyond the hill on the other side of the synagogue is Lebanon mentioned in the "Song of Songs." The women and girls standing in the courtyard washing and ironing and koshering for Passover—they are the daughters of Jerusalem who are mentioned in the "Song of Songs." Everything, everything is from the "Song of Songs."

I walk, hands in my pockets, and the nuts rattle. Buzi walks beside me step for step. I cannot go slowly, I am borne upward on the air. I long to fly, to float, to soar like an eagle. I begin to run. Buzi runs with me. I leap on the pile of logs, jump from one to the next. Buzi jumps with me. I jump up, she jumps up. I jump down, she jumps down. Who will tire first? I guess right.

"How long can we do this?" Buzi says to me and I answer her in the language of the "Song of Songs":

"'*Until the day dawns and the shadows fade.*' Ha! You tired and I didn't!"

G

I am pleased that Buzi cannot keep up with me. At the same time I feel sorry for her. My heart aches for her. I imagine she is sorrowful. She has this way about her—one minute she is happy and the next she will hide in a corner, weeping silently. No matter how much my mother consoles her, no matter how much my father kisses her, nothing seems to help. She simply must cry it out. For whom? For her father who died so young? For her mother who married and left her without so much as a goodbye? Ah, her mother, her mother! If you mention her mother, her face turns all colors. She does not hold with her mother. She never says a bad word about her but neither does she feel kindly towards her. I know that for certain. I cannot bear it when Buzi is unhappy. I sit down next to her on the logs and try to take her mind off her sorrows.

H

I hold my hands in my pockets, knock the nuts together and say to her:

"Guess what I can do if I want to."

"What can you do?"

"If I want, all your nuts will belong to me."

"Would you win them from me?"

"No. We won't play at all."

"What? Would you take them away from me by force?"

"No. They would come to me of their own will."

She raises her lovely eyes and gazes at me, with her lovely "Song of Songs" eyes. I say to her:

"You think I'm joking? I have this magic phrase that I say . . ."

She opens her eyes wide. I feel very confident and explain it to her, like a grown-up, like a man of the world:

"We boys know everything. I have a friend in *cheder*, Sheike the Blind is his name (he is blind in one eye), and he knows everything. There is nothing in the world that Sheike doesn't know. Even Kabbalah. Do you know what Kabbalah is?"

No, how would she know? I am in seventh heaven because I can give her a lesson on Kabbalah.

"Kabbalah, silly, is something that can come in very handy. With Kabbalah it is possible for me to see you and for you not to see me. With Kabbalah I can draw wine from a stone and gold from a wall. With Kabbalah I can arrange it so that right from the spot where we are sitting, we will both rise up to the clouds and even higher than the clouds!"

I

One of my favorite dreams was to use the Kabbalah to rise up to the clouds and even higher than the clouds with Buzi and to fly away to the other side of the ocean. There, on the other side of the ocean, is the land of the dwarfs who are descended from the heroes of King David's times. The dwarfs are by nature good little people. They live solely on sweets and almond milk, play all day on little fifes and dance in a circle, are not afraid of anything, and love to have visitors. When one of us comes to visit them, the dwarfs give him food and silver utensils and before he leaves they stuff his pockets with diamonds and jewels that are strewn on the ground like trash is strewn in our town.

"Like trash on the ground? Really?"

That's what Buzi once said to me when I told her about the dwarfs.

"You don't believe it?"

"And you believe it?"

"Why not?"

"Where did you hear that?"

"Where else? In *cheder*."

"Ah, in *cheder*."

Lower and lower sinks the sun, tinting the sky with the color of fine gold. The gold is reflected in Buzi's eyes. They swim in gold.

J

I want very much for Buzi to be impressed with Sheike's magic tricks that I can perform with Kabbalah. But Buzi isn't impressed at all. On the contrary, I get the feeling she is making fun of me. Otherwise why is she flashing her pearly teeth at me? I begin to feel resentful and say to her:

"You don't believe me?"

Buzi laughs.

"You think I'm exaggerating? That I'm making up lies?"

Buzi laughs harder. Eh! If that's the case, I have to get even with her! And I know how. I say to her:

"The trouble is that you don't know what Kabbalah is. If you knew what Kabbalah was you wouldn't laugh that way. With Kabbalah, if I want, I can bring your mother here. Yes-yes. And if you beg me very hard, I can bring her here this very night, riding on a stick."

In an instant she stops laughing. A little cloud crosses her lovely bright face and I feel the sun has suddenly disappeared. No more sun. No more day. I fear I have gone too far. I should not have touched upon her pain—her mother. I regret telling her that story. I must make up for it. I must ask for forgiveness. I move closer to her. She turns away. I try to take her hand. I want to speak to her in the words of the "Song of Songs": *Return, return, O Shulamite!*"—Or Buzi. Suddenly I hear a voice calling from the house:

"Shimek! Shimek?"

Shimek—that's my name. It's my mother calling me to go to synagogue with my father.

K

Going to synagogue on Passover eve with my father—what greater joy can there be? What can be better than being dressed from head to toe in spanking new clothes to show off to your friends? Not to mention the service, the very first evening service and benediction of Passover. Ah! What pleasures our great God has prepared for his Jewish children!

"Shimek! Shimek?"

My mother is impatient. "I'm coming, I'm coming right away, here I come! I just want to say two words to Buzi, no more than two words."

I admit that what I have just said is not true. Kabbalah cannot make someone fly. But I myself—yes, I can fly and I will show her that. Right after Passover I will make my first flight. I will ascend right in front of her, from these logs, right before her eyes. In no time I will be above the clouds. And then I will turn right, and go—do you see?—to where the world ends and the Frozen Sea begins.

L

Buzi listens intently. The sun sends its last rays to kiss the earth goodbye.

"What is the Frozen Sea?" asks Buzi.

"You don't know about the Frozen Sea? It's called the Frozen Sea because its waters are thick as liver and salty as brine. No vessels can sail on it, and if a person loses his way there he can never return."

Buzi stares at me wide-eyed.

"Then why do you want to go there?"

"I'm not *going* there, little silly, I'm *flying* there. I'll fly above the sea like an eagle. And very soon I'll be back on dry land where the twelve high mountains erupt with fire, and on the twelfth mountain, at the very peak, I will alight and go by foot for seven miles until I reach a dense forest. Then I will walk through the forest until I come to a little stream. I will cross the stream and count seven times seven and before my eyes there will appear a little old man with a long beard who asks me: "What is your wish?" I will say to him: "Take me to the queen's daughter."

"Which queen's daughter?"

This is what Buzi says to me and she seems to be frightened.

"The queen's daughter, that beautiful princess who was snatched from under the wedding canopy, enchanted, carried off far away, and has been imprisoned in a crystal palace for seven years."

"But what has that to do with you?"

"What do you mean what has that to do with me? I must free her."

"You must free her?"

"Who else, then?"

"You don't have to fly so far away. Listen to me, you don't have to!"

M

Buzi takes my hand and her small hand feels cold. I look deep into her eyes and see reflected in them the pure gold of the sun as it bids farewell to the day, that first bright warm Passover day. Slowly the day is dying. Like a candle the sun is going out. The din that sounded all day is dying. Hardly a person can be found on the street. In the windows of the houses flicker the little flames of the holiday candles. A strange, a holy silence surrounds us, me and Buzi, and we feel ourselves at one with this holy silence.

"Shimek! Shimek?"

N

This is the third time my mother has called for me to go to synagogue with my father. Doesn't she think I know that we need to go to synagogue? I'll stay here just one minute, one minute, no more. When Buzi hears that I'm being called, she tears her hand out of mine, jumps up and hurries me along:

"Shimek, they're calling you. Go, go. It's getting late. Go, go."

I get ready to go. The day has vanished. The sun has gone out. The gold has turned blood red. A little breeze, light and cool, wafts by. Buzi urges me to go. I cast one last look at her. It isn't the same Buzi as before. In my eyes she has acquired a different face with a different charm in this enchanted twilight. "The enchanted princess," flashes through my mind. But Buzi does not allow me to dwell on my thoughts. She pushes me, pushes me to go. I start to leave, looking back at the enchanted princess who has become one with the enchanted Passover evening and I feel myself to be enchanted too. But she motions to me with her hand that I must go! I must go! And I imagine I hear her voice speaking to me in the words of the "Song of Songs":

"Make haste, my beloved! Be thou like a young hart upon the mountains of Bether!"

Buzi and I
Pick Greens

A

"Faster, Buzi, faster!" I say to Buzi a day before Shevuos, taking her hand and running quickly up the hill with her. "The day won't last forever, silly. We have to go over a hill and after that, a little stream. And after the stream we'll come to the 'the Little Bridge,' the footbridge. The stream will be running under it, the frogs will be croaking, the boards of the footbridge will shake and rock and then there, on the other side of the footbridge—that's where the real Garden of Eden begins, Buzi! That's where my estates begin."

"Your estates?"

"I mean the big meadow. A huge field that stretches endlessly, boundlessly. It's covered with a green blanket, decorated with yellow blossoms and little reddish beet-leaves. And the delicious aromas you will smell there—the finest scents in the world! And I have trees there, numberless, tall, thickly branched! And I have a little hill on which I can sit. If I wish, I sit on it as much as I please. If I wish, I rise through the magical power of God and soar like an eagle, higher than the clouds, over field and forest, over sea and desert, until I arrive at the legendary 'mountains of darkness'."

"And from there," Buzi interrupts me, "you walk seven miles until you come to a stream."

"No, to a thick forest. First into the forest, then out of the forest and only then do I come to a river."

"You swim across the river and count seven times seven . . ."

"And a little old man with a long beard appears before me."

"He asks you: 'What is your wish?'"

"I say to him: 'Take me to the princess.'"

Buzi tears her hand from mine and starts to run downhill. I run after her.

"Buzi, why are you running away?"

Buzi doesn't answer. She is angry. She doesn't like the princess. She likes all my stories but not the one about the princess.

B

You remember who Buzi is. I told you about her before. But if you've forgotten, I'll tell you again.

I had an older brother, Benny, who drowned. He left a water-mill, a young widow, two horses, and a child. The mill was abandoned, the horses sold, the widow married and went far away. And the child was brought to us. That's Buzi.

Ha-ha-ha! Everyone thinks Buzi and I are brother and sister. She calls my father Papa, she calls my mother Mama, and we live like brother and sister and love one another like brother and sister.

Like brother and sister? Why then is Buzi shy with me?

It happened one time that the two of us were alone in the whole house. It was in the evening, already getting dark. My father had gone to the synagogue to say Kaddish for my brother Benny and my mother to buy matches. Buzi and I crept into a corner and I told her stories. Buzi loves when I tell her stories, fine stories about *cheder*, stories from a thousand and one nights. She moved very close to me. Her hand was in mine.

"Tell, Shimek, tell!"

Night came quietly. Slowly the shadows crept up the walls, quivering, falling back to the ground and dissolving. We could barely see one another. But I felt her hand trembling and I heard her heart beating and I saw her eyes glowing in the darkness. Suddenly she tore her hand from mine. "What's the matter, Buzi?" "We mustn't." "What mustn't we?" "Hold hands." "Why? Who told you that?" "I just know." "Are we strangers? Aren't we brother and sister?" "Ah! If we were only brother and sister!" Buzi said slowly and I heard in what she said the words of the "Song of Songs":

"Why art thou not my brother?"

It is always like this. When I speak of Buzi, I am reminded of the "Song of Songs."

C

Where were we? Ah, the day before Shevuos. We are running down the hill. First Buzi, then I. Buzi is angry at me because of the princess. She likes all my stories but not the ones about the princess. But you needn't worry. Buzi's anger doesn't last as long as it takes for me to tell you about it. Already she is looking at me with her large, bright, pensive eyes. She tosses her hair back and says to me:

"Shimek! Oh, Shimek! Just look. Look at that sky. Don't you see what a beautiful sky is up there!"

"I see, silly. Don't you think I see it? I see the sky, I feel a warm breeze, I hear birds chirping and twittering and flying over our heads. It's our sky, it's our breeze, they're our birds—everything is ours, ours, ours! Give me your hand, Buzi!"

No. She doesn't give me her hand. She is shy. Why is Buzi shy with me? Why is she blushing?

"Let's go!" says Buzi and runs on ahead of me, "Come on, let's go to the other side of the little footbridge . . ." and I imagine she is speaking to me in the words of Shulamith in the "Song of Songs": *L'kha dodi . . .*

Come, my beloved! Let us go forth into the field;
Let us lodge in the villages!
Let us get up early in the vineyards!
Let us see whether the vine hath budded, and its blossom be
  open,
And the pomegranates be in flower.

And soon we are at the little footbridge.

D

The stream is flowing, the frogs croaking, and the boards of the footbridge shake and rock, and Buzi trembles.

"Oh, Buzi, you're . . . what are you frightened of, silly? Hold on to me, or here, let me hold you. We'll hold on to one another. See? That's the way, that's the way."

We cross the footbridge.

Our arms around one another, we continue walking, just the two of us in this Garden of Eden. Buzi holds on to me hard, very hard. She is silent, but I imagine she is speaking to me in the words of the "Song of Songs": *Ani l'dodi v'dodi li . . .*

"I am my beloved's and my beloved is mine. . . ."

The meadow is huge. It stretches endlessly, boundlessly, covered with a green blanket, decorated with yellow blossoms and reddish beetleaves. The scents here are the sweetest, of the finest spices in the world! And we both walk with our arms around one another, just the two of us, together in this Garden of Eden.

"Shimek!" Buzi says to me and gazes right into my eyes, moving still closer to me, "When will we start picking greens for Shevuos?"

"The day is still young, silly!" I say to her and I am burning. I don't know where to look first—at the cap of blue sky? At the green blanket of the broad meadow? At the horizon where the sky blends with the earth? Or at Buzi's radiant face, into Buzi's large beautiful eyes that seem to me as deep as the sky and as pensive as the night? Her eyes are always pensive. A profound sorrow lies hidden in them. A mute sadness clouds them. I know her sorrow, I am familiar with her sadness. She bears a great ache in her heart. A resentment against her mother who married a strange man and left her forever, for always, as if she were nothing but a stranger.

At home her mother's name cannot be mentioned, as if her mother never existed. My mother—*she* is her mother. My father—*he* is her father. And they love her as one of their own, dote on her, give her her heart's desire. Nothing is too good for Buzi. Buzi said she wanted to go with me to pick greens for Shevuos (*I* put her up to that), and my father said to my mother: "What do you think?" as he peered over his silver-rimmed spectacles, stroking the silver hairs of his beard. A discussion followed between my parents about our going out alone beyond the town to pick greens for Shevuos:

MY FATHER: What do you say?
MY MOTHER: What do *you* say?
MY FATHER: Should we let them go?
MY MOTHER: Why *shouldn't* we let them go?
MY FATHER: Am I saying no?
MY MOTHER: What then are you saying?
MY FATHER: I'm just asking should they go?
MY MOTHER: Why *shouldn't* they go?

And so on. I know what was bothering them. My father told me at least twenty times, and so did my mother, that there's a footbridge, and under the footbridge there is water, a river, a river, a river . . .

E

Buzi and I have long put the footbridge, the water, and the river behind us. We are traipsing across the wide open meadow, under the wide open sky. We run across the green field, throw ourselves on the ground, and roll around in the fragrant grass. We stand up, fall down, and roll around again and again, and we still haven't picked greens for Shevuos. I lead Buzi over the length and breadth of the meadow. I boast to her about my estate.

"Do you see these trees? Do you see this sand? Do you see this hill?"

"Is this all yours?" Buzi says to me, her eyes laughing. I resent her laughter. She has this habit of laughing at me. I begin to sulk and turn away from Buzi for a moment. Buzi realizes I am offended. She steps in front of me, looks into my eyes, takes my hand and says: "Shimek!" My anger flees and all is forgotten. I take her by the hand and lead her to my hill where I always like to sit all through the year. If I wish, I sit there as long as I please. If I wish, I rise through the magical power of God and soar like an eagle, higher than the clouds, over field and forest, over sea and desert.

F

There on the hill we sit, Buzi and I (we still haven't picked greens for Shevuos), and tell stories. That is, I tell and she listens. I tell her that some day, some day when I am a grown-up and she is a grown-up, we will be together forever. We will rise through the magical power of God above the clouds and circle the globe. First we will visit all the countries where Alexander of Macedonia ruled. Then we will fly over to the Holy Land. There we will visit the hills of sweet-smelling spices and all the vineyards, stuff our pockets full with carob, figs, dates, and olives and from there we will fly off further and further. And in each place we will play a new trick because no one will be able to see us.

"No one will be able to see us?" Buzi asks and grabs me by the hands.

"No one, no one! We will be able to see everyone but no one will be able to see us!"

"If that's so, Shimek, I have a favor to ask of you."

"A favor?"

"A little favor . . ."

But I already know what the favor will be. She wants us to visit the place where her mother was married and to play a trick on her stepfather.

"Why not?" I say to her. "With the greatest pleasure! You can count on me, silly. I can play a trick on them that they'll never forget!"

"Not them, just *him, only him*," Buzi begs me. But I'm not going to agree to that so quickly. When I get angry, watch out! Does she think her mother can get off so easily? The gall of that hussy, marrying another man, going off to who-knows-where and abandoning a child, not writing her so much as a letter! How is it possible? Whoever heard of such an outrage?!

G

I regret my fury. I am as sorry as sorry can be. But it's too late. Buzi covers her face with both hands. Is she crying? I could tear myself apart! Why did I have to touch on her sorest spot—her mother? Deep in my heart I call myself the ugliest names: ass! ox! big mouth! I move closer to her. I take her hand in mine:

"Buzi! Buzi!"

I want to speak to her in the words of the "Song of Songs":

Let me see thy countenance, let me hear thy voice.

Suddenly—how did my father and mother get here?

H

My father's silver-rimmed spectacles gleam from the distance. The silver hairs of his beard are blown about by the wind. And my mother is waving with her handkerchief at us from afar. Both of us, Buzi and I, sit stunned. What are my parents doing here?

They have come to check if anything had happened to us, heaven forbid, some calamity. After all, a footbridge, water, a river, a river, a river . . .

Strange parents!

"And where are your greens?"

"What greens?"

"The greens you were going to pick for Shevuos?"

Both of us, Buzi and I, look at one another. I understand what her eyes are saying. I understand her expression. And I imagine I hear her speaking to me in the words of the "Song of Songs":

Oh, that thou wert my brother! Why art thou not my brother?

* * *

"Oh, well, we'll just have to make do with whatever greens we have at hand for Shevuos," my father says with a smile, the silver hairs of his beard glinting in the bright rays of the golden sun, "So long as the children are safe, praise God, and no harm has come to them."

"Praise God!" my mother repeats, dabbing at her red, perspiring face with her handkerchief. And they look at us tenderly, their faces beaming with pride.

Strange, strange parents!

Bandits

A

s he still snoring?"

"Boy, is he snoring!"

"What's wrong with him!"

"Wake him up! Wake him up!"

"Leib-Dreib-Obdirik!"

"Wake up, sweetie-pie!"

"Open up your little eyes."

Barely managing to open my eyes, I raised my head, looked around, and saw the whole gang of good-for-nothings, my *cheder* classmates. The window was open and along with their sparkling eyes I saw the the first rays of the bright warm morning sun. I kept looking around.

"What's he looking at us like that for?"

"Like he's done something!"

"Don't you recognize us?"

"Have you forgotten it's Lag B'Omer today?"

Ach! Lag B'Omer? . . . Like a flash of lightning those

words coursed through my body. In a split second I bolted out of bed and was on my feet. In another minute I was dressed, washed, ready, and looking for my mother. She was busy serving breakfast to the younger children.

"Mama, today is Lag B'Omer."

"Happy holiday to you. What do you want?"

"I need something for our Lag B'Omer party."

"What should I give you? My troubles? Or my pains?" said my mother, but still and all she was willing to give me something for the party. We bargained. I wanted more, she gave me less. I asked for two eggs, she said she would give me a headache instead. I became angry. For that, instead of two eggs, she gave me two smacks. I cried, she relented and gave me an apple. I wanted an orange, she called me an unkosher pest, "What else will you come up with?"

My friends, waiting impatiently outside, began to clamor: "Are you coming or not?"

"Leib-Dreib-Obdirik!"

"Time isn't standing still!"

"Hurry! Come on!"

"Make like a whirlwind!"

After more negotiation my mother and I came to an agreement. I grabbed some breakfast and my contribution to the party and sped out of the house to my friends, fresh, eager, and happy, into the bright, warm outdoors and all of us raced off to *cheder*.

B

The *cheder* was alive and noisy with excitement. Twenty throats were all shouting at the same time. The table was piled high with good food. We had never had a Lag B'Omer party like this one before—imagine, a party with whisky and wine!

For this, we had to thank our friend, Berl, Yossl the winemaker's boy. He brought a bottle of good whisky and two bottles of wine, real vintage wine made by Yossl himself. His father gave him the whisky but he took the two bottles of wine.

"What do you mean, you took them?"

"What don't you understand, stupid head? I took them from the shelf when no one was looking."

"But doesn't that mean you stole them?"

"You're a genius! What of it?"

"What do you mean, what of it? And what about, 'Thou shalt not steal'?"

"I took it in honor of our holiday party, dope!"

"You mean stealing is a good deed?"

"Absolutely! What do you say to this wiseacre?"

"Show me where it says it's allowed."

"He wants us to tell him where it says it's allowed."

"Tell him it's written in the 'Book of Tomfoolery'!"

"In the chapter, 'And he took'."

"On page twelve, bim-bom!"

"The first day of the month Kremenitz."

"Ha-ha-ha!"

"Be quiet, kids, here comes Mazeppe!"

Suddenly it grew as quiet as if we were praying the silent Eighteen Benedictions. We sat up straight at the table like well-behaved sissies, mutes, model children, innocent lambs.

C

Mazeppe—that was our rebbe's name. His real name was Borukh-Moishe but as he had recently come to us from Mazepevka, our town had dubbed him, "The Mazepevker," and we schoolboys shortened it to Mazeppe. Incidentally, when students crown a rebbe with a fine name, you can be sure he has earned it. Let me introduce him to you:

Short, wizened, skinny—almost grotesque. You could hardly make out a sign of a beard, a mustache, or eyebrows, not because he shaved them, God forbid, but because it was their nature to get together and decide not to grow. But that was made up for by the size of his lips and nose—what a nose! A loaf, a horn, a shofar. He had a voice that clanged like a bell, roared like a lion! How did a tiny creature like this acquire such a fearful voicebox? And where did he get his physical strength? When he grabbed your arm with his thin, clammy fingers, you saw stars, and if he let you have one of his slaps, you felt it for three days on end. He hated lengthy discussions. For the least little thing, guilty or not, his sentence was: "Lie down for a whipping!"

"Rebbe! Yossl-Yaakov-Yossl hit me."

"Lie down!"

"Rebbe, it's a lie! He kicked me in the side first!"

"Lie down!"

"Rebbe! Khayim-Berl-Lappe's stuck out his tongue at me."

"Lie down!"

"Rebbe! Lies! All lies! It was he who thumbed his nose."

"Lie down!"

And you had to lie down. Nothing would help you. Even Eli the Redhead, who was already a *bar mitzvah* boy, a bridegroom-to-be who wore a silver watchpiece—do you think he got out of a whipping? Oho! And what whippings! Eli vowed that one day he would get revenge on Mazeppe for those whippings so that he would remember him the rest of his life! That's what Eli kept telling us after each whipping and we would add:

"Amen, may it be so, from your mouth into God's ears."

D

After the usual prayers led by the rebbe (he wouldn't let us pray by ourselves; he knew that without him present we would skip more than half the prayers), Mazeppe announced to us in his lion-voice:

"So, children, wash up and sit down to the table for the party and after the blessing I'll let you out for a walk."

In the past we had the Lag B'Omer party on the other side of town, out in the open air, on the bare ground. Under God's sky, we could toss bits of bread to the birds, let them also enjoy the holiday. But with Mazeppe you didn't argue too long. If Mazeppe said: "Sit down," you had better sit down or else he could tell you to *lie* down.

"Blessed are the seated!" the rebbe said after we had made the blessing over the bread.

"Come eat with us!" we said to him out of courtesy.

"Eat in good health!" he said to us, "I won't join you but I wouldn't mind making a blessing over the wine. What do you have there in that bottle? Whisky?" he said, reaching his dried-out arm and skinny fingers toward the bottle of whisky and poured himself a glassful, tasted it, and puckered up his lips so that we had to be stronger than iron not to burst out laughing.

"Who does this strong stuff belong to?" he said, taking another sip. "Not bad, not bad at all," and took another sip, drinking to our health.

"*L'khayim*, children, may God grant us another year of life and . . . and . . . you don't happen to have a little something to eat, do you? Oh, well, I'll go wash up and in honor of Lag B'Omer I'll join you for the party."

What was happening to our rebbe? Not the same Mazeppe! In high spirits, talkative, cheeks flushed, nose red, eyes glistening. Chewing and talking at the same time, he pointed to the bottles of wine.

"What kind of wine do you have there? Passover wine?" He sampled some and puckered his lips. "Psss! Now *that* is special!" He drank. "It's been a long time since I've drunk such wine, I tell you!" he said to Yossl the winemaker's son with a little laugh. "There's a devil in your father's wine cellar, ha-ha! I have seen barrels down there, barrel upon barrel of the best vintages made from pure raisins, ha-ha! *L'khayim*, children! May God grant that you grow up to be honest, righteous Jews and that you . . . that you . . . open the other bottle . . . here, have a drop, why don't you take some? And drink *l'khayim*. May God grant that . . ." He licked his lips and his eyes started to shut. ". . . that . . . that . . . all good things come to Israel . . ."

E

After eating and grace, Mazeppe tried to address us but his tongue was thick and his speech muddled:

"Well then, uh, uh, I suppose we've fulfilled our duty, our *mitzvah*, of having a Lag B'Omer party, right? Soooo . . . what's next? Ah?"

"Next we're going for our walk."

"Ah? For a walk? Excellent. Where to?"

"To the dark woods."

"Ah? To the dark woods? Most excellent! I'm coming along with you. Walking in the woods is very good, very healthy, because a woods . . . ah? I am going to teach you about the woods . . ."

And we all set out with our rebbe and walked past the town limits. At first we felt a bit awkward walking with the rebbe who walked among us waving his arms as he spoke and giving us a lecture on the woods:

"The nature of the woods, you must understand, is that the Almighty so created it so that it would be full of trees, and on them, on the trees that is, there would be branches, and on the branches leaves would be growing, green ones, you see, and they would give off aromas, the leaves, fragrant aromas, sweet yet pungent . . ."

Saying this the rebbe inhaled deeply the sweet yet pungent aromas although we were still far from the woods and the aromas were hardly sweet or pungent.

"Here! Why are you all so quiet?" our rebbe said to us. "Say something nice, sing a little song, hah? Look, I was once a boy, a prankster like you, heh-heh, I also had a rebbe like you do, heh-heh . . ."

That Mazeppe had once been a prankster like us and had a rebbe like us seemed hard to believe, almost unimaginable. Mazeppe a prankster?! We looked at one another and snickered quietly. We pictured our rebbe Mazeppe as the prankster he might have been, with a rebbe of his own who used to . . . we were afraid to go on picturing more. But good old Eli wasn't afraid and came right out and asked him:

"Rebbe! Did your rebbe whip you like you whip us?"

"Hah? And what whippings, heh-heh!"

We looked at the rebbe and then at each other and we understood each other. We laughed along with him, "Heh-heh," until we were far outside the town, in the wide open meadow not far from the dark woods.

F

The meadow was as pleasant as paradise itself. Green sweet-smelling grass, white flowers, yellow blossoms, gossamer flies. Above us the blue cap of sky spread out infinitely. And ahead of us was the woods, dressed in its holiday best. In the trees chirping birds hopped from branch to branch, welcoming us in honor of our beloved Lag B'Omer. We sought out a shady spot under a thick tree to protect us from the burning sun and all of us stretched out on the ground, the rebbe in the middle.

The rebbe was exhausted from the walk. He dropped to the ground and lay face up. His eyes were shutting, his tongue could barely get the words out:

"You are darling, golden chi-children . . . Jewish children . . . saints . . . I love you all and you all love me . . . Isn't it true you all lo-love me?"

"Like a pain in the eyes!" Eli answered him.

"Hah? I know you all lo-love me," the rebbe said to him.

"May God love you as much as we do!" said Eli to him.

We became frightened and said to Eli: "God be with you, what are you saying!"

"Idiots!" Eli answered, laughing, "Why are you afraid? Don't you see he's drunk?"

"Hah?" the rebbe said to him, one eye open, the other already asleep, "What are you saying? Saints? All of you are saints . . . then again . . . either way . . . guardians of Israel . . . Hup-hup-hup . . . hrrrrrssss . . ."

Our rebbe dropped off into a deep sleep and the sound of his snoring through his nose was like the sound of the shofar, and could be heard deep in the woods. We all sat around him feeling very gloomy:

"This is our rebbe? This is the one we're terrified of? This is Mazeppe?"

G

"Kids!" cried Eli, "Why are we sitting around like a bunch of dimwits? Let's come up with a punishment for Mazeppe."

We were stricken with dread.

"Why are you afraid, silly asses?" Eli said again, "He's like a dead man now, a corpse."

The feeling of dread became even stronger as Eli went on:

"Now we can do whatever we want to him. All winter he's whipped us like sheep. Let's have our revenge on him this one time."

"What do you want to do to him?"

"Nothing. I just want to scare him."

"How are you going to scare him?"

"You'll soon see," Eli said to us. He stood up, went over to the rebbe, removed the rebbe's rope belt and called out to us:

"See? We'll tie him to the tree with his own belt so he won't be able to get loose. Then one of us will go up to him and shout right in his ear: "Rebbe, bandits!"

"What will happen then?"

"Nothing. We'll run away and he'll shout, *Sh'ma Yisroel*—Hear O Israel."

"How long will he shout?"

"Until he gives up."

Without thinking too long, Eli took the belt, tied the rebbe's hands and feet to the tree while we looked on, quaking in our shoes:

"This is our rebbe? This is the one we are terrified of? This is Mazeppe?"

"Why are you all standing around like a bunch of nit-wits?" Eli said to us, "If God has performed a miracle for us and delivered Mazeppe in our hands, let's celebrate and dance!"

We all joined hands in a circle and danced wildly like madmen, jumping and singing and spinning around.

"And this brings our service to an end," said Eli and we stopped. Eli went over to the rebbe, bent down close to him and shouted loudly into his ear in a voice that would wake the dead:

"Help! Rebbe! Bandits! Bandits!! Bandits!!!"

H

As one we shot away from there like arrows, afraid of stopping to look back. We were in a panic, even Eli, though he didn't stop shouting at us:

"Fools! Nitwits! Idiots! Why are you running?"

"Why are *you* running?"

"You're running, so I'm running."

We burst into town screaming: "Bandits! . . . Bandits! . . ."

People saw us running and ran after us. Seeing people running, more people joined in.

"Why are people running?"

"How should we know? They're all running so we're running too."

Finally one of us ran out of breath and came to a halt. This was the signal for the rest of us to stop although we kept on shouting, "Bandits! Bandits! Bandits!"

"Where? Where? Where?"

"There, in the dark woods. Bandits attacked us, tied the rebbe to a tree, God knows if he's still alive . . ."

I

If you are envious that we are free from *cheder* (our rebbe is sick), your envy is wasted. Wasted. No one knows how it feels when the shoe pinches someone else. No one, no one knew who the real bandits were. We hardly saw one another but when we did meet, the first thing we said was: "How's the rebbe?" (No more Mazeppe!) And when we were at our prayers, we prayed to God for the rebbe's health and wept silently: Lord Almighty! Lord Almighty! And Eli? Don't ask about Eli. May his name be eradicated, that Eli!

EPILOGUE

When the rebbe recovered (for six weeks he lay in a fever and muttered about bandits) and we returned to *cheder*, we barely recognized him, that's how much he had changed. What had become of his lion-voice? He had thrown away the whip. No more, "Lie down." No more Mazeppe. A gentle, subdued melancholy had spread like a shadow over his face. A feeling of regret stole into our hearts and suddenly Mazeppe became very dear to us, close to our hearts. Ah, if he would only scold us again, say nasty things as before, as if nothing had ever happened. Instead, he would suddenly stop in the middle of a lesson and ask us to tell him again what had happened with the bandits that Lag B'Omer. We didn't hesitate and repeated over and over the rehearsed story by heart—how bandits had run out of the woods, attacked him, tied him up and threatened to cut his throat and how we had escaped and fled back to town and with our cries for help we had saved him.

The rebbe heard us out to the end, his eyes shut. Then he heaved a sigh and asked again:

"Are you absolutely certain they were bandits?"

"What else could they have been?"

"Maybe a band of pranksters . . . ?"

The rebbe's eyes gazed far into the distance and we imagined that flitting across his thick lips was a sly little smile.

Getzel

"Sit down, I'll tell you a story about nuts."

"About what? About nuts?"

"About nuts!"

"Now? While there's a war on?"

"Especially because there's a war on and your heart is heavy. I want to take your mind off your worries. By the way, crack open a nut and you find a nutmeat."

A

His name was Getzel, but he was called Goyetzel and was considered a simpleton. Everyone made fun of him and ridiculed him. He was an overgrown lad who sat among the younger *cheder* boys, awkward, with freakishly large hands and unusually thick lips. His voice sounded as if it were echoing in a barrel and he wore overly wide trousers and outsized boots, giving him a bearish look. His large head

329

rested on his shoulders like a kneading trough that was stuffed with hemp, hay, or feathers, please forgive me for saying this. That's what our rebbe, Reb Yenkel, said of him in *cheder*, repeatedly insulting him with references to his size: "Goyetzel," "Monster," "Klutz," "Grotesque Oaf," and other fine nicknames. And he? No reaction. It never seemed to bother him in the least! He would sit in a corner, cram his cheeks full of food and chew like a calf on its cud. You must understand that Goyetzel loved food. Eating was more important to him than anything else. "A bottomless stomach," his friends said of him. "A glutton," the rebbe said to his face, but Goyetzel didn't so much as flinch! The minute he saw food, it went right into his mouth and was devoured eagerly. Lunch was delivered to him in *cheder*, always the best of everything—cheese knishes and plenty of stuffed dumplings! To his mother, a wealthy woman, this clumsy oaf of a boy was a beloved only child and so she fed him, stuffed him with food day and night as one would stuff a goose, always complaining that "the child doesn't eat a thing."

"That's how she tries to avert the the Evil Eye from him," our rebbe, Reb Yenkel, would say, naturally behind his mother's back.

"A plague on his mother!" his wife would add her support in a sing-song while screwing up her face so that it was impossible not to laugh. "In my home town such children are kept out of sight, may my pains be his!"

"May I outlive him!" the rebbe completed the diatribe as he pulled down Getzel's hat over his ears.

The whole *cheder* laughed as Goyeztel sat sulking in silence; he was angry, but he kept silent. It was difficult to rile him up but once he got angry—watch out! An enraged bear was not as dangerous as he. In a fit of rage he would prance about and bite his own hands with his strong white teeth. And if he gave someone a slap, it was really felt and appreciated. His classmates knew this all too well, their backs having felt his blows, and they were scared to death of him, afraid of having anything to do with him. For blows, as you know, Jewish children have respect. In order to protect themselves from Getzel's fists, all ten *cheder* students united—ten boys against one. And that was how two sides formed in Reb Yenkel's *cheder*: on one side was Getzel and on the other side were the rest of the students. The students sharpened their minds, Getzel his fists. The students studied, Getzel stuffed himself with knishes and dumplings.

B

One day, a holiday, the boys gathered together to play at nuts. The game of nuts, like all games, was not much better than *dreydl* and no worse than cards. There are different ways of playing at nuts: "in the hole," "in the bank," and "in the cap." And the game would end, of course, as all games: someone lost, another won. And, as everywhere, the winner was considered clever, shrewd, and a fine fellow while the loser was a fool, lamebrain, and a dunce, just like in those clubs where people sit day and night playing cards.

The ten of us classmates got together in *cheder* to play at nuts. We laid out a row of nuts on the ground and rolled nuts toward the row; whoever knocked the most nuts out of the row, won. Suddenly the door burst open and there stood Getzel with full pockets, as usual.

"Come in!" one of the boys said.

"Speaking of the Messiah!" said another.

"And in comes Haman!" said a third.

"And Rashi says: 'The devil brought him!'" said a fourth.

"What are you playing, 'In the bank'? I'll play with you too. I have nuts," said Getzel and was immediately told:

"No way!"

"Why not?"

"Because!"

"All right, then I'll bust up your game!"

And without a moment's hesitation, he kicked the row of nuts with his bear-like feet all over the room. The boys were not too happy with this. The nerve of that hooligan!

"Kids, why don't we do something?" one of us said.

"Let's think of something!" said another.

"Let's break his bones!" a third shouted.

"Go on, try it!" said Getzel and rolled up his sleeves, ready to go to work.

And a war broke out. On one side was the whole *cheder*, on the other side—Getzel.

Although ten is more than one, they felt the sting of his strong fists that gave them several swellings on foreheads and a few black eyes. But they were also able to leave a few marks on Getzel with their sharp fingernails and teeth or however they could manage to assail him from front or back or from the side, scratching, pinching, plucking, tearing, biting. In short, ten is more than one. They triumphed and Getzel had to take to his heels and flee. And that's where the real story of the nuts begins.

C

Bloodied, scratched, with torn trousers, Getzel remained standing a while outside in deep thought. Then he slapped his pockets so hard that the nuts rattled loudly.

"So, you don't want to play at nuts with me? Then let the Angel of Death play with you! I have no use for you! As far as I'm concerned, the two of us can play," Getzel said to himself and ran as far as his legs would take him until he stopped in the middle of the road and said aloud as if he were with someone else:

"Where do you think we should go, Getzel?" And he immediately answered himself:

"Far away, past the town, on the other side of the mills. No one is there. There the two of us can be alone, no one will bother us. And if someone tries, we'll break his bones, mess him up . . ."

And Getzel, seeming to be talking to himself, felt as if he was not one person but two, with the strength of two! Just let his classmates come and he would make mincemeat of them, make limp dishrags of them! These thoughts gave him enormous pleasure and he did not cease talking to himself as if he were speaking to someone else.

"Listen now, how far do you think we have to go?" he said to himself and answered himself right away: "Well, it depends on you."

"Maybe we had better sit down and play at nuts right here? Eh? What do you say, Getzel?"

"That's fine with me."

And Getzel sat down on the ground, far beyond the town, on the other side of the mills. He took out and counted the nuts and divided them exactly in half. He put one half in his right pocket, the other half in his left pocket, removed his cap, threw a few nuts into it from the right pocket and said to himself:

"They think that I can't get along without them. Listen, Getzel, what game are we playing?"

"I don't know. Whatever game you want."

"Let's play 'Odds or Even'."

"That's fine with me."

He shook his cap and said, "Now guess! Odds or even?"

"Well, guess!" he said to himself, ramming his elbow into his side.

"Even."

"Even, you say? You got whipped! You've lost three nuts. Give them here."

He removed three nuts from his left pocket and put them into his right pocket. Again he shook the cap and again asked:

"Now what is it? Odds or even?"

"Odds."

"Odds, you say? What an idiot! Give it here, you've lost four nuts!"

He transfered four nuts from his left pocket to his right, shook the cap and said to himself:

"Maybe you can guess right this time. Odds or even?"

"Even."

"Even, you say? May your limbs fail you! Give me five nuts, you dope!"

"It's bad enough I'm losing, do you have to curse me too?"

"Whose fault is it if you're a nincompoop and guess like a blind man feeling around in a hole? Go on now, guess: Odds or even? Now you'll surely guess right."

"Even."

"Even? Keep it up and you won't live long! Hand me seven nuts, you idiot, and try again: Odds or even?"

"Even."

"Again even? You're really generous with your nuts! Hand me five nuts, *shlimazel*, and guess again. Maybe you'll guess right just once: Odds or even? Well, why aren't you saying anything?"

"I don't have any more nuts."

"It's lie! You do have!"

"As I am a Jew, I don't have anymore."

"Take a good look deep in your pocket! That's the way."

"None."

"None? Lost all your nuts? So? What good did they do you? Aren't you an ass?"

"Enough, you've won all my nuts and now you're rubbing it in?"

"Serves you right! You wanted to beat me and I beat you."

Goyetzel was deliriously happy about this turn of events and that he, Goyetzel, had won and Getzel had lost. He felt a surge of power. He was now ready to win all the nuts in the world. "Where are they now, those classmates of mine? I'd really get even with them! I wouldn't leave them a single nut even if they were dying for it! If they would stretch out on the ground and beg, I would leave them to die a miserable death!"

And Getzel grew full of rage, clenched his fists, ground his teeth and spoke to himself as if there were someone else with him:

"Go ahead, try to start up with me! Now I'm not alone! Now there are two of us! So, Getzel, why are you sitting there like a snot-nose? Why don't we play at some more nuts?"

"Nuts? Where will I get nuts? I told you I don't even have one nut left."

"Ach! I forgot that you don't have any more nuts. I tell you what, Getzel."

"What?"

"Do you have any money?"

"I do. What of it?"

"Buy nuts from me."

"What do you mean, buy nuts from you?"

"Birdbrain, don't you know what buy means? Give me money and I'll give you nuts. Hah?"

"Well, all right. That's fine with me."

He removed a silver coin from his purse, arrived at a price, counted out twenty nuts from his right pocket to the left and the game continued.

D

An experienced cardplayer, they say, once called in his son, also a cardplayer, half an hour before his death and said to him:

"My child! I am leaving this world. We will never see one another again. I know that you play cards, you have my faults. You can play as much as you like, but God help you, never bet everything!"

Those words are, forgive the comparison, like scripture. There is nothing in the world worse than to bet everything. Experienced cardplayers say you can lose your shirt that way! It can drive you to desperation and lead you on a path to hell from which there is no return! That's what everyone says, and that's what happened to our young man. He worked that cap so long, odds or even, moving nuts from one pocket to the next until the left pocket remained without a single nut.

"Well, why aren't you playing?"

"I don't have any nuts."

"You're out of nuts again, *shlimazel*?"

"You say I'm a *shlimazel*, and I say you're a cheat."

"If you say that word once more, I'll smack your face."

"Just go ahead and try it!"

Getzel remained sitting quietly a few minutes, scratching the ground with his fingers, digging a hole and quietly muttering a tune under his breath. Then he said:

"Damn it! Let's play at nuts."

"Where will I get nuts?"

"Do you have any more money? I'll sell you another ten."

"Money? Where will I get money? I don't have a groshen."

"No nuts and no money? That's great! Oy, I can't stand it! Ha-ha-ha!"

That "Ha-ha-ha!" rang out across the field and echoed through the distant thick woods and Getzel rolled on the ground with laughter.

"Why this laughter of yours, you Goyetzel you?" he said to himself and quickly answered himself:

"I'm laughing at *you, shlimazel*. It's enough that you lost all your nuts to me, but what good did it do you to lose all your money as well, so much money, you moron, you imbecile? Oy, I can't stand it! Ha-ha-ha!"

"It was your idea that I do it, you fiend, you lout, you good-for-nothing!"

"Aren't you smart! If I tell you to cut off your nose, do you have to listen to me? You numbskull! You nincompoop! You ass! Ha-ha-ha!"

"Shut your mouth, you Goyetz, and don't let me look at your unkosher face!"

He turned away from himself, sat a few minutes brooding, digging at the ground with his fingers, poured the earth back in the hole and hummed a little song under his breath.

E

"Do you know what I think, Getzel?" he announced to himself a bit later. "Let's make up, let's be friends. God helped me and I was lucky enough to win all the nuts, why shouldn't we allow ourselves to enjoy a few of them? I don't suppose they're too bad. Hah? What do you think, Getzel?"

"Yes, I think so too, they can't be too bad," he answered himself and threw one nut and then another and then a third into his mouth, each time cracking the nut with his teeth. After cracking the shell and removing a fat nutmeat, he cleaned it off, threw it back in his mouth and chewed it with his large white teeth, munching it with gusto like a horse munching oats and said:

"Would you like a nutmeat, Getzel? Don't be shy, speak up!"

"Why not?" he answered himself, stretched out his left hand but quickly slapped it with his right:

"And how about a punch instead?"

"I'll give *you* a punch!"

"I'll give you *two*."

He did not stop cracking nuts and chewing the fat nutmeats, munching like a horse munching oats. It bothered him that he was gobbling up nutmeats while the other one sat and looked, and he said to him:

"Listen, Getzel, I'm going to ask you something. What's it like to watch me eating?"

"What's it like for me? Why don't you find out!"

"Eh, I see you're angry? Here's a nutmeat for you."

And Getzel's right hand started to give his left hand a nutmeat. As the left hand reached for the nutmeat, the right hand pinched it. So the left hand gave the right hand a slap, then the right hand gave the left hand a slap. The left hand hurled a punch at the right cheek, then the right hand hauled off and punched the left cheek twice. The left hand grabbed the right lapel and the right hand tore off the left lapel from top to bottom. The left hand then grabbed the right earlock followed by the right hand pulling the left ear.

"Let go of my earlock, Getzi. You'd better let go of my earlock!"

"Let go of my ear, and I'll let go of your earlock!"

"To hell with you!"

"All right, then you'll be without an earlock, Getzi!"

"And you'll be without an ear, Goyetz!"

"Ay!"

"Ay-ay!"

EPILOGUE

For several minutes our Getzel rolled on the ground. Now he was lying *right* side up, now he was lying *left* side up, holding on to his pocket of nuts with both hands. One minute Goyetzl was winning, the next Getzel was winning. At last Getzel-Goyetzel stood up, covered with mud like a pig, tattered, with a bloodied ear and a torn earlock. He yanked out all the nuts from his pocket and flung them in the mud, far away as the mill, muttering angrily:

"There! Serves you right! Not for me, not for you!"

Glossary

Ahashuerosh—King of Persia in the Book of Esther.

Bar Mitzvah—Confirmation ceremony of a male reaching his thirteenth birthday, when a boy comes of age and assumes religious responsibility.

Bris—Circumcision ceremony of an eight-day-old baby boy, according to the covenant between God and Abraham.

Challah—The braided holiday or Sabbath egg bread.

Cheder—Religious elementary school in the home of the teacher, the rebbe, where children were taught Hebrew, prayers, and the Bible.

Dreydl—Four-sided spinning top, played with by children during Chanukah.

Farfel—Pellet-shaped dough.

Gehenim—Hell, inferno.

Gemara—The part of the Talmud that comments on the Mishnah.

Goot yontev—Happy Holiday!

Goy—Gentile, non-Jew; Jew ignorant of Jewish traditions.

Groshen—Small Polish coin.

Haggadah—Book of the Passover home service read during the two consecutive seders of the first two nights of Passover. It consists of the narrative of the Jewish exodus from Egypt.

Haman—In the Book of Esther, chief minister to Ahashuerosh, King of Persia. The villain whose name children try to drown out with their *groggers*, or noisemakers, during Purim.

Hamantash—Three-cornered, filled pastry eaten during Purim.

Haroses—Mixture of apples, nuts, and wine used in the Passover ritual to symbolize the mortar Jews made as slaves in Egypt.

Kabbalah—A body of Jewish mystical lore and interpretations of scripture, an attempt to fathom the mysteries of God and creation.

Kaddish—Prayer recited by mourners after the death of a close relative.

Kayn Eyn Horeh—Literally, no Evil Eye; the equivalent of knocking on wood for fear of retribution for being presumptuous, for excessive praise, or when one hopes there is truth in one's words.

Kiddush—Blessing recited over the wine at the beginning of the Sabbath or holiday evening meal.

Klezmer—Musician.

Kosher—Food or drink that Jews are permitted to eat when proper regulations have been observed in its preparation.

Kvass—A frothy sour brew made from fermenting rye flour, malt, and sugar.

Lag B'Omer—A joyous, minor spring holiday commemorating the end of a plague in the second century C.E. Celebrated by outings, picnics, and appreciation of nature.

L'khayim—To life! Used as a toast.

Lulav—Palm branch, tied together with sprigs of myrtle and willow, used together with the *esrog*, a large, lemonlike citrus fruit, during Sukkos to symbolize the harvest.

Maftir—Concluding section of the Torah portion read on Sabbaths and holidays. It is an honor to be called up to the Torah for *Maftir*.

Matzo—Traditional unleavened flatbread eaten during Passover to commemorate the years Jews spent wandering through the desert.

Mazel tov—Congratulations, literally, good luck.

Megillah—The Book of Esther, the story of Purim, written on a scroll and read aloud.

Mezuzah—A rolled piece of parchment containing passages from Deuteronomy, inserted in a wooden or metal case and affixed in a slanting position on the right side of the door-post of Jewish homes and synagogues. A devout Jew will kiss his fingers and touch the *mezuzah* upon entering a building.

Minkha—Afternoon daily prayer recited before sunset, usually combined with the *maariv*, or evening prayer.

Mitzvah—A Torah commandment, a good deed.

Passover—Spring festival celebrated for eight days, commemorating the Jews' exodus from Egypt where they were slaves.

Purim—Feast of Lots, celebrating the downfall of Haman, persecutor of the Jews; marked by parades, exchanges of pastry gift trays, costume parties, and dramatic renditions of the Purim story.

Rebbe—Chasidic rabbi, teacher.

Rosh Hashanah—Jewish New Year; with Yom Kippur, the High Holidays.

Sabbath—or **Shabbos**,starting at sundown Friday night and ending at sundown Saturday night. The day of rest and worship for Jews.

Seder—Passover supper table. See *Haggadah*.

Shemini Atzeres—A festival that comes on the eighth day of Sukkos, on the day before *Simkhas Torah*.

Shevuos—The Festival of Weeks, celebrated seven weeks after Passover, celebrates the giving of the Law on Mount Sinai and the gathering of the first fruits. Dairy food is eaten.

Shiva—Weeklong period of mourning following the funeral of a close relative.

Shlimazel—An unlucky person whose life is a series of misfortunes, perpetual bad luck.

Sh'ma Yisroel—"Hear O Israel," the credo of Jews, prayer recited daily. Jews' affirmation of faith in one God.

Shofar—Ram's horn blown in synagogues on Rosh Hashanah and Yom Kippur.

Sholem Aleykhem—Traditional Jewish greeting meaning, "peace be with you," but used to say, "Hello," or "Goodbye."

Shtetl—Jewish towns in the Pale of Settlement in eastern Europe.

Shul—Synagogue, prayer house.

Simkhas Torah—Holiday after *Sukkos* celebrating the completion of a year's reading of the Torah and beginning anew. The joyous holiday is marked with the carrying of the Torahs in a procession in the synagogue and by flags that children decorate with biblical drawings and top with an apple and a lit candle.

Slikhes—Penitential prayers recited the week before Rosh Hashanah.

Sukkah—Homemade shed or lean-to behind the house, made of crude lumber and topped with green branches, in which the family eats its meals during Sukkos. It symbolizes the dwellings used by the Jews during their wanderings in the desert.

Sukkos, or **Succos**—The Feast of Tabernacles, fall harvest festival, lasting seven days.

Talmud—A compilation of the religious, ethical, and legal teachings and decisions of the rabbis interpreting the Bible.

Talmud-Torah—Tuition-free elementary school maintained by the community for the poorest children.

Tanakh—The Bible.

Tefillin—Phylacteries; square leather boxes containing scriptural passages worn on the left arm and forehead during weekday morning prayers by observant male Jews over thirteen.

Tisha B'Av—A fast day commemorating the day the first and second Temples in Jerusalem were destroyed.

Treyf—Unclean, ritually impure.

Vey iz mir!—Woe is me, alas!

Yarmulke—Prayer cap worn by Jewish males.

Yahrtzeit—Anniversary of the death of a close relative.

Yom Kippur—Day of Atonement, holiest day for Jews, a day of fasting and solemn prayer.

Zloty—Standard monetary unit of Poland.

ABOUT THE TRANSLATOR

Aliza Shevrin has translated and published four novels and three collections of children's short stories by Sholom Aleichem as well as a novel by I. B. Singer. She teaches and lectures about Yiddish and was a Rockefeller Scholar in Bellagio, Italy, in 1982. Ms. Shevrin holds degrees from Cornell University and Washburn University as well as a master's degree in social work from the University of Kansas. She is currently director of Jewish Family Services in Ann Arbor, Michigan, where she lives with her husband, Howard. They have four children and six grandchildren.